WOMAN'S INSTITUTE LIBRARY OF COOKERY

**SOUP
MEAT
POULTRY AND GAME
FISH AND SHELL FISH**

WOMAN'S INSTITUTE
OF DOMESTIC ARTS AND SCIENCES, Inc.
SCRANTON, PA.
1923

Soup: Copyright, 1918, by INTERNATIONAL EDUCATIONAL PUBLISHING COMPANY.
Meat, Parts 1 and 2: Copyright, 1918, by INTERNATIONAL EDUCATIONAL PUBLISHING COMPANY.
Poultry and Game: Copyright, 1918, by INTERNATIONAL EDUCATIONAL PUBLISHING COMPANY.
Fish and Shell Fish: Copyright, 1918, by INTERNATIONAL EDUCATIONAL PUBLISHING COMPANY.

Copyright in Great Britain

All rights reserved

Printed in U. S. A.

Press of
International Textbook Company
Scranton, Pa.

4710

PREFACE

This volume, which is the third of the Woman's Institute Library of Cookery, includes soups and the high-protein foods, meat, poultry, game, and fish. It therefore contains information that is of interest to every housewife, for these foods occupy an important place in the majority of meals.

In her study of *Soup,* she will come to a thorough appreciation of the place that soup occupies in the meal, its chief purposes, and its economic value. All the different kinds of soups are classified and discussed, recipes for making them, as well as the stocks used in their preparation, receiving the necessary attention. The correct serving of soup is not overlooked; nor are the accompaniments and garnishes so often required to make the soup course of the meal an attractive one.

In *Meat,* Parts 1 and 2, are described the various cuts of the different kinds of meat—beef, veal, lamb, mutton, and pork—and the part of the animal from which they are obtained, the way in which to judge a good piece of meat by its appearance, and what to do with it from the time it is purchased until all of it is used. All the methods applicable to the cooking of meats are emphasized in this section. Supplementing the text are numerous illustrations showing the ways in which meat cuts are obtained. Besides, many of them are so reproduced that actual cuts of meat may be readily recognized. Equipped with this knowledge, the housewife need give no concern to the selection, care, and cooking of every variety of meat.

In *Poultry and Game,* the selection and preparation of all kinds of poultry receive attention. While such food is somewhat of a luxury in a great many homes, it helps to relieve the monotony of the usual protein foods, and it often supplies just what is desired for special occasions. Familiarity with poultry and game is a decided asset to any housewife, and success with their cooking and serving is assured through a study of this text, for every step in their preparation is clearly explained and illustrated.

In *Fish and Shell Fish,* the other high-protein food is treated in full as to its composition, food value, purchase, care, and preparation. Such interesting processes as the boning, skinning, and filleting of fish are not only carefully explained but clearly illustrated. In addition to recipes for fresh, salt, smoked, and canned fish are given directions for the preparation of all edible shell fish and recipes for the various stuffings and sauces served with fish.

Too much cannot be said about the importance of the subjects covered in this volume and the necessity for a thorough understanding of them on the part of every housewife. Indeed, a mastery of them will mean for her an acquaintance with the main part of the meal, and when she knows how to prepare these foods, the other dishes will prove a simple matter.

CONTENTS

Soup   *Section*   *Page*

	Section	Page
Value of Soup	9	1
Classification of Soups	9	3
Uses and Varieties of Soup Stock	9	5
The Stock Pot	9	7
Principal Ingredients in Soup	9	9
Processes Involved in Making Stock	9	11
Serving Soup	9	16
Recipes for Soup and Soup Accompaniments	9	18
Stocks and Clear Soups	9	19
Heavy Thick Soups	9	21
Cream Soups	9	25
Purées	9	29
Chowders	9	30
Soup Accompaniments and Garnishes	9	31

Meat

	Section	Page
Value of Meat as Food	10	1
Structure and Composition of Meat	10	3
Purchase and Care of Meat	10	8
Purposes of Cooking Meat	10	11
Methods of Cooking Meat	10	11
Time Required for Cooking Meat	10	15
Beef—General Characteristics	10	17
Cuts of Beef	10	18
Steaks and Their Preparation	10	22
Roasts and Their Preparation	10	31
Preparation of Stews and Corned Beef	10	38
Beef Organs and Their Preparation	10	42

CONTENTS

Meat—*Continued*

	Section	Page
Making Gravy	10	44
Trying Out Suet and Other Fats	10	44
Preparation of Left-Over Beef	10	45
Veal	11	1
Cuts of Veal and Their Uses	11	2
Veal Cuts and Their Preparation	11	4
Veal Organs and Their Preparation	11	9
Preparation of Left-Over Veal	11	10
Mutton and Lamb—Comparison	11	12
Cuts of Mutton and Lamb	11	15
Preparation of Roasts, Chops, and Stews	11	17
Preparation of Left-Over Lamb and Mutton	11	21
Pork	11	23
Cuts of Pork	11	24
Fresh Pork and Its Preparation	11	29
Cured Pork and Its Preparation	11	32
Preparation of Left-Over Pork	11	37
Serving and Carving of Meat	11	38
Sausages and Meat Preparations	11	39
Principles of Deep-Fat Frying	11	40
Application of Deep-Fat Frying	11	41
Timbale Cases	11	44

Poultry and Game

	Section	Page
Poultry as a Food	12	1
Selection of Poultry	12	3
Selection of Chicken	12	6
Selection of Poultry Other Than Chicken	12	9
Composition of Poultry	12	12
Preparation of Chicken for Cooking	12	13
Preparation of Poultry Other Than Chicken for Cooking	12	23
Cooking of Poultry	12	24
Stuffing for Roast Poultry	12	33
Boned Chicken	12	35
Dishes from Left-Over Poultry	12	46
Serving and Carving of Poultry	12	49
Game	12	52
Recipes for Game	12	53

CONTENTS

Soup   *Section*   *Page*

	Section	Page
Value of Soup	9	1
Classification of Soups	9	3
Uses and Varieties of Soup Stock	9	5
The Stock Pot	9	7
Principal Ingredients in Soup	9	9
Processes Involved in Making Stock	9	11
Serving Soup	9	16
Recipes for Soup and Soup Accompaniments	9	18
Stocks and Clear Soups	9	19
Heavy Thick Soups	9	21
Cream Soups	9	25
Purées	9	29
Chowders	9	30
Soup Accompaniments and Garnishes	9	31

Meat

Value of Meat as Food	10	1
Structure and Composition of Meat	10	3
Purchase and Care of Meat	10	8
Purposes of Cooking Meat	10	11
Methods of Cooking Meat	10	11
Time Required for Cooking Meat	10	15
Beef—General Characteristics	10	17
Cuts of Beef	10	18
Steaks and Their Preparation	10	22
Roasts and Their Preparation	10	31
Preparation of Stews and Corned Beef	10	38
Beef Organs and Their Preparation	10	42

CONTENTS

MEAT—*Continued*   *Section*   *Page*

	Section	Page
Making Gravy	10	44
Trying Out Suet and Other Fats	10	44
Preparation of Left-Over Beef	10	45
Veal	11	1
Cuts of Veal and Their Uses	11	2
Veal Cuts and Their Preparation	11	4
Veal Organs and Their Preparation	11	9
Preparation of Left-Over Veal	11	10
Mutton and Lamb—Comparison	11	12
Cuts of Mutton and Lamb	11	15
Preparation of Roasts, Chops, and Stews	11	17
Preparation of Left-Over Lamb and Mutton	11	21
Pork	11	23
Cuts of Pork	11	24
Fresh Pork and Its Preparation	11	29
Cured Pork and Its Preparation	11	32
Preparation of Left-Over Pork	11	37
Serving and Carving of Meat	11	38
Sausages and Meat Preparations	11	39
Principles of Deep-Fat Frying	11	40
Application of Deep-Fat Frying	11	41
Timbale Cases	11	44

POULTRY AND GAME

	Section	Page
Poultry as a Food	12	1
Selection of Poultry	12	3
Selection of Chicken	12	6
Selection of Poultry Other Than Chicken	12	9
Composition of Poultry	12	12
Preparation of Chicken for Cooking	12	13
Preparation of Poultry Other Than Chicken for Cooking	12	23
Cooking of Poultry	12	24
Stuffing for Roast Poultry	12	33
Boned Chicken	12	35
Dishes from Left-Over Poultry	12	46
Serving and Carving of Poultry	12	49
Game	12	52
Recipes for Game	12	53

CONTENTS

FISH AND SHELL FISH	Section	Page
Fish in the Diet	13	1
Composition and Food Value of Fish	13	3
Purchase and Care of Fish	13	7
Cleaning Fish	13	11
Boning Fish	13	14
Skinning Fish	13	14
Filleting Fish	13	15
Methods of Cooking Fish	13	17
Recipes for Fish Sauces and Stuffings	13	18
Recipes for Fresh Fish	13	21
Recipes for Salt and Smoked Fish	13	31
Recipes for Canned Fish	13	33
Recipes for Left-Over Fish	13	35
Shell Fish—Nature, Varieties, and Use	13	36
Oysters and Their Preparation	13	39
Clams and Their Preparation	13	47
Scallops and Their Preparation	13	49
Lobsters and Their Preparation	13	51
Crabs and Their Preparation	13	56
Shrimp and Their Preparation	13	58

SOUP

SOUP AND ITS PLACE IN THE MEAL

VALUE OF SOUP

1. **Soup** is a liquid food that is prepared by boiling meat or vegetables, or both, in water and then seasoning and sometimes thickening the liquid that is produced. It is usually served as the first course of a dinner, but it is often included in a light meal, such as luncheon. While some persons regard the making of soup as difficult, nothing is easier when one knows just what is required and how to proceed. The purpose of this Section, therefore, is to acquaint the housewife with the details of soup making, so that she may provide her family with appetizing and nutritious soups that make for both economy and healthfulness.

2. It is interesting to note the advancement that has been made with this food. The origin of soup, like that of many foods, dates back to practically the beginning of history. However, the first soup known was probably not made with meat. For instance, the mess of pottage for which Esau sold his birthright was soup made of red lentils. Later on meat came to be used as the basis for soup because of the agreeable and appetizing flavor it provides. Then, at one time in France a scarcity of butter and other fats that had been used to produce moistness and richness in foods, brought about such clear soups as bouillon and consommé. These, as well as other liquid foods, found much favor, for about the time they were devised it came to be considered vulgar to chew food. Thus, at various periods, and because of different emergencies, particular kinds of soup have been introduced, until now there are many kinds from which the housewife may choose when she desires a dish that will start a meal in the right way and at the same time appeal to the appetite.

3. Value of Soup in the Meal.—Not all persons have the same idea regarding the value of soup as a part of a meal. Some consider it to be of no more value than so much water, claiming that it should be fed to none but children or sick persons who are unable to take solid food. On the other hand, many persons believe that soup contains the very essence of all that is nourishing and sustaining in the foods of which it is made. This difference of opinion is well demonstrated by the ideas that have been advanced concerning this food. Some one has said that soup is to a meal what a portico is to a palace or an overture to an opera, while another person, who evidently does not appreciate this food, has said that soup is the preface to a dinner and that any work really worth while is sufficient in itself and needs no preface. Such opinions, however, must be reconciled if the true value of this food is to be appreciated.

4. Probably the best way in which to come to a definite conclusion as to the importance of soup is to consider the purposes it serves in a meal. When its variety and the ingredients of which it is composed are thought of, soup serves two purposes: first, as an appetizer taken at the beginning of a meal to stimulate the appetite and aid in the flow of digestive juices in the stomach; and, secondly, as an actual part of the meal, when it must contain sufficient nutritive material to permit it to be considered as a part of the meal instead of merely an addition. Even in its first and minor purpose, the important part that soup plays in many meals is not hard to realize, for it is just what is needed to arouse the flagging appetite and create a desire for nourishing food. But in its second purpose, the real value of soup is evident. Whenever soup contains enough nutritive material for it to take the place of some dish that would otherwise be necessary, its value cannot be overestimated.

If soup is thought of in this way, the prejudice that exists against it in many households will be entirely overcome. But since much of this prejudice is due to the fact that the soup served is often unappetizing in both flavor and appearance, sufficient attention should be given to the making of soup to have this food attractive enough to appeal to the appetite rather than discourage it. Soup should not be greasy nor insipid in flavor, neither should it be served in large quantities nor without the proper accompaniment. A small quantity of well-flavored, attractively served soup cannot fail to meet the approval of any family when it is served as the first course of the meal.

5. General Classes of Soup.—Soups are named in various ways, according to material, quality, etc.; but the two purposes for which soup is used have led to the placing of the numerous kinds into two general classes. In the first class are grouped those which serve as appetizers, such as bouillon, consommé, and some other broths and clear soups. In the second class are included those eaten for their nutritive effect, such as cream soups, purées, and bisques. From these two classes of soup, the one that will correspond with the rest of the meal and make it balance properly is the one to choose. For instance, a light soup that is merely an appetizer should be served with a heavy dinner, whereas a heavy, highly nutritious soup should be used with a luncheon or a light meal.

6. Economic Value of Soup.—Besides having an important place in the meal of which it forms a part, soup is very often an economy, for it affords the housewife a splendid opportunity to utilize many left-overs. With the French people, who excel in the art of soup making chiefly because of their clever adaptation of seasoning to foods, their *pot-au-feu* is a national institution and every kitchen has its stock pot. Persons who believe in the strictest food economy use a stock pot, since it permits left-overs to be utilized in an attractive and palatable way. In fact, there is scarcely anything in the way of fish, meat, fowl, vegetables, and cereals that cannot be used in soup making, provided such ingredients are cared for in the proper way. Very often the first glance at the large number of ingredients listed in a soup recipe creates the impression that soup must be a very complicated thing. Such, however, is not the case. In reality, most of the soup ingredients are small quantities of things used for flavoring, and it is by the proper blending of these that appetizing soups are secured.

CLASSIFICATION OF SOUPS

7. The two general classes of soup already mentioned permit of numerous methods of classification. For instance, soups are sometimes named from the principal ingredient or an imitation of it, as the names potato soup, beef soup, macaroni soup, mock-turtle soup testify. Again, both stimulating and nutritious soups may be divided into thin and thick soups, thin soups usually being clear, and thick soups, because of their nature, cloudy. When the quality of soups is considered, they are placed in still different classes and are called broth, bisque, consommé, purée, and so on. Another important classification of soups results from the nationality of the people who use them. While soups are classified in other ways, it will be sufficient for all practical purposes if the housewife understands these three principal classes.

8. Classes Denoting Consistency.—As has already been pointed out, soups are of only two kinds when their consistency is thought of, namely, *clear soups* and *thick soups*.

Clear soups are those made from carefully cleared stock, or soup foundation, and flavored or garnished with a material from which the soup usually takes its name. There are not many soups of this kind, *bouillon* and *consommé* being the two leading varieties, but in order to be palatable, they require considerable care in making.

Thick soups are also made from stock, but milk, cream, water, or any mixture of these may also be used as a basis, and to it may be added for thickening meat, fish, vegetables, eggs, or grain or some other starchy material. Soups of this kind are often made too thick, and as such soups are not appetizing, care must be taken to have them just right in consistency.

9. Classes Denoting Quality.—When attention is given to the quality of soup, this food divides itself into several varieties, namely, *broth, cream soup, bisque, chowder,* and *purée.*

Broths have for their foundation a clear stock. They are sometimes a thin soup, but other times they are made quite thick with vegetables, rice, barley, or other material, when they are served as a substantial part of a meal.

Cream soups are highly nutritious and are of great variety. They have for their foundation a thin cream sauce, but to this are always added vegetables, meat, fish, or grains.

Bisques are thick, rich soups made from game, fish, or shell fish, particularly crabs, shrimp, etc. Occasionally, vegetables are used in soup of this kind.

Chowders are soups that have sea food for their basis. Vegetables and crackers are generally added for thickening and to impart flavor.

Purées are soups made thick partly or entirely by the addition of some material obtained by boiling an article of food and then straining it to form a pulp. When vegetables containing starch, such as beans, peas, lentils, and potatoes, are used for this purpose, it is unnecessary to thicken the soup with any additional starch; but when meat, fish, or watery vegetables are used, other thickening is required. To be right, a purée should be nearly as smooth as thick cream and of the same consistency.

10. Classes Typical of Particular Countries.—Certain kinds of soup have been made so universally by the people of various countries that they have come to be regarded as national dishes and are always thought of as typical of the particular people by whom they are used. Among the best known of these soups are *Borsch,* a soup much used by the Russian people and made from beets, leeks, and sour cream; *Daikan,* a Japanese soup in which radishes are the principal ingredient; *Kouskous,* a soup favored by the people of Abyssinia and made from vegetables; *Krishara,* a rice soup that finds much favor in India; *Lebaba,* an Egyptian soup whose chief ingredients are honey, butter, and raisin water; *Minestra,* an Italian soup in which vegetables are combined; *Mulligatawny,* an Indian rice soup that is flavored with curry; *Potroka,* another kind of Russian soup, having giblets for its foundation; *Soljinka,* an entirely different variety of Russian soup, being made from fish and onions; and *Tarhonya,* a Hungarian soup containing noodles.

STOCK FOR SOUP

USES AND VARIETIES OF STOCK

11. Meaning and Use of Stock.—In order that soup-making processes may be readily grasped by the housewife, she should be thoroughly familiar with what is meant by *stock,* which forms the foundation of many soups. In looking into the derivation of this term, it will be found that the word stock comes from an Anglo-Saxon word meaning to stick, and that while it has many different uses, the idea of fixedness is expressed in every one of them. As is generally known, a stock of anything means a reserve supply of that thing stored away for future use. When applied to soup, stock is similar in meaning, for it refers to material stored or prepared in such a way that it may be kept for use in the making of certain kinds of soup. In a more definite sense, soup stock may be regarded as a liquid containing the juices and soluble parts of meat, bone, and vegetables, which have been extracted by long, slow cooking and which can be utilized in the making of soups, sauces, and gravies.

12. Soups in which stock is utilized include all the varieties made from beef, veal, mutton, and poultry. If clear stock is desired for the making of soup, only fresh meat and bones should be used and all material that will discolor the liquid in any way carefully avoided. For ordinary, unclarified soups, the trimmings and bones of roast, steak, or chops and the carcass of fowl can generally be utilized. However, very strongly flavored meat, such as mutton, or the fat from mutton should be used sparingly, if at all, on account of the strong flavor that it imparts.

13. Varieties of Stock.—Several kinds of stock are utilized in the making of soup, and the kind to employ depends on the soup desired. In determining the kind of stock required for the foundation of a soup, the housewife may be guided by the following classification:

First stock is made from meat and bones and then clarified and used for well-flavored, clear soups.

Second stock is made from the meat and the bones that remain after the first stock is strained off. More water is added to the remaining material, and this is then cooked with vegetables, which supply the needed flavor. Such stock serves very well for adding flavor to a nutritious soup made from vegetables or cereal foods.

Household stock is made by cooking meat and bones, either fresh or cooked, with vegetables or other material that will impart flavor and add nutritive value. Stock of this kind is used for ordinary soups.

Bone stock is made from meat bones to which vegetables are added for flavor, and it is used for making any of the ordinary soups.

Vegetable stock is made from either dried or fresh vegetables or both. Such stock is employed in making vegetable soups.

Game stock is made from the bones and trimmings of game to which vegetables are added for flavor. This kind of stock is used for making game soups.

Fish stock is made from fish or fish trimmings to which vegetables are added for flavor. Shell fish make especially good stock of this kind. Fish stock is employed for making chowders and fish soups.

14. Additional Uses of Stock.—As has already been shown, stock is used principally as a foundation for certain varieties of soup. This material, however, may be utilized in many other ways, being especially valuable in the use of left-over foods. Any bits of meat or fowl that are left over can be made into an appetizing dish by adding thickened stock to them and serving the combination over toast or rice. In fact, a large variety of made dishes can be devised if there is stock on hand to add for flavor. The convenience of a supply of stock will be apparent when it is realized that gravy or sauce for almost any purpose can be made from the contents of the stock pot.

15. Soup Extracts.—If a housewife does not have sufficient time to go through the various processes involved in making soup, her family need not be deprived of this article of diet, for there are a number of concentrated meat and vegetable extracts on the market for making soups quickly. The *meat extracts* are made of the same flavoring material as that which is drawn from meat in the making of stock. Almost all the liquid is evaporated and the result is a thick, dark substance that must be diluted greatly with water to obtain the basis for a soup or a broth. Some of the *vegetable extracts,* such as Japanese soy and English marmite, are so similar in appearance and taste to the meat extracts as to make it quite difficult to detect any difference. Both varieties of these extracts may be used for sauces and gravies, as well as for soups, but it should be remembered that they are not highly nutritious and are valuable merely for flavoring.

THE STOCK POT

16. Nature, Use, and Care of Stock Pot.—Among the utensils used for cooking there is probably none more convenient and useful than the stock pot. It is nothing more or less than a covered crock or pot like that shown in Fig. 1, into which materials that will make a well-flavored stock are put from time to time. From such a supply, stock can be drawn when it is needed for soup; then, when some is taken out, more water and materials may be added to replenish the pot. The stock pot should be made of either enamel or earthenware, since a metal pot of any kind is liable to impart flavor to the food. Likewise, its lid, or cover, should be tight-fitting, for then it will be an excellent utensil in which the materials may be stored until they are to be heated, when they can be poured or dipped into a saucepan or a kettle.

The stock pot, like any other utensil used for making soup, should receive considerable care, as it must be kept scrupulously clean. No stock pot should ever be allowed to stand from day to day without being emptied, thoroughly washed, and then exposed to the air for a while to dry.

17. Food Suitable for the Stock Pot.—Some one has said that nothing edible is out of place in the stock pot, and, to a great extent, this statement is true. Here should be put the bones from the cooked roast, as well as the trimmings cut from it before it went into the oven; the tough ends and bones of beefsteak; the trimmings or bones sent home by the butcher; the carcasses of fowls, together with any remains of stuffing and tough or left-over bits of meat; any left-over vegetables; the remains of the gravy or any unsweetened sauces used for meats or vegetables; the spoonful of left-over hash, stew, or stuffing; a left-over stuffed tomato or pepper; and the water in which rice, macaroni, or certain vegetables have been cooked. Of course, plain water can be used for the liquid, but the water in which such vegetables as cauliflower, carrots, beans, peas, asparagus, celery, and potatoes have been cooked is especially desirable, for, besides imparting flavor to the soup, it adds valuable mineral salts. However, when such things as left-over cereals, rice, macaroni, and green vegetables are to be utilized in soup, they should not be put in the stock pot; rather, they should be added to the stock after it is removed from the pot.

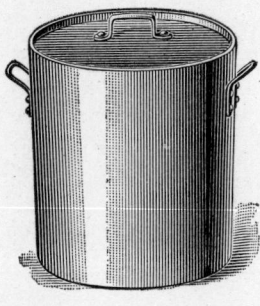

Fig. 1

MAKING OF SOUP

PRINCIPAL INGREDIENTS

18. The making of the stock that is used in soup is the most important of the soup-making processes; in fact, these two things—soup and stock—may be regarded, in many instances, as one and the same. The housewife will do well, therefore, to keep in mind that whenever reference is made to the making of soup usually stock making is also involved and meant. Before the actual soup-making processes are taken up, however, the nature of the ingredients required should be well understood; for this reason, suitable meats and vegetables, which are the principal ingredients in soups, are first discussed.

19. Meat Used for Soup Making.—With the exception of pork, almost every kind of meat, including beef, veal, mutton, lamb, game, and poultry, is used for soup making. Occasionally, ham is employed, but most other forms of pork are seldom used to any extent. When soup stock is made from these meats, they may be cooked separately, or, as a combination is often an improvement over a single variety, several kinds may be combined. For instance, mutton used alone makes a very strongly flavored soup, so that it is usually advisable to combine this kind of meat with another meat that has a less distinctive flavor. On the other hand, veal alone does not have sufficient flavor, so it must be combined with lamb, game, fowl, or some other well-flavored meat.

20. Certain cuts of meats are preferred to others in the making of soups, because of the difference in their texture. The tender cuts, which are the expensive ones, should not be used for soups, as they do not produce enough flavor. The tough cuts, which come from the muscles that the animal uses constantly and that therefore grow hard and tough, are usually cheaper, but they are more suitable, because they contain the material that makes the best soup. The pieces best adapted to soup making are the shins, the shanks, the lower part of the round, the neck, the flank, the shoulder, the tail, and the brisket. The parts of the animal from which these cuts are taken are clearly shown in Fig. 2. Although beef is obtained from the animal shown, the same cuts come from practically the same places in other animals. Stock made from one of these cuts will be improved if a small amount of the fat of the meat is cooked with it; but to avoid soup that is too greasy, any excess fat that remains after cooking should be carefully removed. The marrow of the shin bone is the best fat for soup making.

If soup is to be made from fish, a white variety should be selected. The head and trimmings may be utilized, but these alone are not sufficient, because soup requires some solid pieces of meat. The same is true of meat bones; they are valuable only when they are used with meat, an equal proportion of bone and meat being required for the best stock.

21. Vegetables Used for Soup Making.—In soup making, the housewife has also a large number of vegetables from which

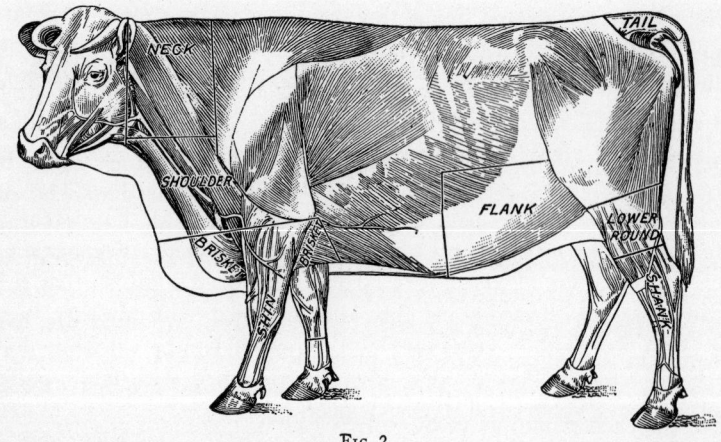

Fig. 2

to select, for any vegetable that has a decided flavor may be used. Among those from which soups can be made successfully are cabbage, cauliflower, asparagus, corn, onions, turnips, carrots, parsnips, tomatoes, beans, peas, lentils, salsify, potatoes, spinach, celery, mushrooms, okra, and even sweet potatoes. These vegetables are used for two purposes: to provide flavoring and to form part of the soup itself as well as to furnish flavor. When they are used simply for flavoring, they are cooked until their flavor is obtained and then removed from the stock. When they are to form part of the soup, as well as to impart flavor, they are left in the soup in small pieces or made into a purée and eaten with the soup.

Attention, too, must be given to the condition of the vegetables that are used in soup. The fresh vegetables that are used should be in perfect condition. They should have no decayed places that might taint or discolor the soups, and they should be as crisp and solid as possible. If they are somewhat withered or faded, they can be freshened by allowing them to stand in cold water for a short time. When dried vegetables are to be used for soup making, they should first be soaked well in cold water and then, before being added to the stock, either partly cooked or entirely cooked and made into a purée.

PROCESSES INVOLVED IN MAKING STOCK

22. Although the making of stock or soup is a simple process, it must necessarily be a rather long one. The reason for this is that all flavor cannot be drawn from the soup materials unless they are subjected to long, slow cooking at a temperature lower than the boiling point. With this point definitely understood, the actual work of soup making may be taken up.

23. Cooking Meat for Soup.—When clear stock is to be made from fresh meat, the required quantity of meat should be cut into small pieces rather than large ones, so as to expose as much of the surface as possible from which the flavor of the meat can be drawn. A little more flavor is obtained and a brown color developed if a small part, perhaps a fourth, of the pieces of meat are first browned in the frying pan. The pieces thus browned, together with the pieces of fresh meat, are put into a kettle and a quart of cold water for each pound of meat is then added.

The reason for using cold rather than hot water will be evident when the action of water on raw meat is understood. The fiber of meat is composed of innumerable thread-like tubes containing the flavor that is to be drawn out into the water in order to make the stock appetizing. When the meat is cut, these tiny tubes are laid open. Putting the meat thus prepared into cold water and allowing it to heat gradually tend to extract the contents of the tubes. This material is known as *extractives,* and it contains in its composition stimulating substances. On the other hand, plunging the meat into hot water and subjecting it quickly to a high temperature will coagulate the protein in the tissue and prevent the extractives from leaving the tubes.

24. To obtain the most flavor from meat that is properly prepared, it should be put over a slow fire and allowed to come gradually to the boiling point. As the water approaches the boiling point, a scum consisting of coagulated albumin, blood, and foreign material will begin to rise to the top, but this should be skimmed off at once and the process of skimming continued until no scum remains. When the water begins to boil rapidly, either the fire should be lowered or the kettle should be removed to a cooler part of the stove so that the water will bubble only enough for a very slight motion to be observed. Throughout the cooking, the meat should not be allowed to boil violently nor to cease bubbling entirely.

The meat should be allowed to cook for at least 4 hours, but longer if possible. If, during this long cooking, too much water evaporates, more should be added to dilute the stock. The salt that is required for seasoning may be added just a few minutes before the stock is removed from the kettle. However, it is better to add the salt, together with the other seasonings, after the stock has been drawn off, for salt, like heat, has a tendency to harden the tissues of meat and to prevent the flavor from being readily extracted.

25. Although, as has been explained, flavor is drawn from the fibers of meat by boiling it slowly for a long time, the cooking of meat for soup does not extract the nourishment from it to any extent. In reality, the meat itself largely retains its original nutritive value after it has been cooked for soup, although a small quantity of protein is drawn out and much of the fat is removed. This meat should never be wasted; rather, it should be used carefully with materials that will take the place of the flavor that has been cooked from it.

26. Flavoring Stock.—It is the flavoring of stock that indicates real skill in soup making, so this is an extremely important part of the work. In fact, the large number of ingredients found in soup recipes are, as a rule, the various flavorings, which give the distinctive flavor and individuality to a soup. However, the housewife whose larder will not produce all of the many things that may be called for in a recipe should not feel that she must forego making a particular kind of soup. Very often certain spices or certain flavoring materials may be omitted without any appreciable difference, or something that is on hand may be substituted for an ingredient that is lacking.

27. The flavorings used most for soup include cloves, peppercorns, red, black, and white pepper, paprika, bay leaf, sage, marjoram, thyme, summer savory, tarragon, celery seed, fennel, mint, and rosemary. While all of these are not absolutely necessary, the majority of them may well be kept on the pantry shelf. In addition, a bottle of Worcestershire sauce should be kept on hand. Celery and parsley, which are also much used for flavoring, can usually be purchased fresh, but as they are scarce at times it is advisable to dry some of the leaves during the season when they can be secured, so as to have a supply when they are not in the market. A small amount of lemon peel often improves soup, so some of this should be kept in store. Another group of vegetables that lend themselves admirably to soup flavoring includes leeks, shallots, chives, garlic, and onions, all of which belong to the same family. They must be used judiciously, however, as a strong flavor of any of them is offensive to most persons.

28. As many of the flavorings used for soup lose their strength when they are exposed to the air, every effort should be made to keep them in good condition. Many of them can be kept an indefinite length of time if they are placed in tightly closed metal boxes or glass jars. Flavorings and spices bought from the grocer or the druggist in paper packages should be transferred to, and enclosed in, a receptacle that will not allow them to deteriorate. If proper attention is given to these materials, the supply will not have to be replenished often; likewise, the cost of a sufficient number to produce the proper flavorings will be very slight.

29. In the use of any of the flavorings mentioned or the strongly flavored vegetables, care should be taken not to allow any one particular flavor to predominate. Each should be used in such quantity that it will blend well with the others. A very good way in which to fix spices and herbs that are to flavor soup is to tie them in a small piece of cheesecloth and drop the bag thus made into the soup pot. When prepared in this way, they will remain together, so that, while the flavor can be cooked out, they can be more readily removed from the liquid than if they are allowed to spread through the contents of the pot. Salt, which is, of course, always used to season soup, should be added in the proportion of 1 teaspoonful to each quart of liquid.

30. Removing Grease From Soup.—A greasy soup is always unpalatable. Therefore, a very important feature of soup making, whether a thin or a thick soup is being made, is the removal of all grease. Various ways of removing grease have been devised, depending on whether the soup is hot or cold. In the case of hot or warm soup, all the grease that it is possible to remove with a spoon may be skimmed from the top, and the remainder then taken up with a piece of clean blotting paper, tissue-paper, or absorbent cotton. Another plan, by which the fat may be hardened and then collected, consists in tying a few small pieces of ice in a piece of cloth and drawing them over the surface of the soup. A very simple method is to allow the soup or stock to become cold, and then remove the fat, which collects on the top and hardens, by merely lifting off the cake that forms.

31. Clearing Soup.—Sometimes it is desired to improve the appearance of soup stock, particularly a small amount of soup that is to be served at a very dainty luncheon or dinner. In order to do this, the stock may be treated by a certain process that will cause it to become clear. After being cleared, it may be served as a thin soup or, if it is heavy enough, it may be made into a clear, sparkling jelly into which many desirable things may be molded for salad or for a dish to accompany a heavy course. Clearing soup is rather extravagant; however, while it does not improve the taste, it does improve the appearance.

A very satisfactory way in which to clear stock is to use egg whites and crushed egg shell. To each quart of cold stock should be added the crushed shell and a slightly beaten egg white. These should be mixed well, placed on the fire, and the mixture stirred constantly until it boils. As the egg coagulates, some of the floating particles in the stock are caught and carried to the top, while others are carried to the bottom by the particles of shell as they settle. After the mixture has boiled for 5 or 10 minutes, the top should be skimmed carefully and the stock then strained through a fine cloth. When it has been reheated, the cleared stock will be ready to serve.

32. Thickening Soup.—Although thin, clear soups are preferred by some and are particularly desirable for their stimulating effect, thick soups find much favor when they are used to form a substantial part of a meal. Besides giving consistency to soup, thickening usually improves the flavor, but its chief purpose is to give nutritive value to this food. In fact, whenever a soup is thickened, its food value is increased by the ingredient thus added. For this reason, it is advisable to thicken soups when they are desired for any other purpose than their stimulating effect.

33. The substance used to thicken soups may be either a starchy material or food or a purée of some food. The starchy materials generally used for this purpose are plain flour, browned flour, corn starch, and arrowroot flour. Any one of these should be moistened with enough cold water to make a mixture that will pour easily, and then added to the hot liquid while the soup is stirred constantly to prevent the formation of lumps. A sufficient amount of this thickening material should be used to make a soup of the consistency of heavy cream.

The starchy foods that are used for thickening include rice, barley, oatmeal, noodles, tapioca, sago, and macaroni. Many unusual and fancy forms of macaroni can be secured, or the plain varieties of Italian pastes may be broken into small pieces and cooked with the soup. When any of these foods are used, they should be added long enough before the soup is removed to be cooked thoroughly.

Purées of beans, peas, lentils, potatoes, and other vegetables are especially desirable for the thickening of soups, for they not only give consistency, but add nutritive value and flavor as well. Another excellent thickening may be obtained by beating raw eggs and then adding them carefully to the soup just before it is to be served. After eggs have been added for thickening, the soup should not be allowed to boil, as it is liable to curdle.

34. Keeping Stock.—Soup stock, like many other foods, spoils quite readily. Therefore, in order to keep it for at least a few days, it must receive proper attention. At all times, the vessel containing stock should be tightly closed and, especially in warm weather, the stock should be kept as cold as possible. Stock that is heavy enough to solidify into a jellylike consistency when it is cold will keep better than stock that remains liquid. The addition of salt or any spicy flavoring also helps to keep stock from deteriorating, because these materials act as preservatives and prevent the action of bacteria that cause spoiling. Bacteria may be kept from entering soup if, instead of removing the grease, it is allowed to form in a solid cake over the top. No matter which of these precautions is taken to prevent stock from spoiling, it should be heated to boiling point once a day when it is to be kept for several days.

SERVING SOUP

35. Soup may be correctly served in several different ways, the method to adopt usually depending on the kind of soup. Thin, clear soups are generally served in bouillon cups, as shown in Fig. 3, which may be placed on the table immediately before the family assembles or passed after the members are seated. Heavier soups may be served at the table from a soup tureen, or each person's portion

Fig. 3

may be served before the family comes to the table. For soups of this kind, the flat soup plate, like that shown in Fig. 4, is found preferable.

The spoon to be served with soup also depends on the kind of soup, but a larger spoon than a teaspoon is always necessary. When soup is served in a soup plate, a dessert spoon is used, as will be observed in Fig. 4. A bouillon spoon is the best kind to use with any thin soup served in bouillon cups. Such a spoon, as shown in Fig. 3, is about the length of a teaspoon, but has a round bowl.

36. To increase the attractiveness of soup and at the same time make it more appetizing and nutritious, various accompaniments and relishes are served with it. When the accompaniment is in the form of crackers, croutons, or bread sticks, they may be passed after the soup is served, or, as shown in Figs. 3 and 4, a few of them may be placed on the bread-and-butter plate at each person's place.

The relishes should be passed while the soup is being eaten. Plain whipped cream or whipped cream into which a little mashed pimiento has been stirred adds much to the flavor and appearance of soup when served on the top of any hot or cold variety. Then, too, many soups, especially vegetable soups, are improved in flavor by the addition of a spoonful of grated cheese, which should be sprinkled into the dish at the time of serving. For this purpose, a

Fig. 4

hard, dry cheese, such as Parmesan, which can often be purchased already grated in bottles, is the most satisfactory.

37. In summer, clear soups are sometimes served cold, as cold soups are found more desirable for warm weather than hot ones. However, when a soup is intended to be hot, it should be hot when it is ready to be eaten, and every effort should be made to have it in this condition if an appetizing soup is desired. This can be accomplished if the soup is thoroughly heated before it is removed from the stove and the dishes in which it is to be served are warmed before the soup is put into them.

RECIPES FOR SOUP AND SOUP ACCOMPANIMENTS

NECESSITY FOR CAREFUL WORK

38. So that the housewife may put into practice the knowledge she has gained about soup making, there are here given recipes for various kinds of soup. As will be observed, these recipes are classified according to the consistency and nature of the soups, all those of one class being placed in the same group. As it is important, too, for the housewife to know how to prepare the various accompaniments and garnishes that are generally served with soup, directions for the making of these are also given and they follow the soup recipes.

39. In carrying out these recipes, it will be well to note that exactness in fulfilling the requirements and care in working out the details of the recipes are essential. These points cannot be ignored in the making of soup any more than in other parts of cookery, provided successful results and excellent appearance are desired. It is therefore wise to form habits of exactness. For instance, when vegetables are to be cut for soups, they should be cut into pieces of equal size, or, if they are to be diced, they should be cut so that the dice are alike. All the pieces must be of the same thickness in order to insure uniform cooking; if this precaution is not observed, some of the pieces are likely to overcook and fall to pieces before the others are done.

Strict attention should also be given to the preparation of other ingredients and the accompaniments. The meat used must be cut very carefully rather than in ragged, uneven pieces. Noodles, which are often used in soup, may be of various widths; but all those used at one time should be uniform in width—that is, all wide or all narrow. If different widths are used, an impression of careless cutting will be given. Croutons and bread sticks, to be most satisfactory, should be cut straight and even, and, in order to toast uniformly, all those made at one time should be of the same size.

STOCKS AND CLEAR SOUPS

40. Stock for Clear Soup or Bouillon.—A plain, but well-flavored, beef stock may be made according to the accompanying recipe and used as a basis for any clear soup served as bouillon without the addition of anything else. However, as the addition of rice, barley, chopped macaroni, or any other such food will increase the food value of the soup, any of them may be supplied to produce a more nutritious soup. When this stock is served clear, it should be used as the first course in a comparatively heavy meal.

STOCK FOR CLEAR SOUP OR BOUILLON

4 lb. beef	6 whole cloves
4 qt. cold water	12 peppercorns
1 medium-sized onion	1 bay leaf
1 stalk celery	Salt
2 sprigs parsley	Pepper

Cut the meat into small pieces. Pour the cold water over it, place on a slow fire, and let it come to a boil. Skim off all scum that rises to the top. Cover tightly and keep at the simmering point for 6 to 8 hours. Then strain and remove the fat. Add the onion and celery cut into pieces, the parsley, cloves, peppercorns, and bay leaf. Simmer gently for about 20 minutes. Add salt and pepper to taste. Strain through a cloth.

41. Household Stock.—If it is desired to make a stock that may be kept on hand constantly and that may be used as a foundation for various kinds of soups, sauces, and gravies, or as a broth for making casserole dishes, household stock will be found very satisfactory. Such stock made in quantity and kept in a sufficiently cool place may be used for several days before it spoils. Since most of the materials used in this stock cannot be put to any other particularly good use, and since the labor required in making it is slight, this may be regarded as an extremely economical stock.

HOUSEHOLD STOCK

3 qt. cold water	4 cloves
3 lb. meat (trimmings of fresh meat, bones, and tough pieces from roasts, steaks, etc.)	6 peppercorns
	Herbs
	Salt
1 medium-sized onion	Pepper

Pour the cold water over the meat and bones and put them on the fire to cook. When they come to a boil skim well. Then cover and simmer 4 to 6 hours. Add the onion, cloves, peppercorns, and herbs and cook for another hour. Add salt and pepper to taste. Strain and set aside to cool. Remove the fat.

42. White Stock.—An especially nice broth having a delicate flavor and generally used for special functions when an attractive meal is being served to a large number of persons is made from veal and fowl and known as white stock. If allowed to remain in a cool place, this stock will solidify, and then it may be used as the basis for a jellied meat dish or salad.

WHITE STOCK

5 lb. veal	2 stalks celery
1 fowl, 3 or 4 lb.	1 blade mace
8 qt. cold water	Salt
2 medium-sized onions	Pepper
2 Tb. butter	

Cut the veal and fowl into pieces and add the cold water. Place on a slow fire, and let come gradually to the boiling point. Skim carefully and place where it will simmer gently for 6 hours. Slice the onions, brown slightly in the butter, and add to the stock with the celery and mace. Salt and pepper to suit taste. Cook 1 hour longer and then strain and cool. Remove the fat before using.

43. Consommé.—One of the most delicious of the thin, clear broths is consommé. This is usually served plain, but any material that will not cloud it, such as finely diced vegetables, green peas, tiny pieces of fowl or meat, may, if desired, be added to it before it is served. As a rule, only a very small quantity of such material is used for each serving.

CONSOMMÉ

4 lb. lower round of beef	5 cloves
4 lb. shin of veal	4 sprigs parsley
¼ c. butter	Pinch summer savory
8 qt. cold water	Pinch thyme
1 small carrot	2 bay leaves
1 large onion	Salt
2 stalks celery	Pepper
12 peppercorns	

Cut the beef and veal into small pieces. Put the butter and meat into the stock kettle, and stir over the fire until the meat begins to brown. Add the cold water, and let come to the boiling point. Skim carefully and let simmer for 6 hours. Cut the vegetables into small pieces and add to the stock with the spices and herbs. Cook for 1 hour, adding salt and pepper to suit taste. Strain and cool. Remove the fat and clear according to directions previously given.

44. Tomato Bouillon.—It is possible to make a clear tomato soup without meat stock, but the recipe here given, which is made with meat stock, has the advantage of possessing a better flavor. The tomato in this bouillon lends an agreeable color and flavor and affords a change from the usual clear soup. Cooked rice, macaroni, spaghetti, or vermicelli may be added to tomato bouillon to provide an additional quantity of nutrition and vary the plain soup.

TOMATO BOUILLON
(Sufficient to Serve Eight)

1 qt. meat stock   ¼ tsp. pepper
1 tsp. salt   1 can tomatoes
1 Tb. sugar

Heat the stock, and to it add the salt, sugar, and pepper. Rub the tomatoes through a fine sieve, and add them to the stock. Cook together for a few minutes and serve.

HEAVY THICK SOUPS

45. Julienne Soup.—A very good way in which to utilize any small quantities of vegetables that may be in supply but are not sufficient to serve alone is to use them in julienne soup. For soup of this kind, vegetables are often cut into fancy shapes, but this is a more or less wasteful practice and should not be followed, as tiny strips or dice cut finely and carefully are quite as agreeable. The vegetables do not add a large amount of nutriment to this soup, but they introduce into the soup mineral salts that the soups would otherwise not have and they also add a variety of flavor.

JULIENNE SOUP
(Sufficient to Serve Six)

1 pt. mixed vegetables   1 qt. stock
½ tsp. salt   ¼ tsp. pepper

Cut into tiny dice or into strips such vegetables as celery, carrots, and turnips, making them as nearly the same size and shape as possible. Put them on to cook in enough boiling salted water to cover well. Cook until they are soft enough to be pierced with a fork, but do not lose their shape. Drain off the water and put the vegetables into the stock. Bring to the boiling point, season with the pepper, and serve.

46. Ox-Tail Soup.—The use of ox tails for soup helps to utilize a part of the beef that would ordinarily be wasted, and, as a rule, ox tails are comparatively cheap. Usually the little bits of meat that cook off the bones are allowed to remain in the soup. Variety may be obtained by the addition of different kinds of vegetables.

Ox-Tail Soup
(Sufficient to Serve Eight)

2 ox tails	1 Tb. mixed herbs
1 large onion	4 peppercorns
1 Tb. beef drippings	1 Tb. salt
4 qt. cold water	

Wash and cut up the ox tails, separating them at the joints. Slice the onion and brown it and half of the ox tails in the beef drippings. When they are browned, put them and the remainder of the ox tails into a kettle. Add the water and the herbs and peppercorns tied in a little piece of cheesecloth. Bring to the boiling point, and then simmer for 3 to 4 hours or until the meat separates from the bones. Add the salt an hour before serving the soup. Remove the fat and serve some of the nicest joints with the soup. If vegetables are desired, they should be diced and added 20 minutes before serving, so that they will be cooked soft.

47. Mulligatawny Soup.—If a highly seasoned soup is desired, mulligatawny, although not a particularly cheap soup, will be found very satisfactory. The curry powder that is used adds an unusual flavor that is pleasing to many people, but if it is not desired, it may be omitted.

Mulligatawny Soup
(Sufficient to Serve Eight)

3 lb. chicken	4 cloves
1 lb. veal	1 stalk celery
4 qt. cold water	1 Tb. curry powder
2 onions	1 tsp. salt
1 Tb. butter	$\frac{1}{4}$ tsp. pepper
4 peppercorns	1 lemon

Cut up the chicken and veal, add the cold water to them, and place over a slow fire. Slice the onions and brown them in the butter. Add them and the peppercorns, cloves, chopped celery, and curry powder stirred to a smooth paste with a little water to the meat.

Simmer together slowly until the chicken is tender. Remove the meat from the bones and cut it into small pieces. Put the bones into the kettle and simmer for another hour. Strain the liquid from the veal and bones and remove the fat. Add the salt, pepper, chicken, and the juice of the lemon. Return to the fire and cook for a few minutes. Serve with a tablespoonful or two of cooked rice in each soup dish.

48. Noodle Soup.—The addition of noodles to soup increases its food value to a considerable extent by providing carbohydrate from the flour and protein from the egg and flour. Noodle soup is a very attractive dish if the noodles are properly made, for then they will not cause the soup to become cloudy when they are put into it. Little difficulty will be experienced if the directions here given for making noodles are followed explicitly.

NOODLE SOUP
(Sufficient to Serve Six)

1 egg   1 qt. household stock
1 Tb. milk   3 sprigs parsley
½ tsp. salt   1 small onion
Flour

To make noodles, beat the egg slightly, add to it the milk, and stir in the salt and enough flour to make a stiff dough. Toss upon a

FIG. 5

floured board and roll very thin. Allow the dough to dry for ½ hour or more, and then, as shown in Fig. 5, cut it into strips about 4 inches wide. Place several strips together, one on top of the other, and roll them up tight, in the manner indicated. Cut each roll into thin slices with a sharp knife, as shown in Fig. 6. When the slices are separated the noodles should appear as shown in the pile at the right. If it is desired not to follow this plan, the dough may be rolled into a thin sheet and cut into strips with a noodle cutter.

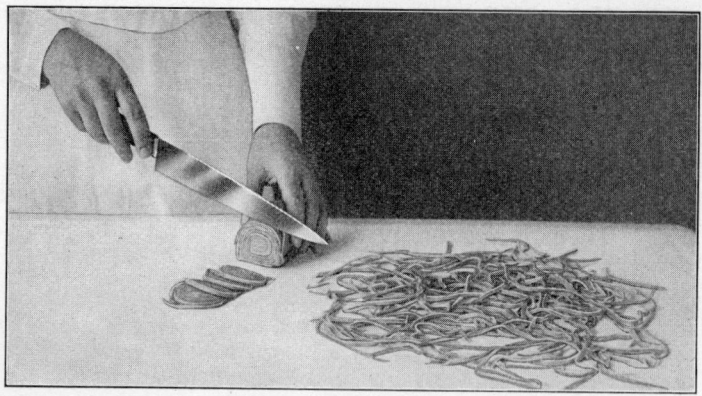

Fig. 6

Such a supply of noodles may be used at once, or they may be dried thoroughly and sealed tightly in a jar for future use. The very dry ones, however, require a little longer cooking than those which are freshly made. With the noodles prepared, heat the stock with the parsley and onion chopped very fine. Add the noodles and cook for 15 or 20 minutes or until the noodles are thoroughly cooked.

Rice, barley, macaroni, and other starchy materials may be added to stock in the same way as the noodles.

49. Vegetable Soup With Noodles.—The combination of noodles and vegetables in soup is a very excellent one, since the vegetables add flavor and the noodles add nutritive value. If the vegetables given in the accompanying recipe cannot be readily obtained, others may be substituted.

VEGETABLE SOUP WITH NOODLES
(Sufficient to Serve Six)

1 carrot
1 onion
1 turnip
1 stalk celery
1 c. boiling water
$\frac{1}{2}$ tsp. salt
$\frac{1}{2}$ c. noodles
2 sprigs parsley
$\frac{1}{8}$ tsp. pepper
1 qt. household stock

Dice the vegetables and put them on to cook with the boiling water and the salt. Cook for a few minutes or until partly soft. Add the noodles, parsley, pepper, and stock and cook for 15 minutes longer. Serve.

CREAM SOUPS

50. Soups classed as cream soups consist of a thin white sauce to which is added a vegetable in the form of a purée or cut into small pieces. Because of their nature, cream soups are usually high in food value; but they are not highly flavored, so their use is that of supplying nutrition rather than stimulating the appetite. Considerable variety can be secured in cream soups, for there are scarcely any vegetables that cannot be used in the making of them. Potatoes, corn, asparagus, spinach, peas, tomatoes, and onions are the vegetables that are used oftenest, but cream soups may also be made of vegetable oysters, okra, carrots, watercress, celery, cabbage, cauliflower, beans, lentils, and dried peas. The

Fig. 7

vegetables may be cooked especially for the soup, or left-over or canned vegetables may be utilized. It is an excellent plan to cook more than enough of some vegetables for one day, so that some will be left over and ready for soup the next day.

If the vegetable is not cut up into small pieces, it must be put through a sieve and made into the form of a purée before it can be added to the liquid. Two kinds of sieves for this purpose are shown in Fig. 7. It will be observed that with the large, round sieve, a potato masher must be used to mash the vegetables, the pulp of which is caught by the utensil in which the sieve is held. In making use of the smaller sieve, or ricer, the vegetable is placed in it and then mashed by pressing the top down over the contents with the aid of the handles.

51. Thin White Sauce.—The liquid for cream soups should be thin white sauce made entirely of milk or of milk and cream. The flavor of the soup will be improved, however, by using with the milk some meat stock, or the stock that remains from cooking celery, asparagus, or any vegetables that will lend a good flavor to the soup. The recipe here given makes a sauce that may be used for any kind of cream soup.

THIN WHITE SAUCE

1 pt. milk, or milk and cream or stock	2 Tb. butter
1 tsp. salt	2 Tb. flour

Heat the liquid, salt, and butter in a double boiler. Stir the flour and some of the cold liquid that has been reserved to a perfectly smooth, thin paste and add to the hot liquid. Stir constantly after adding the flour, so that no lumps will form. When the sauce becomes thick, it is ready for the addition of any flavoring material that will make a palatable soup. If thick material, such as any vegetable in the form of a purée, rice, or potato, is used without additional liquid, only half as much flour will be required to thicken the sauce.

52. Cream-of-Potato Soup.—Because of the large quantity of carbohydrate derived from the potato, cream-of-potato soup is high in food value. For persons who are fond of the flavor of the potato, this makes a delicious soup and one that may be served as the main dish in a light meal.

CREAM-OF-POTATO SOUP
(Sufficient to Serve Four)

2 slices of onion	1 Tb. flour
1 sprig parsley	2 Tb. butter
2 medium-sized potatoes	1 tsp. salt
1 c. milk	$\frac{1}{8}$ tsp. pepper
1 c. potato water	

Cook the onion and parsley with the potatoes, and, when cooked soft, drain and mash. Make a sauce of the milk, potato water, flour, and butter. Season with the salt and pepper, add the mashed potato, and serve.

53. Cream-of-Corn Soup.—The flavor of corn is excellent in a cream soup, the basis of the soup being milk, butter, and flour. Then, too, the addition of the corn, which is comparatively high in food value, makes a very nutritious soup.

CREAM-OF-CORN SOUP
(Sufficient to Serve Four)

1 pt. milk	1 c. canned corn
1 Tb. butter	1 tsp. salt
1 Tb. flour	$\frac{1}{8}$ tsp. pepper

Make a white sauce of the milk, butter, and flour. Force the corn through a colander or a sieve, and add the purée to the white sauce. Season with the salt and pepper, and serve.

54. Cream-of-Asparagus Soup.—The asparagus used in cream-of-asparagus soup adds very little besides flavor, but this is of sufficient value to warrant its use. If a pinch of soda is used in asparagus soup, there is less danger of the curdling that sometimes occurs. In making this soup, the asparagus should be combined with the white sauce just before serving.

CREAM-OF-ASPARAGUS SOUP
(Sufficient to Serve Four)

1 pt. milk	1 c. asparagus purée
2 Tb. flour	1 tsp. salt
2 Tb. butter	$\frac{1}{8}$ tsp. pepper

Make white sauce of the milk, flour, and butter. Add to it the cup of purée made by forcing freshly cooked or canned asparagus through a sieve. Season with the salt and pepper, and serve.

55. Cream-of-Spinach Soup.—Although cream-of-spinach soup is not especially attractive in appearance, most persons enjoy its flavor, and the soup serves as another way of adding an iron-containing food to the diet. Children may often be induced to take the soup when they would refuse the spinach as a vegetable.

CREAM-OF-SPINACH SOUP
(Sufficient to Serve Four)

1 pt. milk	$\frac{1}{2}$ c. spinach purée
2 Tb. flour	1 tsp. salt
2 Tb. butter	$\frac{1}{8}$ tsp. pepper

Make white sauce of the milk, flour, and butter. Add the spinach purée, made by forcing freshly cooked or canned spinach through a sieve. Season with the salt and pepper, heat thoroughly, and serve.

56. Cream-of-Pea Soup.—Either dried peas or canned green peas may be used to make cream-of-pea soup. If dried peas are used, they must first be cooked soft enough to pass through a sieve. The flavor is quite different from that of green peas. With the use of green peas, a fair amount of both protein and carbohydrate is added to the soup, but more protein is provided when dried peas are used.

CREAM-OF-PEA SOUP
(Sufficient to Serve Four)

1 pt. milk   ½ c. pea purée
1 Tb. flour   1 tsp. salt
2 Tb. butter   ⅛ tsp. pepper

Make white sauce of the milk, flour, and butter. Put enough freshly cooked or canned peas through a sieve to make ½ cupful of purée. Then add the pea purée, the salt, and the pepper to the white sauce. Heat thoroughly and serve.

57. Cream-of-Tomato Soup.—As a rule, cream-of-tomato soup is popular with every one. Besides being pleasing to the taste, it is comparatively high in food value, because its basis is cream sauce. However, the tomatoes themselves add very little else besides flavor and mineral salts.

CREAM-OF-TOMATO SOUP
(Sufficient to Serve Four)

1 c. canned tomatoes   ⅛ tsp. soda
1 pt. milk   1 tsp. salt
3 Tb. flour   ⅛ tsp. pepper
3 Tb. butter

Force the tomatoes through a sieve and heat them. Make white sauce of the milk, flour, and butter. Add the soda to the tomatoes, and pour them slowly into the white sauce, stirring rapidly. If the sauce begins to curdle, beat the soup quickly with a rotary egg beater. Add the salt and pepper and serve.

58. Cream-of-Onion Soup.—Many persons who are not fond of onions can often eat soup made of this vegetable. This is probably due to the fact that the browning of the onions before they are used in the soup improves the flavor very decidedly. In addition, this treatment of the onions gives just a little color to the soup.

CREAM-OF-ONION SOUP
(Sufficient to Serve Four)

4 medium-sized onions   2½ c. milk
4 Tb. butter   1 tsp. salt
2 Tb. flour   ⅛ tsp. pepper

Slice the onions and brown them in a frying pan with 2 tablespoonfuls of the butter. Make white sauce of the flour, the remaining butter, and the milk. Add to this the browned onions, salt, and pepper. Heat thoroughly and serve.

PURÉES

59. Chestnut Purée.—There are many recipes for the use of chestnuts in the making of foods, but probably none is any more popular than that for chestnut purée. The chestnuts develop a light-tan color in the soup. The very large ones should be purchased for this purpose, since chestnuts of ordinary size are very tedious to work with.

Chestnut Purée
(Sufficient to Serve Four)

1 c. mashed chestnuts	1 tsp. salt
1 c. milk	⅛ tsp. pepper
2 Tb. flour	⅛ tsp. celery salt
2 Tb. butter	1 c. white stock

Cook Spanish chestnuts for 10 minutes; then remove the shells and skins and mash the chestnuts. Make white sauce of the milk, flour, and butter. Add to this the mashed chestnuts, salt, pepper, celery salt, and stock. Heat thoroughly and serve.

60. Split-Pea Purée.—Dried peas or split peas are extremely high in food value, and their addition to soup stock makes a highly nutritious soup of very delightful flavor. Such a purée served in quantity does nicely for the main dish in a light meal. Instead of the peas, dried beans or lentils may be used if they are preferred.

Split-Pea Purée
(Sufficient to Serve Four)

¾ c. split peas	⅛ tsp. pepper
1 pt. white stock	2 Tb. butter
1 tsp. salt	2 Tb. flour

Soak the peas overnight, and cook in sufficient water to cover well until they are soft. When thoroughly soft, drain the water from the peas and put them through a colander. Heat the stock and add to it the pea purée, salt, and pepper. Rub the butter and flour together, moisten with some of the warm liquid, and add to the soup. Cook for a few minutes and serve.

CHOWDERS

61. Clam Chowder.—The flavor of clams, like that of oysters and other kinds of sea food, is offensive to some persons, but where this is not the case, clam chowder is a popular dish of high food value. This kind of soup is much used in localities where clams are plentiful.

CLAM CHOWDER
(Sufficient to Serve Eight)

1 c. water	$\frac{1}{2}$ c. diced celery
1 qt. clams	$1\frac{1}{2}$ c. milk
1 small onion	2 Tb. butter
1 c. sliced potatoes	$1\frac{1}{2}$ tsp. salt
$\frac{1}{2}$ c. stewed tomatoes	$\frac{1}{8}$ tsp. pepper
$\frac{1}{2}$ c. diced carrots	

Add the water to the clams, and pick them over carefully to remove any shell. Strain the liquid through cheesecloth, and then scald the clams in it. Remove the clams and cook the vegetables in the liquid until they are soft. Add the milk, butter, salt, and pepper and return the clams. Heat thoroughly and serve over crackers.

62. Fish Chowder.—An excellent way in which to utilize a small quantity of fish is afforded by fish chowder. In addition, this dish is quite high in food value, so that when it is served with crackers, little of anything else need be served with it to make an entire meal if it be luncheon or supper. Cod, haddock, or freshwater fish may be used in the accompanying recipe.

FISH CHOWDER
(Sufficient to Serve Six)

2 lb. fish	$1\frac{1}{2}$ tsp. salt
1 small onion	$\frac{1}{8}$ tsp. pepper
1 c. sliced potatoes	2 Tb. butter
$\frac{1}{2}$ c. stewed tomatoes	$1\frac{1}{2}$ c. milk

Skin the fish, remove the flesh, and cut it into small pieces. Simmer the head, bones, and skin of the fish and the onion in water for $\frac{1}{2}$ hour. Strain, and add to this stock the fish, potatoes, tomatoes, salt, and pepper. Simmer together until the potatoes are soft. Add the butter and milk. Serve over crackers.

63. Potato Chowder.—A vegetable mixture such as the one suggested in the accompanying recipe is in reality not a chowder, for this form of soup requires sea food for its basis. However, when it is impossible to procure the sea food, potato chowder does nicely as a change from the usual soup. This chowder differs in no material way from soup stock in this form.

Potato Chowder
(Sufficient to Serve Four)

1½ c. sliced potatoes	1 tsp. salt
1 small onion, sliced	⅛ tsp. pepper
1 c. water	2 Tb. butter
1½ c. milk	

Cook the potatoes and onion in the water until they are soft, but not soft enough to fall to pieces. Rub half of the potatoes through a sieve and return to the sliced ones. Add the milk, salt, pepper, and butter. Cook together for a few minutes and serve.

64. Corn Chowder.—The addition of corn to potato chowder adds variety of flavor and makes a delicious mixture of vegetables. This dish is rather high in food value, especially if the soup is served over crackers. A small amount of tomato, although not mentioned in the recipe, may be added to this combination to improve the flavor.

Corn Chowder
(Sufficient to Serve Six)

1 c. sliced potatoes	1½ c. milk
1 small onion, sliced	2 Tb. butter
1 c. water	1 tsp. salt
1 c. canned corn	⅛ tsp. pepper

Cook the potatoes and onions in the water until they are soft. Add the corn, milk, butter, salt, and pepper, and cook together for a few minutes. Serve over crackers.

SOUP ACCOMPANIMENTS AND GARNISHES

65. The soup course of a meal is a more or less unattractive one, but it may be improved considerably if some tempting thing in the way of a garnish or an accompaniment is served with it. But whatever is selected to accompany soup should be, in a great measure, a contrast to it in both consistency and color. The reason why a difference in consistency is necessary is due to the nature of soup, which, being liquid in form, is merely swallowed and does not stimulate the flow of the gastric juices by mastication. Therefore, the accompaniment should be something that requires chewing and that will consequently cause the digestive juices, which respond to the mechanical action of chewing, to flow. The garnish may add the color that is needed to make soup attractive. The green and red of olives and radishes or of celery and radishes make a decided contrast, so that when any of these things are served with soup, an appetizing first course is the result. It is not necessary to serve more than one of them, but if celery and radishes or celery, radishes, and olives can be combined in the same relish dish, they become more attractive than when each is served by itself.

FIG. 8

66. Radishes and Celery.—Before radishes and celery are used on the table, whether with soup or some other part of a meal, they should be put into cold water and allowed to stand for some time, so that they will be perfectly crisp when they are served. In the case of radishes, the tops and roots should first be cut from them, and the radishes then scrubbed thoroughly. They may be served without any further treatment, or they may be prepared to resemble flowers, as is shown in Fig. 8. This may be done by peeling the red skin back to show the white inside, and then cutting the sections to look like the petals of a flower. Little difficulty will be

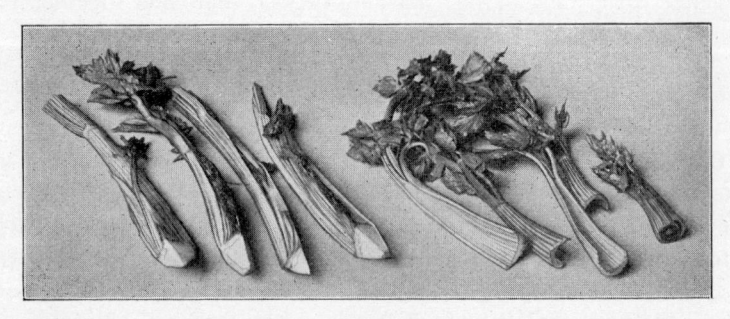

FIG. 9

experienced in preparing radishes in this artistic way if a sharp knife is used, for, with a little practice, the work can be done quickly and skilfully.

67. Celery that is to be served with soup may be prepared in two ways, as Fig. 9 illustrates. The stems may be pulled from the stalk and served separately, as in the group on the right, or the stalk may be cut down through the center with a knife into four or more pieces, as shown at the left of the illustration. The first of these methods is not so good as the second, for by it one person gets all of the tender heart and the coarse outside stems are left for all the others. By the second method, every piece consists of some of the heart and some of the outside stems attached to the root and makes a similar serving for each person. Whichever way is adopted, however, the celery should be scrubbed and cleansed thoroughly. This is often a difficult task, because the dirt sticks tightly between the stems. Still, an effort should be made to have the celery entirely free from dirt before it goes to the table. A few tender yellow leaves may be left on the pieces to improve the appearance of the celery.

68. Crackers.—Various kinds of wafers and crackers can be purchased to serve with soup, and the selection, as well as the serving of them, is entirely a matter of individual taste. One point, however, that must not be overlooked is that crackers of any kind must be crisp in order to be appetizing. Dry foods of this sort absorb moisture from the air when they are exposed to it and consequently become tough. As heat drives off this moisture and restores the original crispness, crackers should always be heated before they are served. Their flavor can be improved by toasting them until they are light brown in color.

69. Croutons.—As has already been learned, croutons are small pieces of bread that have been fried or toasted to serve with soup. These are usually made in the form of cubes, or dice, as is shown in the front group in Fig. 10; but they may be cut into triangles, circles, ovals, hearts, or, in fact, any fancy shape, by means of small cutters that can be purchased for such purposes. The bread used for croutons should not be fresh bread, as such bread does not toast nor fry very well; left-over toast, stale bread, or slices of bread that have been cut from the loaf and not eaten are usually found more satisfactory. If the croutons are not made from slices already cut, the bread should be cut into slices $\frac{1}{4}$ to $\frac{1}{2}$ inch thick, and, after the crusts have been closely trimmed, the slices should be cut into cubes. When the cubes have been obtained, they

WI—C3—4

may be put into a shallow pan and toasted on all sides quickly, placed in a frying basket and browned in deep fat, or put into a frying pan and sautéd in butter. If toast is used, it should merely be cut in the desired shape.

Various methods of serving croutons are in practice. Some housewives prefer to place them in the soup tureen and pour the soup over them, while others like to put a few in each individual serving of soup. A better plan, however, and one that is much followed, is to serve a number of croutons on a small plate or dish at each person's place, as shown in Figs. 3 and 4, for then every one may eat them in the way preferred.

70. Bread Sticks.—A soup accompaniment similar in nature to croutons, and known as *bread sticks,* is made of pieces of bread $\frac{1}{2}$ inch wide, $\frac{1}{2}$ inch thick, and several inches long. These are toasted

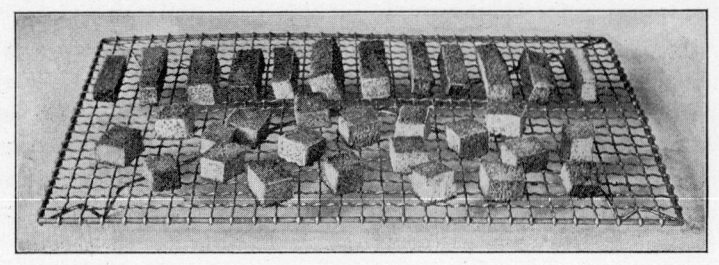

Fig. 10

on each side and are served in place of crackers. A number of them are shown in the back row in Fig. 10. Variety in bread sticks may be secured by spreading butter over them before the toasting is begun or by sprinkling grated cheese over them a few minutes before they are removed from the oven. Bread sticks are usually served on a bread-and-butter plate to the left of each person's place at the table.

71. Pastry Strips.—A very appetizing addition to soup may be made by cutting pastry into narrow strips and then baking these strips in the oven until they are brown or frying them in deep fat and draining them. Strips prepared in this way may be served in place of crackers, croutons, or bread sticks, and are considered delicious by those who are fond of pastry. Details regarding pastry are given in another Section.

72. Soup Fritters.—If an entirely different kind of soup accompaniment from those already mentioned is desired, soup fritters will no doubt find favor. These are made by combining certain ingredients to form a batter and then dropping small amounts of this into hot fat and frying them until they are crisp and brown. The accompanying recipe, provided it is followed carefully, will produce good results.

SOUP FRITTERS

1 egg   ¾ tsp. salt
2 Tb. milk   ½ c. flour

Beat the egg, and to it add the milk, salt, and flour. Drop the batter in tiny drops into hot fat, and fry until brown and crisp. Drain on paper and serve with the soup.

73. Egg Balls.—To serve with a soup that is well flavored but not highly nutritious, egg balls are very satisfactory. In addition to supplying nutrition, these balls are extremely appetizing, and so they greatly improve a course that is often unattractive. Careful attention given to the ingredients and the directions in the accompanying recipe will produce good results.

EGG BALLS

3 yolks of hard-cooked eggs   Salt and pepper
½ tsp. melted butter   1 uncooked yolk

Mash the cooked yolks, and to them add the butter, salt, and pepper, and enough of the uncooked yolk to make the mixture of a consistency to handle easily. Shape into tiny balls. Roll in the white of egg and then in flour and sauté in butter. Serve in the individual dishes of soup.

74. Forcemeat Balls.—Another delicious form of accompaniment that improves certain soups by adding nutrition is forcemeat balls. These contain various nutritious ingredients combined into small balls, and the balls are then either sautéd or fried in deep fat. They may be placed in the soup tureen or in each person's soup.

FORCEMEAT BALLS

½ c. fine stale-bread crumbs   ¼ tsp. salt
½ c. milk   Few grains of pepper
2 Tb. butter   ⅔ c. breast of raw chicken or
White of 1 egg   raw fish

Cook the bread crumbs and milk to form a paste, and to this add the butter, beaten egg white, and seasonings. Pound the chicken or fish to a pulp, or force it through a food chopper and then through a purée strainer. Add this to the first mixture. Form into tiny balls. Roll in flour and either sauté or fry in deep fat. Serve hot.

75. American Forcemeat Balls.—A simple kind of forcemeat balls may be made according to the accompanying recipe. The meat used may be sausage provided especially for the purpose or some that is left over from a previous meal. If it is not possible to obtain sausage, some other highly seasoned meat, such as ham first ground very fine and then pounded to a pulp, may be substituted.

AMERICAN FORCEMEAT BALLS

1 Tb. butter	1 tsp. salt
1 small onion	½ tsp. pepper
1½ c. bread, without crusts	Dash of nutmeg
1 egg	1 Tb. chopped parsley
½ c. sausage meat	

Melt the butter in a saucepan and add the onion finely chopped. Fry for several minutes over the fire. Soak the bread in water until thoroughly softened and then squeeze out all the water. Mix with the bread the egg, salt, pepper, nutmeg, parsley, and meat, and to this add also the butter and fried onion. Form small balls of this mixture and sauté them in shallow fat, fry them in deep fat, or, after brushing them over with fat, bake them in the oven. Place a few in each serving of soup.

SOUP

EXAMINATION QUESTIONS

(1) (*a*) Mention the two purposes that soups serve in a meal. (*b*) What are the qualities of a good soup?

(2) (*a*) Mention the two general classes of soup. (*b*) Explain and illustrate how to choose a soup.

(3) Why is soup an economical dish?

(4) (*a*) Explain in full the meaning of stock as applied to soup. (*b*) For what purposes other than soup making is stock used?

(5) (*a*) What is the value of the stock pot? (*b*) What care should be given to it?

(6) Mention some of the materials that may be put into the stock pot.

(7) (*a*) Why are the tough cuts of meat more suitable for soup than the tender ones? (*b*) Name the pieces that are best adapted to soup making.

(8) (*a*) What proportion of bone to meat should be used in making soup from fresh meat? (*b*) For what two purposes are vegetables used in soup?

(9) Explain briefly the making of stock from meat.

(10) (*a*) Why should the cooking of the meat for stock be started with cold water rather than with hot water? (*b*) What disposal should be made of meat from which stock is made?

(11) (*a*) Of what value are flavorings in the making of soups? (*b*) What precaution should be taken in the use of flavorings?

(12) Explain how grease may be removed from soup.

(13) How may soup be cleared?

(14) (*a*) For what purposes is thickening used in soups? (*b*) Mention the materials most used to thicken soups.

(15) What precaution should be taken to keep soup or stock from spoiling.

(16) What point about the serving of soup should be observed if an appetizing soup is desired?

(17) What kind of dish is used for serving: (*a*) thin soup? (*b*) thick soup?

§9

(18) (a) What is a cream soup? (b) Give the general directions for making soup of this kind.

(19) (a) How may the soup course of a meal be made more attractive? (b) In what ways should soup accompaniments be a contrast to the soup?

(20) (a) Explain the making of croutons. (b) What is the most satisfactory way in which to prepare celery that is to be served with soup?

ADDITIONAL WORK

Plain and prepare a dinner menu from the recipes given in the lessons that you have studied. Submit the menu for this dinner and give the order in which you prepared the dishes. In addition, tell the number of persons you served, as well as what remained after the meal and whether or not you made use of it for another meal. Send this information with your answers to the Examination Questions.

MEAT
(PART 1)

MEAT IN THE DIET

VALUE OF MEAT AS FOOD

1. In its broadest sense, **meat** may be considered as "any clean, sound, dressed or properly prepared edible part of animals that are in good health at the time of slaughter." However, the flesh of carniverous animals—that is, animals that eat the flesh of other animals—is so seldom eaten by man, that the term meat is usually restricted to the flesh of all animals except these. But even this meaning of meat is too broad; indeed, as the term is generally used it refers particularly to the flesh of the so-called domestic animals, and does not include poultry, game, fish, and the like. It is in this limited sense that meat is considered in these Sections, and the kinds to which attention is given are beef, veal, lamb, mutton, and pork. Meat, including these varieties, forms one of the principal sources of the family's food supply. As such, it is valuable chiefly as a food; but, in the form of broths and extracts made from it, meat stimulates the appetite and actually assists the flow of gastric juice. Therefore, so that the outlay for meat will not be greater than it should be and this food will provide the greatest amount of nourishment, every housewife should be thoroughly familiar with the place it occupies in the dietary.

2. In the first place, it should be remembered that the food eaten by human beings comes from two sources—animal and vegetable. The foods of animal origin, which include milk, eggs, and meat, have a certain similarity that causes them to be classed together and this is the fact that they are high-protein foods. Milk is the first protein food fed to the young, but a little later it is partly replaced by eggs, and, finally, or in adult life, meat largely takes the place of both. For this reason, meat has considerable importance in the dietary. In reality, from this food is obtained the greatest amount of protein that the average person eats. However, it will be well to note that milk and eggs, as well as cheese and even cereals and vegetables, can be made to take the place of meat when the use of less of this food is deemed advisable.

3. As the work of protein foods is to build and repair tissue, it is on them that the human race largely depends. Of course, protein also yields energy; but the amount is so small that if one variety of protein food, such as meat, were eaten simply to supply energy to the body, huge quantities of it would be needed to do the same work that a small amount of less expensive food would accomplish. Some persons have an idea that meat produces the necessary strength and energy of those who perform hard work. This is entirely erroneous, because fats and carbohydrates are the food substances that produce the energy required to do work. Some kind of protein is, of course, absolutely necessary to the health of every normal person, but a fact that cannot be emphasized too strongly is that an oversupply of it does more harm than good.

Scientists have been trying for a long time to determine just how much of these tissue-building foods is necessary for individuals, but they have found this a difficult matter. Nevertheless, it is generally conceded that most persons are likely to use too much rather than too little of them. It is essential then, not only from the standpoint of economy, but from the far more important principle of health, that the modern housewife should know the nutritive value of meats.

4. In her efforts to familiarize herself with these matters, the housewife should ever remember that meat is the most expensive of the daily foods of a family. Hence, to get the greatest value for the money expended, meat must be bought judiciously, cared for properly, and prepared carefully. Too many housewives trust the not overscrupulous butcher to give them the kind of meat they should have, and very often they do not have a clear idea as to whether it is the best piece that can be purchased for the desired purpose and for the price that is asked. Every housewife ought to be so familiar with the various cuts of meat that she need not depend on any one except herself in the purchase of this food. She will find that both the buying and the preparation of meats will be a simple matter for her if she learns these three important things: (1) From what part of the animal the particular piece she desires is cut and how to ask for that piece; (2) how to judge a good piece of meat by its appearance; and (3) what to do with it from the moment it is purchased until the last bit of it is used.

5. Of these three things, the cooking of meat is the one that demands the most attention, because it has a decided effect on the quality and digestibility of this food. Proper cooking is just as essential in the case of meat as for any other food, for a tender, digestible piece of meat may be made tough and indigestible by improper preparation, while a tough piece may be made tender and very appetizing by careful, intelligent preparation. The cheaper cuts of meat, which are often scorned as being too tough for use, may be converted into delicious dishes by the skilful cook who understands how to apply the various methods of cookery and knows what their effect will be on the meat tissues.

6. Unfortunately, thorough cooking affects the digestibility of meat unfavorably; but it is doubtless a wise procedure in some cases because, as is definitely known, some of the parasites that attack man find their way into the system through the meat that is eaten. These are carried to meat from external sources, such as dust, flies, and the soiled hands of persons handling it, and they multiply and thrive. It is known, too, that some of the germs that cause disease in the animal remain in its flesh and are thus transmitted to human beings that eat such meat. If there is any question as to its good condition, meat must be thoroughly cooked, because long cooking completely eliminates the danger from such sources.

STRUCTURE AND COMPOSITION OF MEAT

7. An understanding of the physical structure of meat is essential to its successful cooking. Meat consists of muscular tissue, or lean; varying quantities of visible fat that lie between and within the membranes and tendons; and also particles of fat that are too small to be distinguished except with the aid of a microscope. The general nature of the lean part of meat can be determined by examining a piece of it with merely the unaided eye. On close observation, it will be noted that, especially in the case of meat that has been cooked, innumerable threadlike fibers make up the structure. With a microscope, it can be observed that these visible fibers are made up of still smaller ones, the length of which varies in different parts of the animal. It is to the length of these fibers that the tenderness of meat is due. Short fibers are much easier to chew than long ones; consequently, the pieces containing them are the most tender.

These muscle fibers, which are in the form of tiny tubes, are filled with a protein substance. They are held together with a tough, stringy material called *connective tissue*. As the animal grows older and its muscles are used more, the walls of these tubes or fibers become dense and tough; likewise, the amount of connective tissue increases and becomes tougher. Among the muscle fibers are embedded layers and particles of fat, the quantity of which varies greatly in different animals and depends largely on the age of the animal. For instance, lamb and veal usually have very little fat in the tissues, mutton and beef always contain more, while pork contains a greater amount of fat than the meat of any other domestic animal.

8. The composition of meat depends to a large extent on the breed of the animal, the degree to which it has been fattened, and the particular cut of meat in question. However, the muscle fibers are made up of protein and contain more protein, mineral salts, or ash, and certain substances called *extractives,* all of which are held in solution by water. The younger the animal, the greater is the proportion of water and the lower the nutritive value of meat. It should be understood, however, that not all of meat is edible material; indeed, a large part of it is made up of gristle, bones, cartilage, nerves, blood vessels, and connective tissue. The amount of these indigestible materials also varies in different animals and different cuts, but the average proportion in a piece of meat is usually considered to be 15 per cent. of the whole. Because of the variation of both the edible and inedible material of meat, a standard composition for this food cannot readily be given. However, an idea of the average composition of the various kinds can be obtained from Fig. 1.

9. Protein in Meat.—The value of meat as food is due to the proteins that it contains. Numerous kinds of protein occur in meat,

§ 10   MEAT   5

but the chief varieties are myosin and muscle albumin. The *myosin,* which is the most important protein and occurs in the greatest

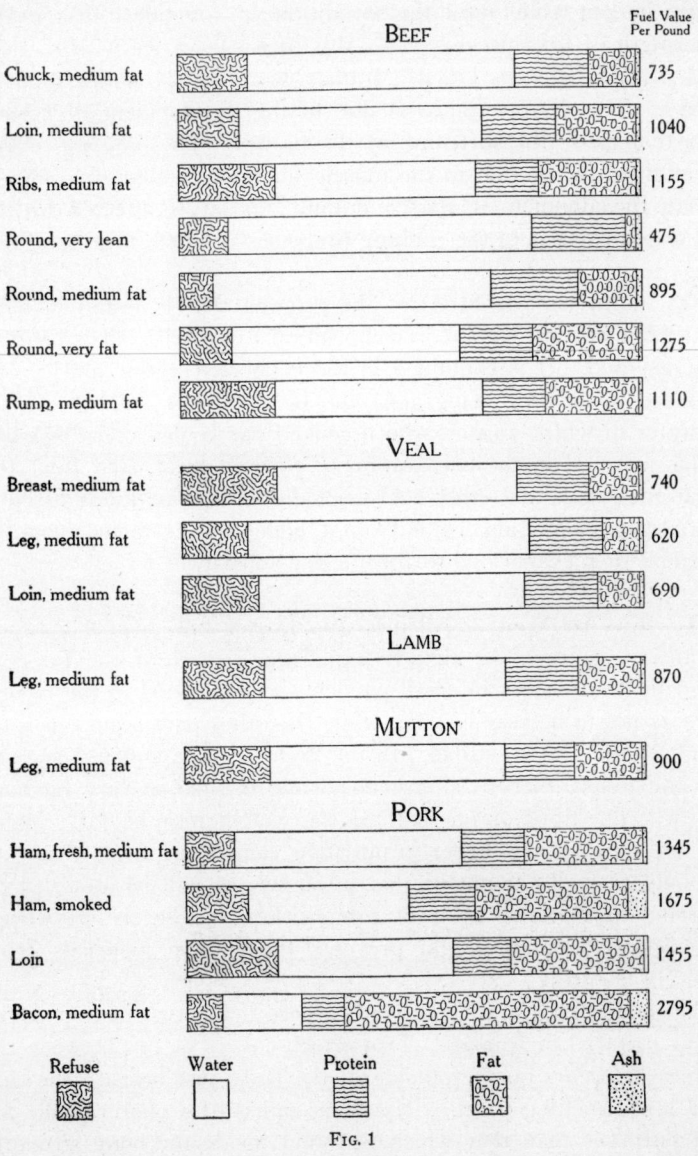

BEEF   Fuel Value
                                                   Per Pound

Chuck, medium fat	735
Loin, medium fat	1040
Ribs, medium fat	1155
Round, very lean	475
Round, medium fat	895
Round, very fat	1275
Rump, medium fat	1110

VEAL

Breast, medium fat	740
Leg, medium fat	620
Loin, medium fat	690

LAMB

| Leg, medium fat | 870 |

MUTTON

| Leg, medium fat | 900 |

PORK

Ham, fresh, medium fat	1345
Ham, smoked	1675
Loin	1455
Bacon, medium fat	2795

Refuse   Water   Protein   Fat   Ash

FIG. 1

quantity, hardens after the animal has been killed and the muscles have become cold. The tissues then become tough and hard, a condition known as *rigor mortis*. As meat in this condition is not desirable, it should be used before rigor mortis sets in, or else it should be put aside until this condition of toughness disappears. The length of time necessary for this to occur varies with the size of the animal that is killed. It may be from 24 hours to 3 or 4 days. The disappearance is due to the development of certain acids that cause the softening of the tissues. The *albumin*, which is contained in solution in the muscle fibers, is similar in composition to the albumen of eggs and milk, and it is affected by the application of heat in the cooking processes in much the same way.

10. Gelatine in Meat.—The gelatine that is found in meat is a substance very similar in composition to protein, but it has less value as food. It is contained in the connective tissue and can be extracted by boiling, being apparent as a jellylike substance after the water in which meat has been cooked has cooled. Use is made of this material in the preparation of pressed meats and fowl and in various salads and other cold-meat dishes. Some kinds of commercial gelatine are also made from it, being first extracted from the meat and then evaporated to form a dry substance.

11. Fat in Meat.—All meat, no matter how lean it appears, contains some fat. As already explained, a part of the fat contained in meat occurs in small particles so embedded in the muscle fibers as not to be readily seen, while the other part occurs in sufficient amounts to be visible. In the flesh of some animals, such as veal and rabbit, there is almost no visible fat, but in very fat hogs or fowls, one-third or one-half of the weight may be fat. Meats that are very fat are higher in nutritive value than meats that contain only a small amount of this substance, as will be observed on referring to the table of meat compositions in Fig. 1. However, an excessive amount of fat prevents the protein materials from digesting normally.

The quality of fat varies greatly, there being two distinct kinds of this material in animals. That which covers or lies between the muscles or occurs on the outside of the body just beneath the skin has a lower melting point, is less firm, and is of a poorer grade for most purposes than that which is found inside the bony structure and surrounds the internal organs. The suet of beef is an example of this internal fat.

Fat is a valuable constituent of food, for it is the most concentrated form in which the fuel elements of food are found. In supplying the body with fuel, it serves to maintain the body temperature and to yield energy in the form of muscular and other power. Since this is such a valuable food material, it is important that the best possible use be made of all drippings and left-over fats and that not even the smallest amount of any kind be wasted.

12. Carbohydrate in Meat.—In the liver and all muscle fibers of animals is stored a small supply of carbohydrate in a form that is called *glycogen,* or *muscle sugar.* However, there is not enough of this substance to be of any appreciable value, and, so far as the methods of cookery and the uses of meat as food are concerned, it is of no importance.

13. Water in Meat.—The proportion of water in meat varies from one-third to three-fourths of the whole, depending on the amount of fat the meat contains and the age of the animal. This water carries with it the flavor, much of the mineral matter, and some food material, so that when the water is removed from the tissues these things are to a great extent lost. The methods of cookery applied to meat are based on the principle of either retaining or extracting the water that it contains. The meat in which water is retained is more easily chewed and swallowed than that which is dry. However, the water contained in flesh has no greater value as food than other water. Therefore, as will be seen in Fig. 1, the greater the amount of water in a given weight of food, the less is its nutritive value.

14. Minerals in Meat.—Eight or more kinds of minerals in sufficient quantities to be of importance in the diet are to be found in meat. Lean meat contains the most minerals; they decrease in proportion as the amount of fat increases. These salts assist in the building of hard tissues and have a decided effect on the blood. They are lost from the tissues of meat by certain methods of cookery, but as they are in solution in the water in which the meat is cooked, they need not be lost to the diet if use is made of this water for soups, sauces, and gravies.

15. Extractives in Meat.—The appetizing flavor of meat is due to substances called *extractives.* The typical flavor that serves to distinguish pork from beef or mutton is due to the difference in the extractives. Although necessary for flavoring, these have no nutritive value; in fact, the body throws them off as waste material when they are taken with the food. In some methods of cookery, such as broiling and roasting, the extractives are retained, while in others, such as those employed for making stews and soups, they are drawn out.

Extractives occur in the greatest quantity in the muscles that the animal exercises a great deal and that in reality have become tough. Likewise, a certain part of an old animal contains more extractives than the same part of a young one. For these reasons a very young chicken is broiled while an old one is used for stew, and ribs of beef are roasted while the shins are used for soup.

Meat that is allowed to hang and ripen develops compounds that are similar to extractives and that impart additional flavor. A ripened steak is usually preferred to one cut from an animal that has been killed only a short time. However, as the ripening is in reality a decomposition process, the meat is said to become "high" if it is allowed to hang too long.

PURCHASE AND CARE OF MEAT

16. Purchase of Meat.—Of all the money that is spent for food in the United States nearly one-third is spent for meat. This proportion is greater than that of any European country and is probably more than is necessary to provide diets that are properly balanced. If it is found that the meat bill is running too high, one or more of several things may be the cause. The one who does the purchasing may not understand the buying of meat, the cheaper cuts may not be used because of a lack of knowledge as to how they should be prepared to make them appetizing, or more meat may be served than is necessary to supply the needs of the family.

Much of this difficulty can be overcome if the person purchasing meat goes to the market personally to see the meat cut and weighed instead of telephoning the order. It is true, of course, that the method of cutting an animal varies in different parts of the country, as does also the naming of the different pieces. However, this need give the housewife no concern, for the dealer from whom the meat is purchased is usually willing to supply any information that is desired about the cutting of meat and the best use for certain pieces.

In fact, if the butcher is competent, this is a very good source from which to obtain a knowledge of such matters.

Another way in which to reduce the meat bill is to utilize the trimmings of bone and fat from pieces of meat. In most cases, these are of no value to the butcher, so that if a request for them is made, he will, as a rule, be glad to wrap them up with the meat that is purchased. They are of considerable value to the housewife, for the bones may go into the stock pot, while the fat, if it is tried out, can be used for many things.

17. The quantity of meat to purchase depends, of course, on the number of persons that are to be served with it. However, it is often a good plan to purchase a larger piece than is required for a single meal and then use what remains for another meal. For instance, a large roast is always better than a small one, because it does not dry out in the process of cookery and the part that remains after one meal may be served cold in slices or used for making some other dish, such as meat pie or hash. Such a plan also saves both time and fuel, because sufficient meat for several meals may be cooked at one time.

In purchasing meat, there are certain pieces that should never be asked for by the pound or by the price. For instance, the housewife should not say to the butcher, "Give me 2 pounds of porterhouse steak," nor should she say, "Give me 25 cents worth of chops." Steak should be bought by the cut, and the thickness that is desired should be designated. For example, the housewife may ask for an inch-thick sirloin steak, a 2-inch porterhouse steak, and so on. Chops should be bought according to the number of persons that are to be served, usually a chop to a person being quite sufficient. Rib roasts should be bought by designating the number of ribs. Thus, the housewife may ask for a rib roast containing two, three, four, or more ribs, depending on the size desired. Roasts from other parts of beef, such as chuck or rump roasts, may be cut into chunks of almost any desirable size without working a disadvantage to either the butcher or the customer, and may therefore be bought by the pound. Round bought for steaks should be purchased by the cut, as are other steaks; or, if an entire cut is too large, it may be purchased as upper round or lower round, but the price paid should vary with the piece that is purchased. Round bought for roasts, however, may be purchased by the pound.

18. Care of Meat in the Market.—Animal foods decompose more readily than any other kind, and the products of their decomposition are extremely dangerous to the health. It is therefore a serious matter when everything that comes in contact with meat is not clean. Regarding the proper care of meat, the sanitary condition of the market is the first consideration. The light and ventilation of the room and the cleanliness of the walls, floors, tables, counters, and other equipment are points of the greatest importance and should be noted by the housewife when she is purchasing meat. Whether the windows and doors are screened and all the meat is carefully covered during the fly season are also matters that should not be overlooked. Then, too, the cleanliness and physical condition of the persons who handle the meat should be of as great concern as the sanitary condition of the market. The housewife who desires to supply her family with the safest and cleanest meat should endeavor to purchase it in markets where all the points pertaining to the sanitary condition are as ideal as possible. If she is at all doubtful as to the freshness and cleanliness of what is sold to her, she should give it thorough cooking in the process of preparation so that no harm will be done to the persons who are to eat it.

19. Care of Meat in the Home.—Because of the perishable nature of meat, the care given it in the market must be continued in the home in order that no deterioration may take place before it is cooked. This is not much of a problem during cold weather, but through the summer months a cool place in which to keep it must be provided unless the meat can be cooked very soon after it is delivered. Meat that must be shipped long distances is frozen before it is shipped and is kept frozen until just before it is used. If such meat is still frozen when it enters the home, it should not be put into a warm place, for then it will thaw too quickly. Instead, it should be put in the refrigerator or in some place where the temperature is a few degrees above freezing point, so that it will thaw slowly and still remain too cold for bacteria to become active.

Even if meat is not frozen, it must receive proper attention after it enters the home. As soon as it is received, it should be removed from the wrapping paper or the wooden or cardboard dish in which it is delivered. If the meat has not been purchased personally, it is advisable to weigh it in order to verify the butcher's bill. When the housewife is satisfied about the weight, she should place the meat in an earthenware, china, or enameled bowl, cover it, and then put it away in the coolest available place until it is used. Some persons put salt on meat when they desire to keep it, but this practice should be avoided, as salt draws out the juices from raw meat and hardens the tissues to a certain extent.

If such precautions are taken with meat, it will be in good condition when it is to be cooked. However, before any cooking method is applied to it, it should always be wiped with a clean, damp cloth. In addition, all fat should be removed, except just enough to assist in cooking the meat and give it a good flavor. Bone or tough portions may also be removed if they can be used to better advantage for soups or stews.

COOKING OF MEAT

PURPOSES OF COOKING MEAT

20. It is in the preparation of food, and of meat in particular, that one of the marked differences between uncivilized and civilized man is evident. Raw meat, which is preferred by the savage, does not appeal to the appetite of most civilized persons; in fact, to the majority of them the idea of using it for food is disgusting. Therefore, civilized man prepares his meat before eating it, and the higher his culture, the more perfect are his methods of preparation.

While it is probably true that most of the methods of cookery render meat less easy to digest than in its raw condition, this disadvantage is offset by the several purposes for which this food is cooked. Meat is cooked chiefly to loosen and soften the connective tissue and thus cause the muscle tissues to be exposed more fully to the action of the digestive juices. Another important reason for cooking meat is that subjecting it to the action of heat helps to kill bacteria and parasites. In addition, meat is cooked to make it more attractive to the eye and to develop and improve its flavor.

METHODS OF COOKING MEAT

21. The result desired when meat is cooked has much to do with the method of cookery to choose, for different methods produce different results. To understand this, it will be necessary to know just what the action of cooking is on the material that meat contains. When raw meat is cut, the tiny meat fibers are laid open, with the result that, in the application of the cooking process, the albuminous material either is lost, or, like the albumen of eggs, is coagulated, or hardened, and thus retained. Therefore, before preparing a piece of meat, the housewife should determine which of these two things she wishes to accomplish and then proceed to carry out the process intelligently.

The methods of cookery that may be applied to meat include broiling, pan broiling, roasting, stewing or simmering, braizing, frying, sautéing, and fricasseeing. All of these methods are explained in a general way in *Essentials of Cookery,* Part 1, but explanations of them as they apply to meat are here given in order to acquaint the housewife with the advantages and disadvantages of the various ways by which this food can be prepared.

22. Broiling and Pan Broiling.—Only such cuts of meats as require short cooking can be prepared by the methods of broiling and pan broiling. To carry out these methods successfully, severe heat must be applied to the surface of the meat so that the albumin in the ends of the muscle fibers may be coagulated at once. This prevents, during the remainder of the preparation, a loss of the meat juices.

Meat to which either of these methods is applied will be indigestible on the surface and many times almost uncooked in the center, as in the case of rare steak. Such meat, however, is more digestible than thin pieces that are thoroughly cooked at the very high temperature required for broiling.

23. Roasting.—The process of roasting, either in the oven or in a pot on top of the stove, to be properly done, requires that the piece of meat to be roasted must first be seared over the entire surface by the application of severe heat. In the case of a pot roast, the searing can be done conveniently in the pot before the pot-roasting process begins. If the meat is to be roasted in the oven, it may be seared first in a pan on top of the stove. However, it may be seared to some extent by placing it in a very hot oven and turning it over so that all the surface is exposed. Then, to continue the roasting process, the temperature must be lowered just a little.

The roasting pan may be of any desirable size and shape that is convenient and sufficiently large to accommodate the meat to be prepared. A pan like that shown in Fig. 2 is both convenient and satisfactory. It is provided with a cover that fits tight. In this cover, as shown, is an opening that may be closed or opened so as to regulate the amount of moisture inside the pan. In the bottom of the pan is a rack upon which the meat may rest.

24. To prepare meat for roasting, flour should be sprinkled or rubbed over its lean surface before it is put in the pan. This forms a paste that cooks into a crust and prevents the loss of juices from the meat. In roasting, the heat is applied longer and more slowly than in broiling or frying, so that there is more possibility for the connective tissue beneath the surface to soften. The surface is, however, as indigestible as that of broiled meat.

An important point for every housewife to remember in this connection is that the larger the roast the slower should be the fire. This is due to the fact that long before the heat could penetrate to the center, the outside would be burned. A small roast, however, will be more delicious if it is prepared with a very hot fire, for then the juices will not have a chance to evaporate and the tissues will be more moist and tasty.

Fig. 2

25. Frying and Sautéing.—When meat is fried or sautéd, that is, brought directly in contact with hot fat, it is made doubly indigestible, because of the hardening of the surface tissues and the indigestibility of the fat that penetrates these tissues. This is especially true of meat that is sautéd slowly in a small quantity of hot fat. Much of this difficulty can be overcome, however, if meat prepared by these methods, like that which is broiled or roasted, is subjected quickly to intense heat. In addition, the fat used for cooking should be made hot before the meat is put into it.

26. Boiling.—To boil meat means to cook it a long time in water at a temperature of 212 degrees Fahrenheit. This method of preparing meat is not strongly advocated, for there is seldom a time when better results cannot be obtained by cooking meat at a lower temperature than boiling point. The best plan is to bring the meat to the boiling point, allow it to boil for a short time, and then reduce the temperature so that the meat will simmer for the remainder of the cooking.

In cooking meat by boiling, a grayish scum appears on the surface just before the boiling point is reached. This scum is caused by the gradual extraction of a part of the soluble albumin that is present in the hollow fibers of the muscle tissue. After its extraction, it is coagulated by the heat in the water. As it coagulates and rises, it carries with it to the top particles of dirt and other foreign material present in the water or on the surface of the meat. In addition, this scum contains a little blood, which is extracted and coagulated and which tends to make it grayish in color. Such scum should be skimmed off, as it is unappetizing in appearance.

27. Whether the meat should be put into cold water or boiling water depends on the result that is desired. It is impossible to make a rich, tasty broth and at the same time have a juicy, well-flavored piece of boiled meat. If meat is cooked for the purpose of making soup or broth, it should be put into cold water and then brought to a boil. By this method, some of the nutritive material and much of the flavoring substance will be drawn out before the water becomes hot enough to harden them. However, in case only the meat is to be used, it should be plunged directly into boiling water in order to coagulate the surface at once, as in the application of dry heat. If it is allowed to boil for 10 minutes or so and the temperature then reduced, the coating that is formed will prevent the nutritive material and the flavor from being lost to any great extent. But if the action of the boiling water is permitted to continue during the entire time of cooking, the tissues will become tough and dry.

28. Stewing or Simmering.—The cheap cuts of meat, which contain a great deal of flavor and are so likely to be tough, cannot be prepared by the quick methods of cookery nor by the application of high temperature, for the result would be a tough, indigestible, and unpalatable dish. The long, slow cooking at a temperature lower than boiling point, which is known as stewing or simmering, should be applied. In fact, no better method for the preparation of tough pieces of meat and old fowl can be found than this process, for by it the connective tissue and the muscle fibers are softened. If the method is carried out in a tightly closed vessel and only a small amount of liquid is used, there is no appreciable loss of flavor except that carried into the liquid in which the meat cooks. But since such liquid is always used, the meat being usually served in it, as in the case of stews, there is no actual loss.

To secure the best results in the use of this method, the meat should be cut into small pieces so as to expose as much surface as possible. Then the pieces should be put into cold water rather than hot, in order that much of the juices and flavoring materials may be dissolved. When this has been accomplished, the temperature should be gradually raised until it nearly reaches the boiling point. If it is kept at this point for several hours, the meat will become tender and juicy and a rich, tasty broth will also be obtained.

29. Braizing.—Meat cooked by the method of braizing, which is in reality a combination of stewing and baking, is first subjected to the intense dry heat of the oven and then cooked slowly in the steam of the water that surrounds it. To cook meat in this way, a pan must be used that will permit the meat to be raised on a rack that extends above a small quantity of water. By this method a certain amount of juice from the meat is taken up by the water, but the connective tissue is well softened unless the cooking is done at too high a temperature.

30. Fricasseeing.—As has already been learned, fricasseeing is a combination of sautéing and stewing. The sautéing coagulates the surface proteins and prevents, to some extent, the loss of flavor that would occur in the subsequent stewing if the surface were not hardened. To produce a tender, tasty dish, fricasseeing should be a long, slow process. This method is seldom applied to tender, expensive cuts of meat and to young chickens, but is used for fowl and for pieces of meat that would not make appetizing dishes if prepared by a quicker method.

TIME REQUIRED FOR COOKING MEAT

31. The length of time required for cooking various kinds of meat is usually puzzling to those inexperienced in cookery. The difference between a dry, hard beef roast and a tender, moist, juicy one is due to the length of time allowed for cooking. Overdone meats of any kind are not likely to be tasty. Therefore, it should be remembered that when dry heat is used, as in baking, roasting, broiling, etc., the longer the heat is applied the greater will be the evaporation of moisture and the consequent shrinkage in the meat.

A general rule for cooking meat in the oven is to allow 15 minutes for each pound and 15 minutes extra. If it is to be cooked by broiling, allow 10 minutes for each pound and 10 minutes extra; by boiling, 20 minutes for each pound and 20 minutes extra; and by simmering, 30 minutes for each pound. In Table I is given the number of minutes generally allowed for cooking 1 pound of each of the various cuts of beef, veal, mutton, lamb, and pork by the different cookery methods. This table should be referred to in studying the two Sections pertaining to meat.

TABLE I
TIME TABLE FOR COOKING MEATS

Name of Cut	Cookery Method	Time Per Pound Minutes
Beef		
Round	Roasting	12 to 15
Ribs	Roasting, well done	12 to 15
Ribs	Roasting, rare	8 to 10
Rump	Roasting	12 to 15
Sirloin	Roasting, rare	8 to 10
Rolled roast	Roasting	12 to 15
Steaks	Broiling, well done	12 to 15
Steaks	Broiling, rare	8 to 10
Fresh beef	Boiling	20 to 25
Corned beef	Boiling	25 to 30
Any cut	Simmering	30
Chuck	Braizing	25 to 30
Veal		
Leg	Roasting	20
Chops or steak	Broiling	8 to 30
Shoulder	Braizing	30 to 40
Mutton		
Leg	Roasting	15 to 20
Shoulder	Roasting	15 to 20
Leg	Braizing	40 to 50
Leg	Boiling	15 to 25
Chops	Broiling	10 to 12
Lamb		
Loin or saddle	Roasting	15 to 20
Leg	Roasting	15 to 20
Chops	Broiling	8 to 10
Pork		
Shoulder or ribs	Roasting	20 to 25
Ham	Boiled	20 to 30
Chops	Broiled	8 to 10

BEEF

GENERAL CHARACTERISTICS OF BEEF

32. As is generally known, **beef** is the flesh of a slaughtered steer, cow, or other adult bovine animal. These animals may be sold to be slaughtered as young as $1\frac{1}{2}$ to 2 years old, but beef of the best quality is obtained from them when they are from 3 to 4 years of age. Ranging from the highest quality down to the lowest, beef is designated by the butcher as prime, extra fancy, fancy, extra choice, choice, good, and poor. In a market where trade is large and varied, it is possible to make such use of meat as to get a higher price for the better qualities than can be obtained in other markets.

33. When the quality of beef is to be determined, the amount, quality, and color of the flesh, bone, and fat must be considered. The surface of a freshly cut piece of beef should be bright red in color. When it is exposed to the air for some time, the action of the air on the blood causes it to become darker, but even this color should be a good clear red. Any unusual color is looked on with suspicion by a person who understands the requirements of good meat. To obtain beef of the best quality, it should be cut crosswise of the fiber. In fact, the way in which meat is cut determines to a great extent the difference between tender and tough meat and, consequently, the price that is charged. This difference can be readily seen by examining the surface of a cut. It will be noted that the tender parts are made up of short fibers that are cut directly across at right angles with the surface of the meat, while the tougher parts contain long fibers that run either slanting or almost parallel to the surface.

34. The amount of bone and cartilage in proportion to meat in a cut of beef usually makes a difference in price and determines the usefulness of the piece to the housewife. Therefore, these are matters that should be carefully considered. For instance, a certain cut of beef that is suitable for a roast may cost a few cents less than another cut, but if its proportion of bone to meat is greater than in the more expensive piece, nothing is gained by purchasing it. Bones, however, possess some value and can be utilized in various ways. Those containing *marrow,* which is the soft tissue found in the cavities of bones and composed largely of fat, are more valuable for soup making and for stews and gravies than are solid bones.

In young beef in good condition, the fat is creamy white in color. However, as the animal grows older, the color grows darker until it becomes a deep yellow.

Besides the flesh, bone, and fat, the general shape and thickness of a piece of beef should be noted when its quality is to be determined. In addition, its adaptability to the purpose for which it is selected and the method of cookery to be used in its preparation are also points that should not be overlooked.

CUTS OF BEEF

METHOD OF OBTAINING CUTS

35. With the general characteristics of beef well in mind, the housewife is prepared to learn of the way in which the animal is

Fig. 3

cut to produce the different pieces that she sees in the butcher shop and the names that are given to the various cuts. The cutting of

§ 10　　　　　　　　　　MEAT　　　　　　　　　　19

the animal, as well as the naming of the pieces, varies in different localities, but the difference is not sufficient to be confusing. Therefore, if the information here given is thoroughly mastered, the housewife will be able to select meat intelligently in whatever section

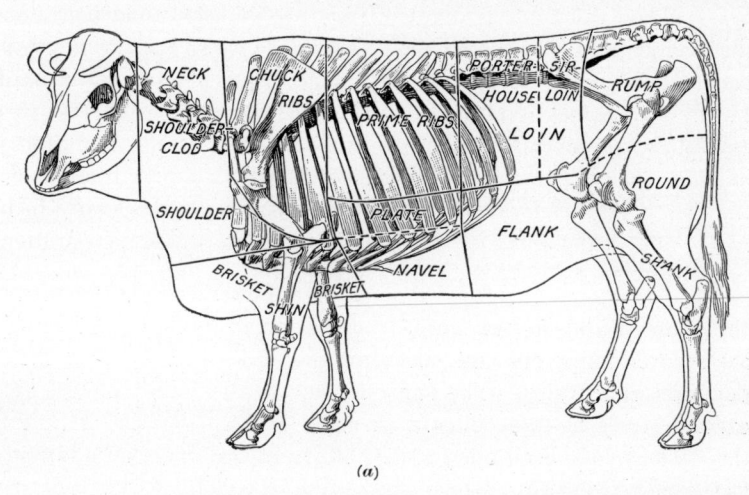

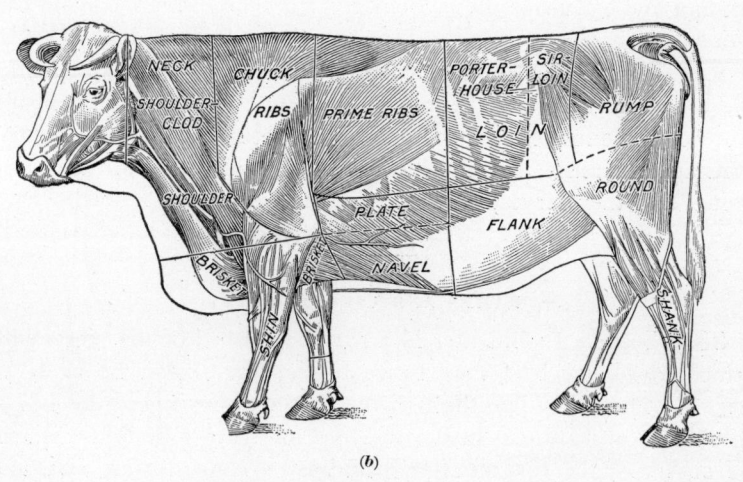

Fig. 4

of the country she may reside. An important point for her to remember concerning meat of any kind is that the cheaper cuts are found near the neck, legs, and shins, and that the pieces increase in price as they go toward the back.

36. The general method of cutting up a whole beef into large cuts is shown in Fig. 3. After the head, feet, and intestines are removed, the carcass is cut down along the spine and divided into halves. Each half includes an entire side and is known as a *side of beef*. Then each side is divided into *fore* and *hind quarters* along the diagonal line that occurs about midway between the front and the back. It is in this form that the butcher usually receives the beef. He first separates it into the large pieces here indicated and then cuts these pieces into numerous smaller ones having names that indicate their location. For instance, the piece marked *a* includes the *chuck; b,* the *ribs; c,* the *loin; d,* the *round; e,* the *flank; f,* the *plate;* and *g,* the *shin.*

37. The cuts that are obtained from these larger pieces are shown in Fig. 4. For instance, from the chuck, as illustrated in (*a*), are secured numerous cuts, including the neck, shoulder clod, shoulder, and chuck ribs. The same is true of the other pieces, as a careful study of these illustrations will reveal. Besides indicating the various cuts, each one of these illustrations serves an additional purpose. From (*a*), which shows the skeleton of the beef, the amount and the shape of the bone that the various cuts contain can be readily observed. From (*b*), which shows the directions in which the surface muscle fibers run, can be told whether the cutting of the pieces is done across the fibers or in the same direction as the fibers. Both of these matters are of such importance to the housewife that constant reference to these illustrations should be made until the points that they serve to indicate are thoroughly understood.

NAMES AND USES OF CUTS

38. So that a still better idea may be formed of the pieces into which a side of beef may be cut, reference should be made to Fig. 5. The heavy line through the center shows where the side is divided in order to cut it into the fore and hind quarters. As will be observed, the fore quarter includes the chuck, prime ribs, and whole plate, and the hind quarter, the loin and the round, each of these large pieces being indicated by a different color.

To make these large pieces of a size suitable for sale to the consumer, the butcher cuts each one of them into still smaller pieces, all of which are indicated in the illustration. The names of these

§ 10   Fig. 5

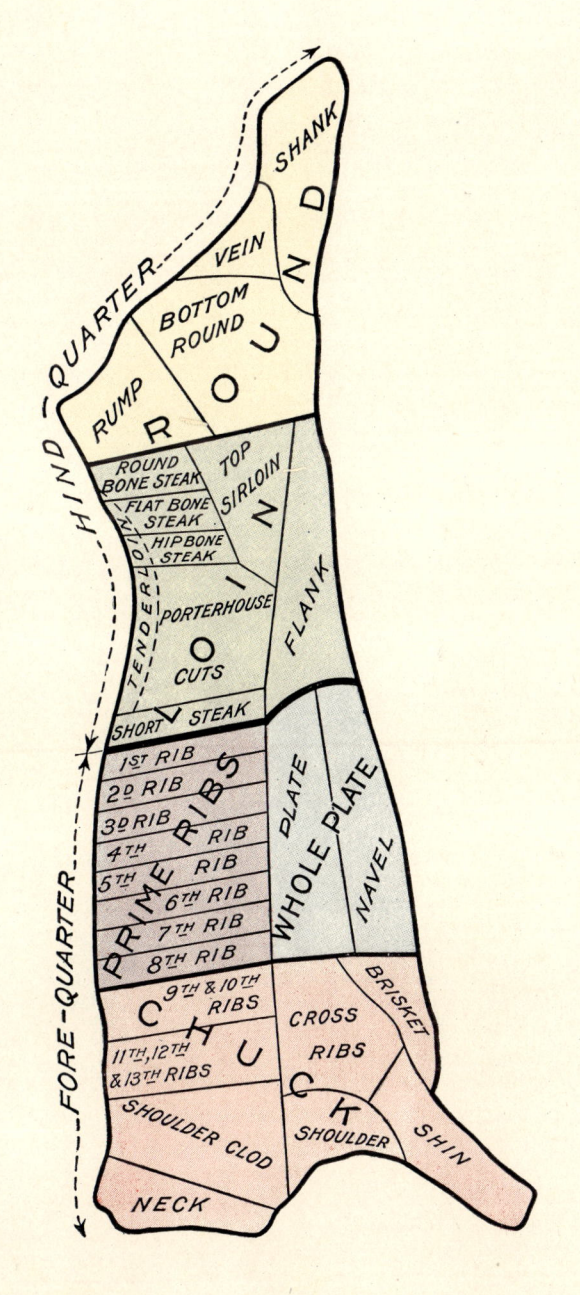

cuts, together with their respective uses, and the names of the beef organs and their uses, are given in Table II.

TABLE II

CUTS OBTAINED FROM A SIDE OF BEEF AND THEIR USES

Name of Large Piece	Name of Cut	Uses of Cuts
Chuck	Neck	Soups, broths, stews
	Shoulder clod	Soups, broths, stews, boiling, corning
	Ribs (11th, 12th, and 13th)	Brown stews, braizing, poor roasts
	Ribs (9th and 10th)	Braizing, roasts
	Shoulder	Soups, stews, corning, roast
	Cross-ribs	Roast
	Brisket	Soups, stews, corning
	Shin	Soups
Prime Ribs	Ribs (1st to 8th, inclusive)	Roasts
Whole Plate	Plate	Soups, stews, corning
	Navel	Soups, stews, corning
Loin	Short steak	Steaks, roasts
	Porterhouse cuts	Steaks, roasts
	Hip-bone steak	Steaks, roasts
	Flat-bone steak	Steaks, roasts
	Round-bone steak	Steaks, roasts
	Sirloin	Steaks
	Top sirloin	Roasts
	Flank	Rolled steak, braizing, boiling
	Tenderloin	Roast
Round	Rump	Roasts, corning
	Upper round	Steaks, roasts
	Lower round	Steaks, pot roasts, stews
	Vein	Stews, soups
	Shank	Soups
Beef Organs	Liver	Broiling, frying
	Heart	Baking, braizing
	Tongue	Boiling, baking, braizing
	Tail	Soup

39. As will be observed from Fig. 5, the ribs are numbered in the opposite direction from the way in which they are ordinarily counted; that is, the first rib in a cut of beef is the one farthest from the head and the thirteenth is the one just back of the neck. The first and second ribs are called the *back ribs;* the third, fourth, fifth, and sixth, the *middle ribs.* To prepare the ribs for sale, they are usually cut into pieces that contain two ribs, the first and second ribs being known as the first cut, the third and fourth as *the second cut*, etc. After being sawed across, the rib bones are either left in to make a *standing rib roast* or taken out and the meat then rolled and fastened together with skewers to make a *rolled roast*. *Skewers,* which are long wooden or metal pins that may be pushed through meat to fasten it together, will be found useful to the housewife in preparing many cuts of meat for cooking. They may usually be obtained at a meat market or a hardware store.

40. Certain of the organs of beef are utilized to a considerable extent, so that while they cannot be shown in Fig. 5, they are included in Table II. The heart and the tongue are valuable both because they are economical and because they add variety to the meat diet of the family. The tongue, either smoked or fresh, may be boiled and then served hot, or it may be pickled in vinegar and served cold. The heart may be prepared in the same way, or it may be stuffed and then baked. The tail of beef makes excellent soup and is much used for this purpose.

COOKING OF BEEF

STEAKS AND THEIR PREPARATION

41. Steaks Obtained From the Loin.—The way in which a loin of beef is cut into steaks is shown in Fig. 6. From a to b are cut *Delmonico steaks;* from b to c, *porterhouse steaks;* from c to d, *hip-bone steaks;* from d to e, *flat-bone steaks;* and from e to f, *sirloin steaks.* The *loin* is cut from the rump at f and from the flank and plate at h to j. When steaks are cut from the flesh of animals in good condition, they are all very tender and may be used for the quick methods of cookery, such as broiling. A very good idea of what each of these steaks looks like can be obtained from Figs. 7 to 11, inclusive. Each of these illustrations shows the entire section of steak, as well as one steak cut from the piece.

Delmonico steak, which is shown in Fig. 7, is the smallest steak that can be cut from the loin and is therefore an excellent cut for a small family. It contains little or no tenderloin. Sometimes this steak is wrongly called a club steak, but no confusion will result

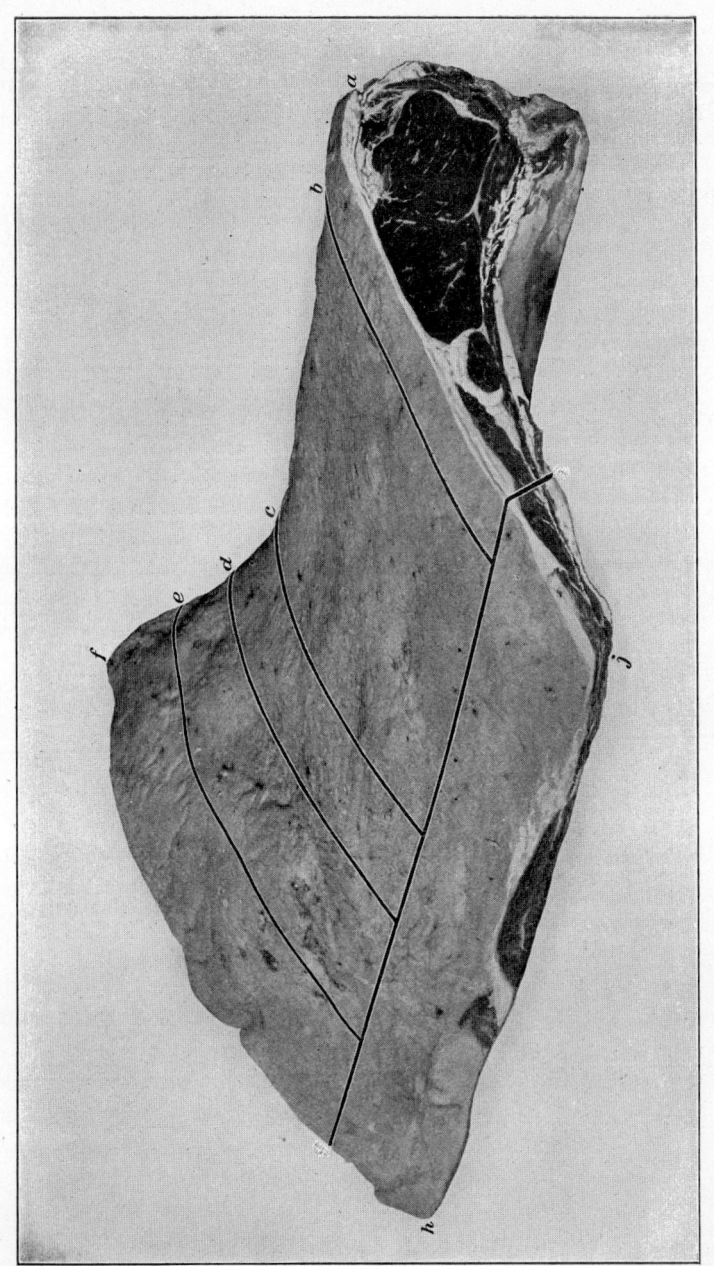

Fig. 6

if it is remembered that a *club steak* is a porterhouse steak that has most of the bone and the flank end, or "tail," removed.

Porterhouse steak, which is illustrated in Fig 8, contains more

Fig. 7

tenderloin than any other steak. This steak also being small in size is a very good cut for a small number of persons.

Hip-bone steak, shown in Fig. 9, contains a good-sized piece of

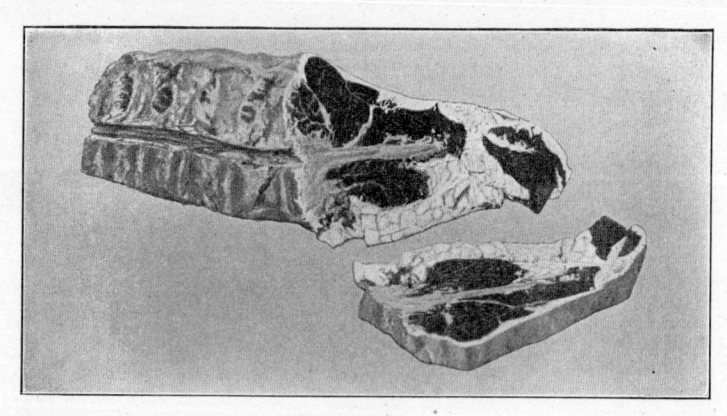

Fig. 8

tenderloin. Steak of this kind finds much favor, as it can be served quite advantageously.

Flat-bone steak, as shown in Fig. 10, has a large bone, but it also contains a considerable amount of fairly solid meat. When a

§ 10 MEAT 25

large number of persons are to be served, this is a very good steak to select.

Sirloin steak is shown in Fig. 11. As will be observed, this steak contains more solid meat than any of the other steaks cut from

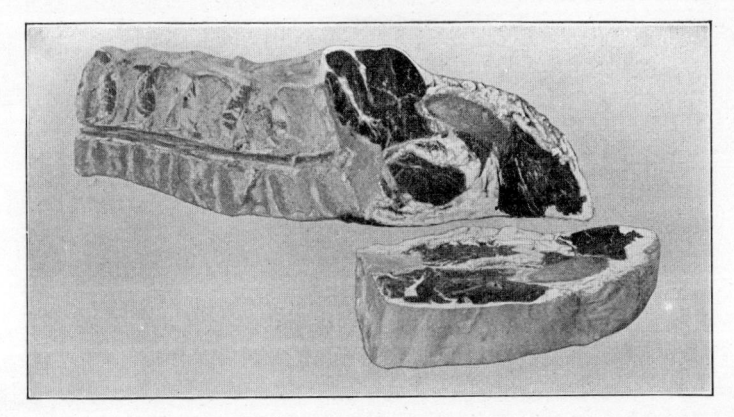

Fig. 9

the loin. For this reason, it serves a large number of persons more advantageously than the others do.

42. Steaks Obtained From the Round.—While the steaks

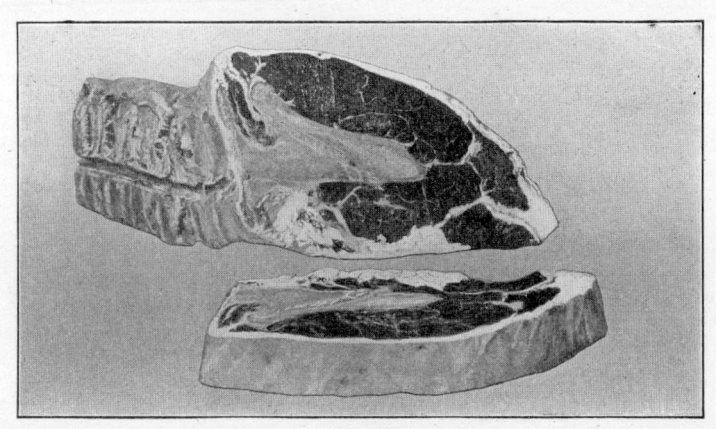

Fig. 10

cut from the loin are usually preferred because of their tenderness, those cut from the upper round and across the rump are very desirable for many purposes. If these are not so tender as is desired, the surface may be chopped with a dull knife in order to make tiny cuts through the fibers, or it may be pounded with some blunt object, as, for instance, a wooden potato masher. In Fig. 12, the entire round

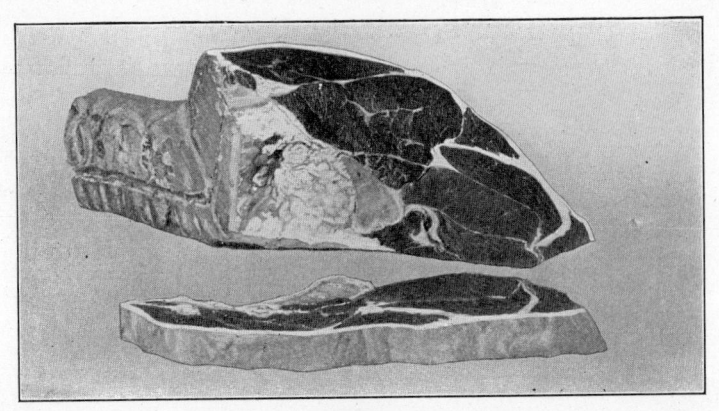

Fig. 11

and the way it is sometimes subdivided into the upper and lower round are shown. What is known as a **round steak** is a slice that is cut across the entire round. However, such a steak is often cut

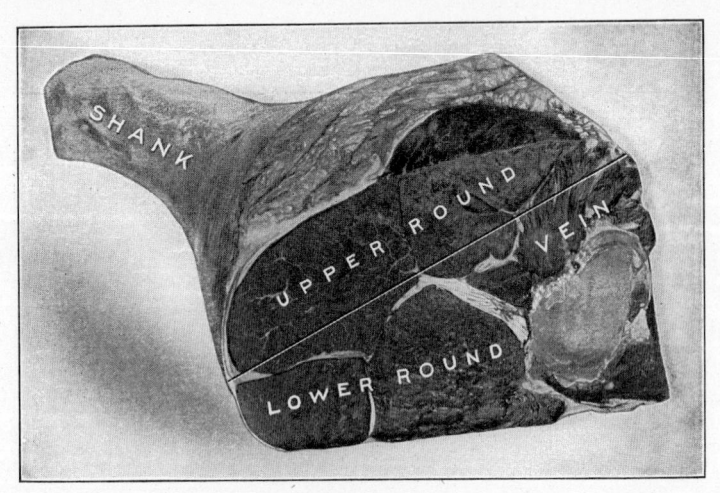

Fig. 12

into two parts where the line dividing the round is shown, and either the upper or the lower piece may be purchased. The upper round is the better piece and brings a higher price than the whole round or the lower round including the vein. The quick methods of cookery may be applied to the more desirable cuts of the round, but the lower round or the vein is generally used for roasting, braizing, or stewing.

43. Broiled Beefsteak.—As has already been explained, the steaks cut from the loin are the ones that are generally used for broiling. When one of these steaks is to be broiled, it should never be less than 1 inch thick, but it may be from 1 to $2\frac{1}{2}$ inches in thickness, according to the preference of the persons for whom it is prepared. As the flank end, or "tail," of such steaks is always tough, it should be cut off before cooking and utilized in the making of soups and such dishes as require chopped meats. In addition, all superfluous fat should be removed and then tried out. Beef fat, especially if it is mixed with lard or other fats, makes excellent shortening; likewise, it may be used for sautéing various foods.

When a steak has been prepared in this manner, wipe it carefully with a clean, damp cloth. Heat the broiler very hot and grease the rack with a little of the beef fat. Then place the steak on the rack, expose it directly to the rays of a very hot fire, and turn it every 10 seconds until each side has been exposed several times to the blaze. This is done in order to sear the entire surface and thus prevent the loss of the juice. When the surface is sufficiently seared, lower the fire or move the steak to a cooler place on the stove and then, turning it frequently, allow it to cook more slowly until it reaches the desired condition. The broiling of a steak requires from 10 to 20 minutes, depending on its thickness and whether it is preferred well done or rare. Place the broiled steak on a hot platter, dot it with butter, season it with salt and pepper, and serve at once.

44. Pan-Broiled Steak.—If it is impossible to prepare the steak in a broiler, it may be pan-broiled. In fact, this is a very satisfactory way to cook any of the tender cuts. To carry out this method, place a heavy frying pan directly over the fire and allow it to become so hot that the fat will smoke when put into it. Grease the pan with a small piece of the beef fat, just enough to prevent the steak from sticking fast. Put the steak into the hot pan and turn it as soon as it is seared on the side that touches the pan. After it is seared on the other side, turn it again and continue to turn it frequently until it has broiled for about 15 minutes. When it is cooked sufficiently to serve, dot it with butter and season it with salt and pepper. Serve hot.

45. Rolled Steak, or Mock Duck.—To have a delicious meat, it is not always necessary to secure the tender, expensive cuts, for excellent dishes can be prepared from the cheaper pieces. For instance, steaks cut from the entire round or thin cuts from the rump can be filled with a stuffing and then rolled to make rolled steak, or mock duck. This is an extremely appetizing dish and affords the housewife a chance to give her family a pleasing variety in the way of meat. The steak used for this purpose should first be broiled in the way explained in Art. **43.** Then it should be filled with a stuffing made as follows:

STUFFING FOR ROLLED STEAK

1 qt. stale bread crumbs	1 c. stewed tomatoes
1 small onion	1 Tb. salt
2 Tb. butter	¼ Tb. pepper
1 c. hot water	

Mix all together. Pile on top of the broiled steak and roll the steak so that the edges lap over each other and the dressing is

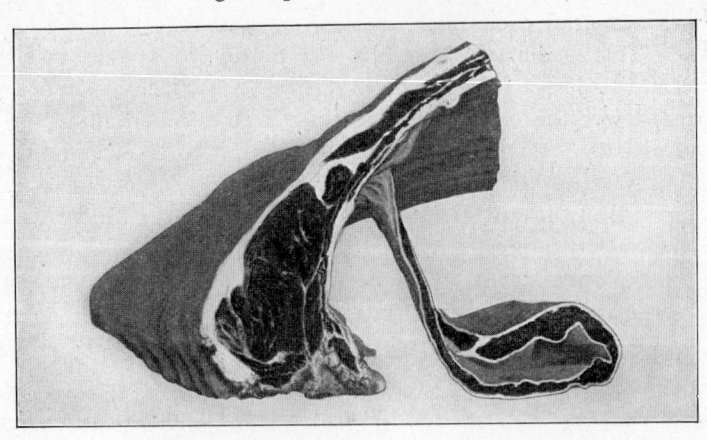

FIG. 13

completely covered. Fasten together with skewers or tie by wrapping a cord around the roll. Strips of bacon or salt pork tied to the outside or fastened with small skewers improve the flavor of the meat. Place in a roasting pan and bake in a hot oven until the steak is thoroughly baked. This will require not less than 40 minutes. Cut into slices and serve hot.

46. Skirt Steak.—Lying inside the ribs and extending from the second or third rib to the breast bone is a thin strip of muscle known as a *skirt steak*. This is removed before the ribs are cut for roasts, and, as shown in Fig. 13, is slit through the center with a long, sharp knife to form a pocket into which stuffing can be put. As a skirt steak is not expensive and has excellent flavor, it is a very desirable piece of meat.

To prepare such a steak for the table, stuff it with the stuffing given for rolled steak in Art. **45,** and then fasten the edges together with skewers. Bake in a hot oven until the steak is well done. Serve hot.

47. Swiss Steak.—Another very appetizing dish that can be made from the cheaper steaks is Swiss steak. To be most satisfactory, the steak used for this purpose should be about an inch thick.

Pound as much dry flour as possible into both sides of the steak by means of a wooden potato masher. Then brown it on both sides in a hot frying pan with some of the beef fat. When it is thoroughly browned, pour a cup of hot water over it, cover the pan tight, and remove to the back of the stove. Have just enough water on the steak and apply just enough heat to keep it simmering very slowly for about $\frac{1}{2}$ hour. As the meat cooks, the water will form a gravy by becoming thickened with the flour that has been pounded into the steak. Serve the steak with this gravy.

48. Hamburger Steak.—The tougher pieces of beef, such as the flank ends of the steak and parts of the rump, the round, and the chuck, may be ground fine by being forced through a food chopper. Such meat is very frequently combined with egg and then formed into small cakes or patties to make Hamburger steak. Besides providing a way to utilize pieces of meat that might otherwise be wasted, this dish affords variety to the diet.

HAMBURGER STEAK
(Sufficient to Serve Four)

1 lb. chopped beef   1 small onion, chopped
1½ tsp. salt   1 egg (if desired)
¼ tsp. pepper

Mix the ingredients thoroughly and shape into thin patties. Cook by broiling in a pan placed in the broiler or by pan-broiling in a hot, well-greased frying pan. Spread with butter when ready to serve.

49. Planked Steak.—A dish that the housewife generally considers too complicated for her, but that may very readily be prepared in the home, is planked steak. Such a steak gets its name from the fact that a part of its cooking is done on a hardwood plank, and that the steak, together with vegetables of various kinds, is served on the plank. Potatoes are always used as one of the vegetables that are combined with planked steak, but besides them almost any combination or variety of vegetables may be used as a garnish. Asparagus tips, string beans, peas, tiny onions, small carrots, mushrooms, cauliflower, stuffed peppers, and stuffed tomatoes are the vegetables from which a selection is usually made. When a tender steak is selected for this purpose and is properly cooked, and when the vegetables are well prepared and artistically arranged, no dish can be found that appeals more to the eye and the taste.

To prepare this dish, broil or pan-broil one of the better cuts of steak for about 8 minutes. Butter the plank, place the steak on the center of it and season with salt and pepper. Mash potatoes and to each 2 cupfuls use 4 tablespoonfuls of milk, 1 tablespoonful of butter, and one egg. After these materials have been mixed well into the potatoes, arrange a border of potatoes around the edge of the plank. Then garnish the steak with whatever vegetables have been selected. Care should be taken to see that these are properly cooked and well seasoned. If onions, mushrooms, or carrots are used, it is well to sauté them in butter after they are thoroughly cooked. With the steak thus prepared, place the plank under the broiler or in a hot oven and allow it to remain there long enough to brown the potatoes, cook the steak a little more, and thoroughly heat all the vegetables.

50. Vegetables Served With Steak.—If an attractive, as well as a tasty, dish is desired and the housewife has not sufficient time nor the facilities to prepare a planked steak, a good plan is to sauté a vegetable of some kind and serve it over the steak. For this purpose numerous vegetables are suitable, but onions, small mushrooms, and sliced tomatoes are especially desirable. When onions are used, they should be sliced thin and then sautéd in butter until they are soft and brown. Small mushrooms may be prepared in the same way, or they may be sautéd in the fat that remains in the pan after the steak has been removed. Tomatoes that are served over steak should be sliced, rolled in crumbs, and then sautéd.

ROASTS AND THEIR PREPARATION

51. Fillet of Beef.—A large variety of roasts can be obtained from a side of beef, but by far the most delicious one is the tenderloin, or fillet of beef. This is a long strip of meat lying directly

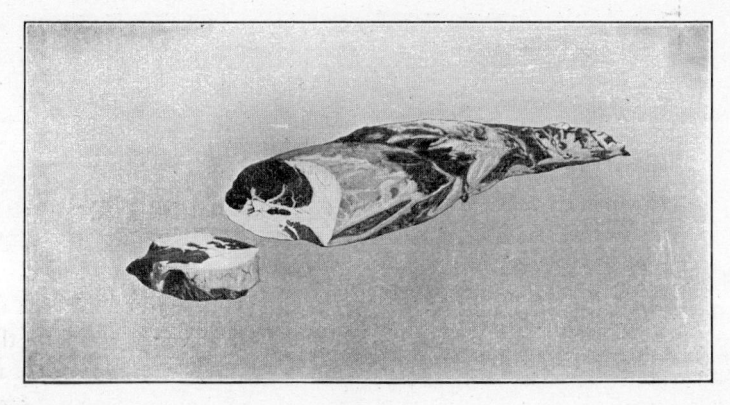

Fig. 14

under the chine, or back bone. It is either taken out as a whole, or it is left in the loin to be cut as a part of the steaks that are obtained from this section. When it is removed in a whole piece, as shown in Fig. 14, the steaks that remain in the loin are not so desirable

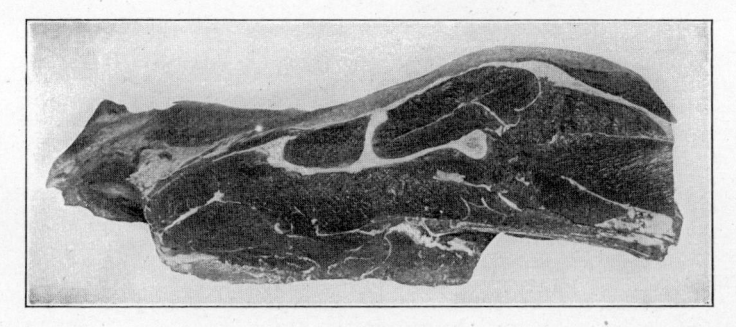

Fig. 15

and do not bring such a good price, because the most tender part of each of them is removed.

Two different methods of cookery are usually applied to the tenderloin of beef. Very often, as Fig. 14 shows, it is cut into slices about 2 inches thick and then broiled, when it is called *broiled fillet*, or *fillet mignon*. If it is not treated in this way, the whole tenderloin is roasted after being rolled, or larded, with salt pork to supply the fat that it lacks. Whichever way it is cooked, the tenderloin always proves to be an exceptionally tender and delicious cut of

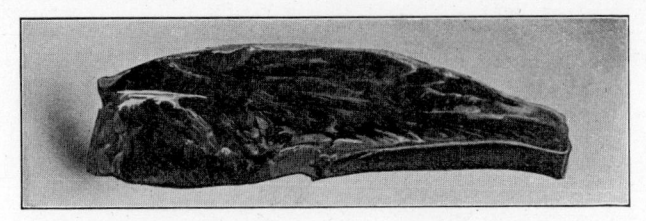

Fig. 16

beef. However, it is the most expensive piece that can be bought, and so is not recommended when economy must be practiced.

52. Chuck Roasts.—While the pieces cut from the chuck are not so desirable as those obtained from the loin or as the prime ribs, still the chuck yields very good roasts, as Figs. 15 and 16 show. The roast shown in Fig. 15 is the piece just back of the shoulder, and that illustrated in Fig. 16 is cut from the ribs in the chuck. These pieces are of a fairly good quality and if a roast as

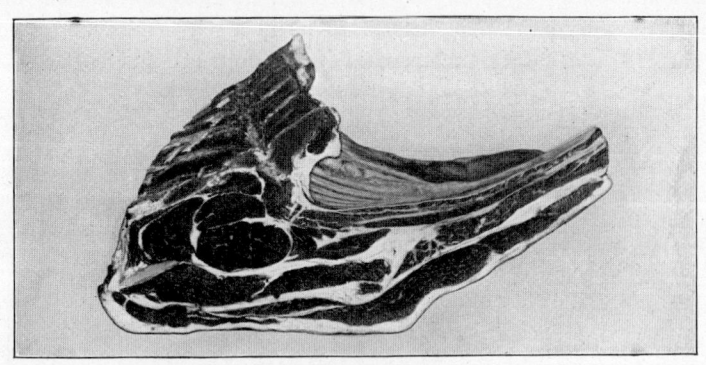

Fig. 17

large as 8 or 10 pounds is desired, they make an economical one to purchase.

53. Rib Roasts.—Directly back of the chuck, as has already been learned, are the prime ribs. From this part of the beef, which is shown in Figs. 17 and 18, the best rib roasts are secured. Fig. 17 shows the ribs cut off at about the eighth rib and Fig. 18 shows the same set turned around so that the cut surface is at about the first

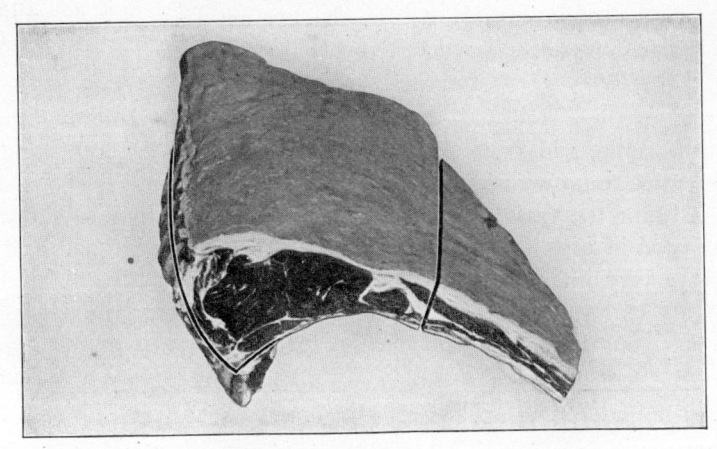

FIG. 18

rib, where the best cuts occur. To prepare this piece for roasting, it is often cut around the dark line shown in Fig. 18, and after the

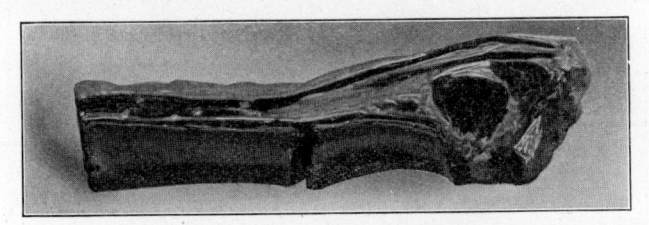

FIG. 19

back bone and ribs have been removed, is rolled into a roll of solid meat. The thin lower part that is cut off is used for boiling.

54. When only a small roast is wanted, a single rib, such as is shown in Fig. 19, is often used. In a roast of this kind, the bone is not removed, but, as will be observed, is sawed in half. Such a roast is called a *standing rib roast*. Another small roast, called a *porterhouse roast,* is illustrated in Fig. 20. This is obtained by cutting a porterhouse steak rather thick. It is therefore a very tender and

FIG. 20

delicious, although somewhat expensive, roast. Other parts of the loin may also be cut for roasts, the portion from which sirloin steaks are cut making large and very delicious roasts.

55. Rump Roasts.—Between the loin and the bottom round lies the rump, and from this may be cut roasts of different kinds. The entire rump with its cut surface next to the round is shown in Fig. 21, and the various pieces into which the rump may be cut are illustrated in Figs. 22 to 25. These roasts have a very good flavor and are very juicy, and if beef in prime condition can be obtained, they are extremely tender. Besides these advantages, rump roasts are economical, so they are much favored. To prepare them for

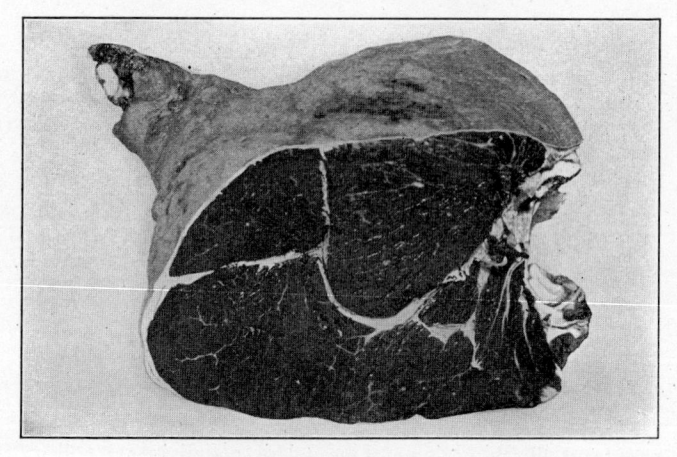

Fig. 21

cooking, the butcher generally removes the bone and rolls them in the manner shown in Fig. 26.

56. Roast Beef.—The usual method of preparing the roasts that have just been described, particularly the tender ones, is to cook them in the oven. For this purpose a roasting pan, such as the one previously described and illustrated, produces the best results, but if one of these cannot be obtained, a dripping pan may be substituted. When the meat is first placed in the oven, the oven temperature should be 400 to 450 degrees Fahrenheit, but after the meat has cooked for about 15 minutes, the temperature should be lowered so that the meat will cook more slowly.

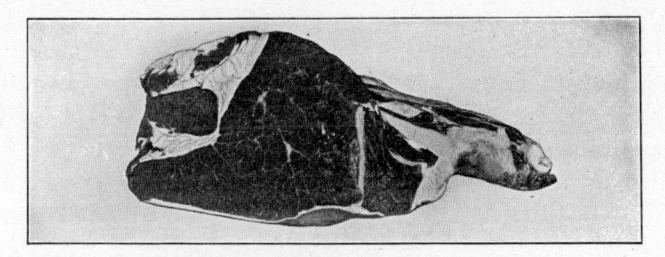

Fig. 22

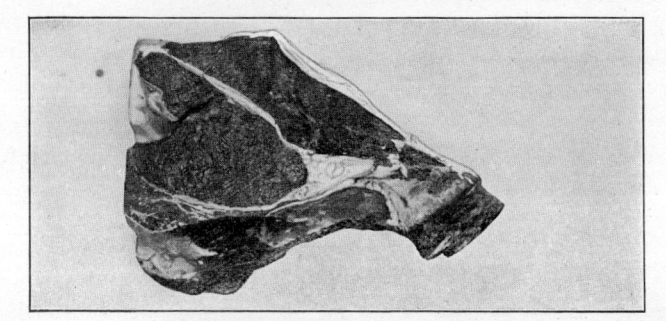

Fig. 23

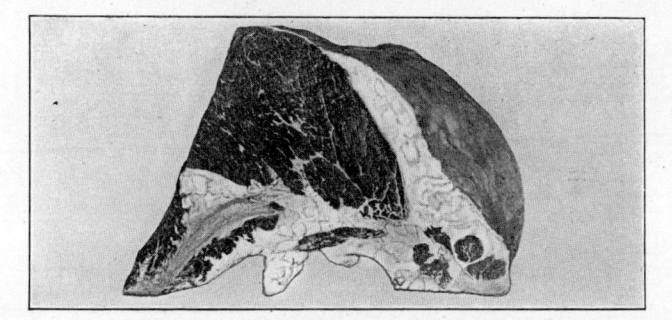

Fig. 24

Fig. 25

Before putting the roast in the oven, wipe it thoroughly with a damp cloth. If its surface is not well covered with a layer of fat, place several pieces of salt pork on it and tie or skewer them fast. Then, having one of the cut sides up so that it will be exposed to the heat of the oven, set the piece of meat in a roasting pan or the utensil that is to be substituted. Dredge, or sprinkle, the surface with flour, salt, and pepper, and place the pan in the oven, first making sure that the oven is sufficiently hot. Every 10 or 15 minutes *baste* the meat with the fat and the juice that cooks out of it; that is, spoon up this liquid and pour it over the meat in order to improve the flavor and to prevent the roast from becoming dry. If necessary, a little water may be added for basting, but the use of water for this purpose should generally be avoided. Allow the meat to roast until it is either well done or rare, according to the way it is preferred. The length of time required for this process depends so much on the size of the roast, the temperature of the oven, and the preference of the persons who are to eat the meat, that definite directions cannot well be given. However, a general idea of this matter can be obtained by referring to the Cookery Time Table given in *Essentials of Cookery,* Part 2, and also to Table I of this Section, which gives the time required for cooking each pound of meat. If desired, gravy may be made from the juice that remains in the pan, the directions for making gravy being given later.

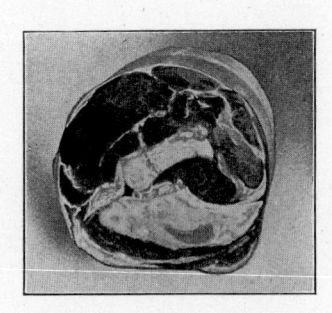

FIG. 26

57. Braized Beef.—An excellent way in which to cook a piece of beef that is cut from the rump or lower round is to braize it. This method consists in placing the meat on a rack over a small quantity of water in a closed pan and then baking it in the oven for about 4 hours. Vegetables cut into small pieces are placed in the water and they cook while the meat is baking. As meat prepared in this way really cooks in the flavored steam that rises from the vegetables, it becomes very tender and has a splendid flavor; also, the gravy that may be made from the liquid that remains adds to its value. In serving it, a spoonful of the vegetables is generally put on the plate with each piece of meat.

Braized Beef
(Sufficient to Serve Six)

3 lb. beef from rump or lower round	¼ c. diced carrots
Flour	¼ c. diced turnips
Salt	¼ c. diced onions
Pepper	¼ c. diced celery
2 thin slices salt pork	3 c. boiling water

Wipe the meat with a damp cloth, and dredge, or sprinkle, it with the flour, salt, and pepper. Try out the pork and brown the entire surface of the meat in the fat thus obtained. Then place the meat on a rack in a deep granite pan, an earthen bowl, or a baking dish, and surround it with the diced vegetables. Add the boiling water, cover the dish tight, and place in a slow oven. Bake for about 4 hours at a low temperature. Then remove the meat to a hot platter, strain out the vegetables, and make a thickened gravy of the liquid that remains, as explained later.

58. Pot-Roasted Beef.—The usual, and probably the most satisfactory, method of preparing the cheaper cuts of beef is to cook them in a heavy iron pot over a slow fire for several hours. If the proper attention is given to the preparation of such a roast, usually called a pot roast, it will prove a very appetizing dish. Potatoes may also be cooked in the pot with the meat. This is a good plan to follow for it saves fuel and at the same time offers variety in the cooking of potatoes.

When a piece of beef is to be roasted in a pot, try out in the pot a little of the beef fat. Then wipe the meat carefully and brown it on all sides in the fat. Add salt, pepper, and ½ cupful of boiling water and cover the pot tightly. Cook over a slow fire until the water is evaporated and the meat begins to brown; then add another ½ cupful of water. Continue to do this until the meat has cooked for several hours, or until the entire surface is well browned and the meat tissue very tender. Then place the meat on a hot platter and, if desired, make gravy of the fat that remains in the pan, following the directions given later. If potatoes are to be cooked with the roast, put them into the pot around the meat about 45 minutes before the meat is to be removed, as they will be cooked sufficiently when the roast is done.

59. Beef Loaf.—Hamburger steak is not always made into small patties and broiled or sautéd. In fact, it is very often combined with cracker crumbs, milk, and egg, and then well seasoned to make a beef loaf. Since there are no bones nor fat to be cut away in serving, this is an economical dish and should be used occasionally to give variety to the diet. If desired, a small quantity of salt pork may be combined with the beef to add flavor.

Beef Loaf
(Sufficient to Serve Ten)

3 lb. beef
¼ lb. salt pork
1 c. cracker crumbs
1 c. milk
1 egg

2 Tb. salt
¼ Tb. pepper
1 small onion
2 Tb. chopped parsley

Put the beef and pork through the food chopper; then mix thoroughly with the other ingredients. Pack tightly into a loaf-cake pan. Bake in a moderate oven for 2½ to 3 hours. During the baking, baste frequently with hot water to which a little butter has been added. Serve either hot or cold, as desired.

PREPARATION OF STEWS AND CORNED BEEF

60. Cuts Suitable for Stewing and Corning.—Because of the large variety of cuts obtained from a beef, numerous ways of cooking this meat have been devised. The tender cuts are, of course, the most desirable and the most expensive and they do not require the same preparation as the cheaper cuts. However, the poorer cuts, while not suitable for some purposes, make very good stews and corned beef. The cuts that are most satisfactory for stewing and corning are shown in Figs. 27 to 30. A part of the chuck that is much used for stewing and corning is shown in Fig. 27, *a* being the upper chuck, *b* the shoulder, and *c* the lower chuck. Fig. 28 shows a piece of the shoulder cut off just at the leg joint, Fig. 29, the neck, and Fig. 30, a piece of the plate called a flat-rib piece. Besides these pieces, the brisket, the lower part of the round, and any of the other chuck pieces that do not make good roasts are excellent for this purpose. In fact, any part that contains bone and fat, as well as lean, makes well-flavored stew.

61. Beef Stew.—Any of the pieces of beef just mentioned may be used with vegetables of various kinds to make beef stew. Also left-over pieces of a roast or a steak may be utilized with other meats in the making of this dish. If the recipe here given is care-

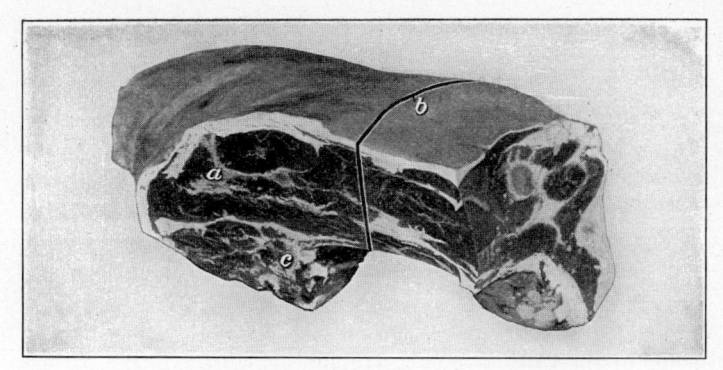

Fig. 27

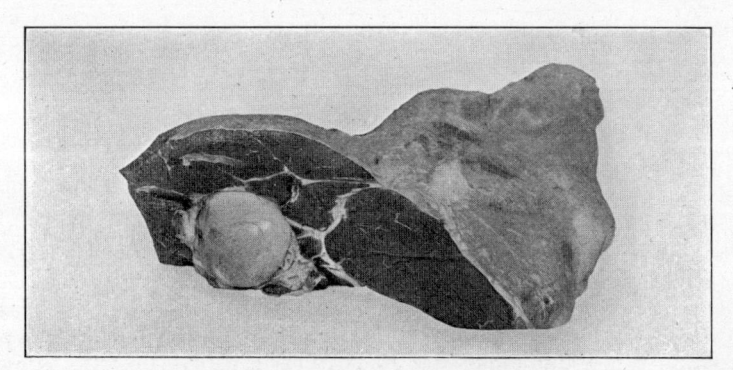

Fig. 28

Fig. 29

Fig. 30

fully followed, a very appetizing as well as nutritious stew will be the result.

Beef Stew
(Sufficient to Serve Eight)

4 lb. beef	$\frac{2}{3}$ c. diced carrots
2 Tb. salt	1 small onion, sliced
$\frac{1}{4}$ Tb. pepper	3 c. potatoes cut into $\frac{1}{4}$-in. slices
$\frac{2}{3}$ c. diced turnips	2 Tb. flour

Wipe the meat and cut it into pieces about 2 inches long. Try out some of the fat in a frying pan and brown the pieces of meat in it, stirring the meat constantly so that it will brown evenly. Put the browned meat into a kettle with the remaining fat and the bone, cover well with boiling water, and add the salt and pepper. Cover the kettle with a tight-fitting lid. Let the meat boil for a minute or two, then reduce the heat, and allow it to simmer for about 2 hours. For the last hour, cook the diced turnips, carrots, and onions with the meat, and 20 minutes before serving, add the potatoes. When the meat and vegetables are sufficiently cooked, remove the bones, fat, and skin; then thicken the stew with the flour moistened with enough cold water to pour. Pour into a deep platter or dish and serve with or without dumplings.

62. When dumplings are to be served with beef stew or any dish of this kind, they may be prepared as follows:

Dumplings

2 c. flour	2 Tb. fat
$\frac{1}{2}$ Tb. salt	$\frac{3}{4}$ to 1 c. milk
4 tsp. baking powder	

Mix and sift the flour, salt, and baking powder. Chop in the fat with a knife. Add the milk gradually and mix to form a dough. Toss on a floured board and roll out or pat until it is about 1 inch thick. Cut into pieces with a small biscuit cutter. Place these close together in a buttered steamer and steam over a kettle of hot water for 15 to 18 minutes. Serve with the stew.

If a softer dough that can be cooked with the stew is preferred, $1\frac{1}{8}$ cupfuls of milk instead of $\frac{3}{4}$ to 1 cupful should be used. Drop the dough thus prepared by the spoonful into the stew and boil for about 15 minutes. Keep the kettle tightly covered while the dumplings are boiling.

63. Corned Beef.—It is generally the custom to purchase corned beef, that is, beef preserved in a brine, at the market; but this is not necessary, as meat of this kind may be prepared in the home. When the housewife wishes to corn beef, she will find it an advantage to procure a large portion of a quarter of beef, part of which may be corned and kept to be used after the fresh beef has been eaten. Of course, this plan should be followed only in cold weather, for fresh meat soon spoils unless it is kept very cold.

To corn beef, prepare a mixture of 10 parts salt to 1 part saltpeter and rub this into the beef until the salt remains dry on the surface. Put the meat aside for 24 hours and then rub it again with some of the same mixture. On the following day, put the beef into a large crock or stone jar and cover it with a brine made by boiling 2½ gallons of water into which have been added 2 quarts salt, 2 ounces saltpeter, and ¾ pound brown sugar. Be careful to cool the brine until it entirely cold before using it. Allow the beef to remain in the brine for a week before attempting to use it. Inspect it occasionally, and if it does not appear to be keeping well, remove it from the brine, rub it again with the salt mixture, and place it in fresh brine. Beef that is properly corned will keep an indefinite length of time, but it should be examined every 2 or 3 days for the first few weeks to see that it is not spoiling.

64. Boiled Corned Beef.—The usual way to prepare beef corned in the manner just explained or corned beef bought at the market is to boil it. After it becomes sufficiently tender by this method of cooking, it may be pressed into a desired shape and when cold cut into thin slices. Meat of this kind makes an excellent dish for a light meal such as luncheon or supper.

To boil corned beef, first wipe it thoroughly and roll and tie it. Then put it into a kettle, cover it with boiling water, and set it over the fire. When it comes to the boiling point, skim off the scum that forms on the top. Cook at a low temperature until the meat is tender enough to be pierced easily with a fork. Then place the meat in a dish or a pan, pour the broth over it, put a plate on top that will rest on the meat, and weight it down with something heavy enough to press the meat into shape. Allow it to remain thus overnight. When cold and thoroughly set, remove from the pan, cut into thin slices, and serve.

65. Boiled Dinner.—Corned beef is especially adaptable to what is commonly termed a boiled dinner. Occasionally it is advisable for the housewife to vary her meals by serving a dinner of this kind. In addition to offering variety, such a dinner affords her an opportunity to economize on fuel, especially if gas or electricity is used, for all of it may be prepared in the same pot and cooked over the same burner.

BOILED DINNER
(Sufficient to Serve Six)

3 lb. corned beef
1 small head of cabbage cut into eighths
1 c. sliced carrots
1 c. sliced turnips
1 c. sliced potatoes
Pepper and salt

Cook the corned beef in the manner explained in Art. **64.** When it has cooked sufficiently, remove it from the water. Into this water, put the cabbage, carrots, turnips, and potatoes; then add the salt and pepper, seasoning to taste. Cook until the vegetables are tender. Remove the vegetables and serve them in vegetable dishes with some of the meat broth. Reheat the meat before serving.

BEEF ORGANS AND THEIR PREPARATION

66. Boiled Tongue.—The tongue of beef is much used, for if properly prepared it makes a delicious meat that may be served hot or cold. It is usually corned or smoked to preserve it until it can be used. In either of these forms or in its fresh state, it must be boiled in order to remove the skin and prepare the meat for further use. If it has been corned or smoked, it is likely to be very salty, so that it should usually be soaked overnight to remove the salt.

When boiled tongue is desired, put a fresh tongue or a smoked or a corned tongue from which the salt has been removed into a kettle of cold water and allow it to come to a boil. Skim and continue to cook at a low temperature for 2 hours. Cool enough to handle and then remove the skin and the roots. Cut into slices and serve hot or cold.

67. Pickled Tongue.—A beef tongue prepared in the manner just explained may be treated in various ways, but a method of preparation that meets with much favor consists in pickling it. Pickled tongue makes an excellent meat when a cold dish is required for a light meal or meat for sandwiches is desired. The pickle required for one tongue contains the following ingredients:

PICKLE

1½ c. vinegar   ¼ Tb. pepper
2 c. water   6 cloves
¼ c. sugar   1 stick cinnamon
1 Tb. salt

Boil all of these ingredients for a few minutes, then add the tongue, and boil for 15 minutes. Remove from the stove and let stand for 24 hours. Slice and serve cold.

68. Braized Tongue.—The process of braizing may be applied to tongue as well as to other parts of beef. In fact, when tongue is cooked in this way with several kinds of vegetables, it makes a delicious dish that is pleasing to most persons.

BRAIZED TONGUE
(Sufficient to Serve Eight)

1 fresh tongue   1 c. stewed tomatoes
⅓ c. diced carrots   2 c. water in which tongue is
⅓ c. diced onions   boiled
⅓ c. diced celery

Boil the tongue as previously directed, and then skin it and remove the roots. Place it in a long pan and pour over it the carrots, onions, celery, stewed tomatoes, and the water. Cover tight and bake in a slow oven for 2 hours. Serve on a platter with the vegetables and sauce.

69. Stuffed Heart.—If a stuffed meat is desired, nothing more appetizing can be found than stuffed heart. For this purpose the heart of a young beef should be selected in order that a tender dish will result.

After washing the heart and removing the veins and the arteries, make a stuffing like that given for rolled beefsteak in Art. **45.** Stuff the heart with this dressing, sprinkle salt and pepper over it, and roll it in flour. Lay several strips of bacon or salt pork across the top, place in a baking pan, and pour 1 cupful of water into the pan. Cover the pan tight, set it in a hot oven, and bake slowly for 2 or 3 hours, depending on the size of the heart. Add water as the water in the pan evaporates, and baste the heart frequently. When it has baked sufficiently, remove to a platter and serve at once.

MAKING GRAVY

70. To meats prepared in various ways, gravy—that is, the sauce made from the drippings or juices that cook out of steaks, roasts, and stews, or from the broth actually cooked from the meat as for soup—is a valuable addition, particularly if it is well made and properly seasoned. A point to remember in this connection is that gravy should be entirely free from lumps and not too thick. It will be of the right thickness if 1 to 2 level tablespoonfuls of flour is used for each pint of liquid. It should also be kept in mind that the best gravy is made from the brown drippings that contain some fat.

To make gravy, remove any excess of fat that is not required, and then pour a little hot water into the pan in order to dissolve the drippings that are to be used. Add the flour to the fat, stirring until a smooth paste is formed. Then add the liquid, which may be water or milk, and stir quickly to prevent the formation of lumps. Season well with salt and pepper. Another method that also proves satisfactory is to mix the flour and liquid and then add them to the fat that remains in the pan in which the meat has been cooked.

TRYING OUT SUET AND OTHER FATS

71. The suet obtained from beef is a valuable source of fat for cooking, and it should therefore never be thrown away. The process of obtaining the fat from suet is called *trying,* and it is always practiced in homes where economy is the rule.

To try out suet, cut the pieces into half-inch cubes, place them in a heavy frying pan, and cover them with hot water. Allow this to come to a boil and cook until the water has evaporated. Continue the heating until all the fat has been drawn from the tissue. Then pour off all the liquid fat and squeeze the remaining suet with a potato masher or in a fruit press. Clean glass or earthen jars are good receptacles in which to keep the fat thus recovered from the suet.

To try out other fats, proceed in the same way as for trying out suet. Such fats may be tried by heating them in a pan without water, provided the work is done carefully enough to prevent them from scorching.

PREPARATION OF LEFT-OVER BEEF

72. As has been shown, meat is both an expensive and a perishable food. Therefore, some use should be made of every left-over bit of it, no matter how small, and it should be disposed of quickly in order to prevent it from spoiling. A point that should not be overlooked in the use of left-over meats, however, is that they should be prepared so as to be a contrast to the original preparation and thus avoid monotony in the food served. This variation may be accomplished by adding other foods and seasonings and by changing the appearance as much as possible. For instance, what remains from a roast of beef may be cut in thin slices and garnished to make an attractive dish; or, left-over meat may be made very appetizing by cutting it into cubes, reheating it in gravy or white sauce, and serving it over toast or potato patties. Then there is the sandwich, which always finds a place in the luncheon. The meat used for this purpose may be sliced thin or it may be chopped fine, and then, to increase the quantity, mixed with salad dressing, celery, olives, chopped pickles, etc. An excellent sandwich is made by placing thin slices of roast beef between two slices of bread and serving hot roast-beef gravy over the sandwich thus formed. Still other appetizing dishes may be prepared from left-over beef as the accompanying recipes show.

73. Mexican Beef.—An extremely appetizing dish, known as Mexican beef, can be made from any quantity of left-over beef by serving it with a vegetable sauce. Such a dish needs few accompaniments when it is served in a light meal, but it may be used very satisfactorily as the main dish in a heavy meal.

MEXICAN BEEF

2 Tb. butter	$\frac{1}{2}$ tsp. salt
1 onion, chopped	$\frac{1}{8}$ tsp. pepper
1 red pepper	1 tsp. celery salt
1 green pepper	Thin slices roast beef
$\frac{3}{4}$ c. canned tomatoes	

Brown the butter, add the chopped onion, and cook for a few minutes. Then add the chopped peppers, tomatoes, salt, pepper, and celery salt. Cook all together for a few minutes and add the thinly sliced roast beef. When the meat has become thoroughly heated, it is ready to serve.

74. Cottage Pie.—A very good way to use up left-over mashed potatoes as well as roast beef is to combine them and make a cottage pie. In this dish, mashed potatoes take the place of the crust that is generally put over the top of a meat pie. If well seasoned and served hot, it makes a very palatable dish.

To make a cottage pie, cover the bottom of a baking dish with a 2-inch layer of well-seasoned mashed potatoes. Over this spread left-over roast beef cut into small pieces. Pour over the meat and potatoes any left-over gravy and a few drops of onion juice made by grating raw onion. Cover with a layer of mashed potatoes 1 inch deep. Dot with butter and place in a hot oven until the pie has heated through and browned on top. Serve hot.

75. Beef Pie.—No housewife need be at a loss for a dish that will tempt her family if she has on hand some left-over pieces of beef, for out of them she may prepare a beef pie, which is always in favor. Cold roast beef makes a very good pie, but it is not necessary that roast beef be used, as left-over steak or even a combination of left-over meats, will do very well.

Cut into 1-inch cubes whatever kinds of left-over meats are on hand. Cover with hot water, add a sliced onion, and cook slowly for 1 hour. Thicken the liquid with flour and season well with salt and pepper. Add two or three potatoes, cut into $\frac{1}{4}$-inch slices, and let them boil for several minutes. Pour the mixture into a buttered baking dish and cover it with a baking-powder biscuit mixture. Bake in a hot oven until the crust is brown. Serve hot.

76. Beef Hash.—One of the most satisfactory ways in which to utilize left-over roast beef or corned beef is to cut it into small pieces and make it into a hash. Cold boiled potatoes that remain from a previous meal are usually combined with the beef, and onion is added for flavor. When hash is prepared to resemble an omelet and is garnished with parsley, it makes an attractive dish.

To make beef hash, remove all skin and bone from the meat, chop quite fine, and add an equal quantity of chopped cold-boiled potatoes and one chopped onion. Season with salt and pepper. Put the mixture into a well-buttered frying pan, moisten with milk, meat stock, or left-over gravy, and place over a fire. Let the hash brown slowly on the bottom and then fold over as for an omelet. Serve on a platter garnished with parsley.

77. Frizzled Beef.—While the dried beef used in the preparation of frizzled beef is not necessarily a left-over meat, the recipe for this dish is given here, as it is usually served at a meal when the preceding left-over beef dishes are appropriate. Prepared according to this recipe, frizzled beef will be found both nutritious and appetizing.

FRIZZLED BEEF
(Sufficient to Serve Four)

2 Tb. butter	1 c. milk
¼ lb. thinly sliced dried beef	4 slices of toast
2 Tb. flour	

Brown the butter in a frying pan and add the beef torn into small pieces. Allow it to cook until the beef becomes brown. Add the flour and brown it. Pour the milk over all, and cook until the flour thickens the milk. Serve over the toast.

MEAT
(PART 1)

EXAMINATION QUESTIONS

(1) (*a*) What is meat? (*b*) What substance in meat makes it a valuable food?

(2) (*a*) What do protein foods do for the body? (*b*) How does meat compare in cost with the other daily foods?

(3) What harm may occur from eating meat that is not thoroughly cooked?

(4) (*a*) Describe the structure of meat. (*b*) How do the length and the direction of the fibers affect the tenderness of meat?

(5) (*a*) How may gelatine be obtained from meat? (*b*) What use is made of this material?

(6) (*a*) Describe the two kinds of fat found in meat. (*b*) What does this substance supply to the body?

(7) (*a*) What is the value of water in the tissues of meat? (*b*) How does its presence affect the cookery method to choose for preparing meat?

(8) (*a*) What are extractives? (*b*) Why are they of value in meat?

(9) (*a*) Name the ways by which the housewife may reduce her meat bill. (*b*) How should meat be cared for in the home?

(10) Give three reasons for cooking meat.

(11) (*a*) Describe the effect of cooking on the materials contained in meat. (*b*) How does cooking affect the digestibility of meat?

(12) What methods of cookery are used for: (*a*) the tender cuts of meat? (*b*) the tough cuts? (*c*) Mention the cuts of meat that have the most flavor.

(13) (*a*) How should the temperature of the oven vary with the size of the roast to be cooked? (*b*) Give the reason for this.

(14) Describe beef of good quality.

(15) In what parts of the animal are found: (*a*) the cheaper cuts of beef? (*b*) the more expensive cuts?

(16) (*a*) Name the steaks obtained from the loin? (*b*) Which of these is best for a large family? (*c*) Which is best for a small family?

(17) Describe the way in which to broil steak.

(18) (*a*) What is the tenderloin of beef? (*b*) Explain the two ways of cooking it.

(19) (*a*) Name the various kinds of roasts. (*b*) Describe the roasting of beef in the oven.

(20) (*a*) What cuts of beef are most satisfactory for stews? (*b*) Explain how beef stew is made.

MEAT
(PART 2)

VEAL

NATURE OF VEAL

1. Veal is the name applied to the flesh of a slaughtered calf. This kind of meat is at its best in animals that are from 6 weeks to 3 months old when killed. Calves younger than 6 weeks are sometimes slaughtered, but their meat is of poor quality and should be avoided. Meat from a calf that has not reached the age of 3 weeks is called *bob veal*. Such meat is pale, dry, tough, and indigestible and, consequently, unfit for food. In most states the laws strictly forbid the sale of bob veal for food, but constant vigilance must be exercised to safeguard the public from unscrupulous dealers. A calf that goes beyond the age of 3 months without being slaughtered must be kept and fattened until it reaches the age at which it can be profitably sold as beef, for it is too old to be used as veal.

2. The nature of veal can be more readily comprehended by comparing it with beef, the characteristics of which are now understood. Veal is lighter in color than beef, being more nearly pink than red, and it contains very little fat, as reference to Fig. 1, *Meat, Part 1*, will show. The tissues of veal contain less nutriment than those of beef, but they contain more gelatine. The flavor of veal is less pronounced than that of beef, the difference between the age of animals used for veal and those used for beef being responsible for this lack of flavor. These characteristics, as well as the difference in size of corresponding cuts, make it easy to distinguish veal from beef in the market.

COPYRIGHTED BY INTERNATIONAL EDUCATIONAL PUBLISHING COMPANY. ALL RIGHTS RESERVED

§ 11

CUTS OF VEAL AND THEIR USES

3. The slaughtered calf from which veal is obtained is generally delivered to the butcher in the form shown in Fig. 1; that is, with

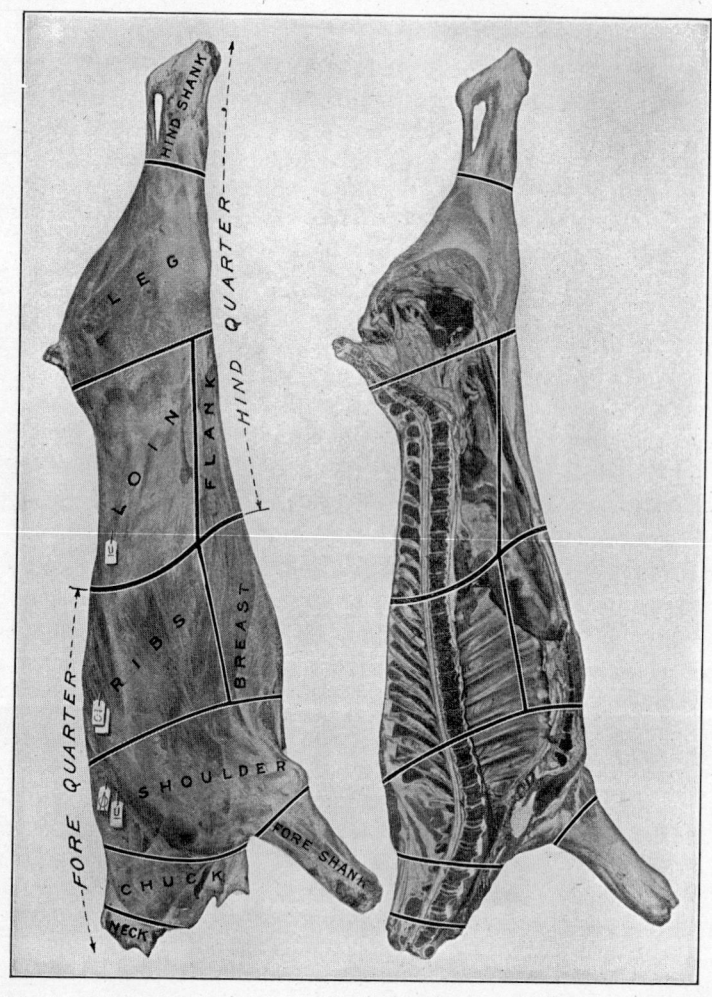

Fig. 1

the head, feet, and intestines removed and the carcass split into halves through the spine. He divides each half into quarters, known as the *fore quarter* and the *hind quarter,* and cuts these into smaller pieces.

4. Fore Quarter.—The fore quarter, as shown in Fig. 1, is composed of the neck, chuck, shoulder, fore shank, breast, and ribs. Frequently, no distinction is made between the neck and the chuck, both of these pieces and the fore shank being used for soups and stews. The shoulder is cut from the ribs lying underneath, and it is generally used for roasting, often with stuffing rolled inside of it. The breast, which is the under part of the fore quarter and corresponds to the plate in beef, is suitable for either roasting or stewing. When the rib bones are removed from it, a pocket that will hold stuffing can be cut into this piece. The ribs between the shoulder and the loin are called the *rack;* they may be cut into chops or used as one piece for roasting.

5. Hind Quarter.—The hind quarter, as Fig. 1 shows, is divided into the loin, flank, leg, and hind shank. The loin and the flank are located similarly to these same cuts in beef. In some localities, the part of veal corresponding to the rump of beef is included with the loin, and in others it is cut as part of the leg. When it is part of the leg, the leg is cut off just in front of the hip bone and is separated from the lower part of the leg, or hind shank, immediately below the hip joint. This piece is often used for roasting, although cutlets or steaks may be cut from it. The hind shank, which, together with the fore shank, is called a *knuckle,* is used for soup making. When the loin and flank are cut in a single piece, they are used for roasting.

6. Veal Organs.—Certain of the organs of the calf, like those of beef animals, are used for food. They include the heart, tongue, liver, and kidneys, as well as the thymus and thyroid glands and the pancreas. The heart and tongue of veal are more delicate in texture and flavor than those of beef, but the methods of cooking them are practically the same. The liver and kidneys of calves make very appetizing dishes and find favor with many persons. The thymus and thyroid glands and the pancreas are included under the term *sweetbreads*. The thymus gland, which lies near the heart and is often called the *heart sweetbread,* is the best one. The thyroid gland lies in the throat and is called the *throat sweetbread.* These two glands are joined by a connecting membrane, but this is often broken and each gland sold as a separate sweetbread. The pancreas, which is the *stomach sweetbread,* is used less often than the others.

7. Table of Veal Cuts.—The various cuts of veal, together with their uses, are arranged for ready reference in Table I. Therefore, so that the housewife may become thoroughly familiar with these facts about veal, she is urged to make a careful study of this table.

TABLE I
NAMES OF VEAL CUTS AND ORGANS AND THEIR USES

Name of Large Cut	Name of Small Cut	Uses of Cuts
Fore Quarter...	Head	Soup, made dishes, gelatine
	Breast	Stew, made dishes, gelatine
	Ribs	Stew, made dishes, chops
	Shoulder	Stew, made dishes
	Neck	Stew or stock, made dishes
Hind Quarter...	Loin	Chops, roasts
	Leg	Cutlets or fillet, sautéing, or roasting
	Knuckle	Stock, stews
Veal Organs....	Brains	Made dishes, chafing dish
	Liver	Broiling, sautéing
	Heart	Stuffed, baked
	Tongue	Boiled, braised
	Sweetbreads	Made dishes, chafing dish
	Kidneys	Boiled, stew

COOKING OF VEAL

VEAL CUTS AND THEIR PREPARATION

8. In the preparation of veal, an important point to remember is that meat of this kind always requires thorough cooking. It should never be served rare. Because of the long cooking veal needs, together with the difficulty encountered in chewing it and its somewhat insipid flavor, which fails to excite the free flow of gastric juice, this meat is more indigestible than beef. In order to render it easier to digest, since it must be thoroughly cooked, the long, slow methods of cookery should be selected, as these soften the connective tissue. Because of the lack of flavor, veal is not so good as beef when the extraction of flavor is desired for broth. However, the absence of flavor makes veal a valuable meat to combine with chicken and the more expensive meats, particularly in highly seasoned made dishes or salads. Although lacking in flavor, veal contains more gelatine than other meats. While this substance is not very valuable as a food, it lends body to soup or broth and assists in the preparation of certain made dishes. To supply the flavor needed in dishes of this kind, pork is sometimes used with the veal.

9. Veal Steaks or Cutlets.—Strictly speaking, veal cutlets are cut from the ribs; however, a thin slice cut from the leg, as shown in Fig. 2, while in reality a steak, is considered by most housewives and butchers as a cutlet. A piece cut from the leg of veal corresponds to a cut of round steak in beef.

10. Pan-Broiled Veal Steak or Cutlets.—Several methods of preparing veal steak or cutlets are in practice, but a very satis-

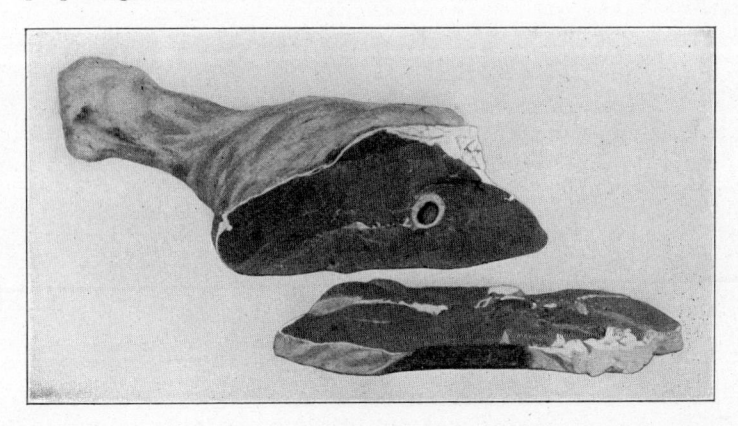

Fig. 2

factory one is to pan-broil them. This method prevents the juices from being drawn out of the meat and consequently produces a tender, palatable dish.

To pan-broil veal steak or cutlets, grease a hot frying pan with fat of any desirable kind, place the pieces of meat in it, and allow them to sear, first on one side and then on the other. When they are completely seared, lower the temperature, and broil for 15 to 20 minutes, or longer if necessary. Season well with salt and pepper. When cooked, remove to a platter and, just before serving, pour melted butter over the meat.

11. Veal Cutlets in Brown Sauce.—To improve the flavor of veal cutlets, a brown sauce is often prepared and served with them. In fact, the cutlets are cooked in this sauce, which becomes thickened by the flour that is used to dredge the meat.

To cook cutlets in this way, dredge them with flour, season them with salt and pepper, and sauté them in hot fat until the flour is quite brown. Then pour 1 cupful of milk and 1 cupful of water over the meat, cover the pan securely, and allow to cook slowly for about ¾ hour. The sauce should be slightly thick and quite brown. Serve the cutlets in the brown sauce.

12. Veal Roasts.—Several different cuts of veal make very good roasts. The most economical one is a 5- or 6-inch slice cut from the leg of veal in the same way as the steak shown in Fig. 2.

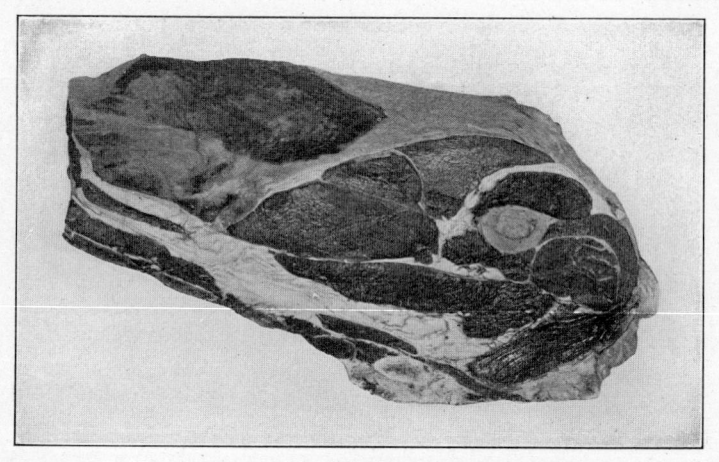

Fig. 3

Both the loin and the best end of the neck are excellent for roasting. The shoulder of veal, which is shown in Fig. 3, is sometimes roasted, but it is more often used for stew. Veal breast from which the ribs have been removed and veal rack, which is the portion of the ribs attached to the neck, may also be used for roasting. When they are, they are usually cut so as to contain a deep slit, or pocket, that may be filled with stuffing. In fact, whenever it is possible, the bone is removed from a piece of roasting veal and stuffing is put in its place.

To roast any of these pieces, wipe the meat, dredge it with flour, and season it with salt and pepper. Place it in a roasting pan and put it into a hot oven. Bake for 15 minutes; then lower the temperature of the oven and continue to bake slowly until the meat is well

§ 11 MEAT 7

done, the length of time depending on the size of the roast. Baste frequently during the roasting. Remove the roast to a hot platter. Then place the roasting pan over the flame, and make gravy by browning 2 tablespoonfuls of flour in the fat that it contains, adding to this 1½ cupfuls of water, and cooking until the flour has thickened the water. Serve the gravy thus prepared in a gravy bowl.

13. Stuffed Veal Breast.—A breast of veal in which a pocket has been cut for stuffing is shown in Fig. 4. When such a piece is

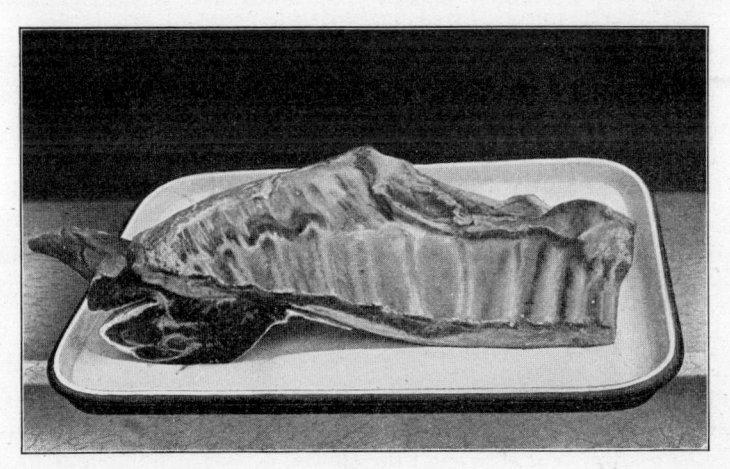

Fig. 4

desired for roasting, it is advisable to have the butcher prepare it. The stuffing required should be made as follows:

STUFFING FOR VEAL

4 Tb. butter or bacon or ham fat
½ Tb. salt
⅛ Tb. pepper
1 Tb. celery salt
2 sprigs of parsley, chopped
1 pimiento, chopped
1½ c. water
1 qt. stale bread crumbs

Melt the fat, and to it add the salt, pepper, celery salt, parsley, pimiento, and water. Pour this mixture over the crumbs, and mix all thoroughly. Stuff into the opening in the breast. Place the meat thus stuffed in a baking pan and bake in a moderately hot oven for 1 to 1½ hours.

14. Veal Potpie.—A good way in which to impart the flavor of meat to a starchy material and thus not only economize on meat, but also provide an appetizing dish, is to serve meat with dumplings in a veal potpie. For such a dish, a piece of veal from the shoulder, like that shown in Fig. 3, is the best cut. To give variety, potatoes may be used, and to improve the flavor at least one onion is cooked with the meat.

To prepare a veal potpie, wipe the meat, cut it into pieces of the right size for serving, and to it add a few pieces of salt pork or bacon. Put these over the fire in enough cold water to cover the meat well and add a small onion, sliced. Bring to the boiling point and skim; then simmer until the meat is tender. Season with salt and pepper a few minutes before the meat has finished cooking. Next, make a baking-powder biscuit dough, roll it $\frac{1}{4}$ inch thick, and cut it into $1\frac{1}{2}$-inch squares. Then examine the meat to see how much of the liquid has evaporated. If the liquid is too thick, add boiling water to thin it. Drop in the squares of dough, cover the pot tight, and boil for 15 minutes without uncovering.

If potatoes are desired in a pie of this kind, cut them into thick slices and add the slices about 10 minutes before the dough is to be put into the broth, so that they will have sufficient time in which to cook.

15. Veal Stew.—The cheaper cuts of veal can be used to advantage for making veal stew. Such a dish is prepared in the same way as beef stew, which is explained in *Meat,* Part 1, except that veal is substituted for the beef. Vegetables of any desired kind may be used in veal stew, and the stewed or boiled dumplings mentioned in the beef-stew recipe may or may not be used. As the vegetables and the dumplings, provided dumplings are used, increase the quantity of meat-flavored food, only small portions of the meat need be served.

16. Jellied Veal.—The large amount of gelatine contained in veal may be utilized in the preparation of jellied veal. The most satisfactory piece for making jellied veal is the knuckle, or shank. No more attractive meat dish than this can be found for luncheon or supper, for it can be cut into thin slices and served on a nicely garnished platter.

Jellied Veal
(Sufficient to Serve Six)

Knuckle of veal 1 Tb. chopped parsley
1 Tb. salt 1 Tb. chopped onion
$\frac{1}{4}$ c. chopped celery

Put the knuckle in a pot and add enough water to cover it. Add the salt, celery, parsley, and onion. Cook until the meat is very tender and then strain off the liquid. Cut the meat from the bones and chop it very fine. Boil the liquid until it is reduced to 1 pint, and then set aside to cool. Place the meat in a mold and when cold pour the broth over it. Keep in a cool place until it has set. Slice and serve cold.

VEAL ORGANS AND THEIR PREPARATION

17. Getting Sweetbreads Ready for Cooking.—The throat glands and the pancreas of calves, which, as has already been learned, are called sweetbreads, can be cooked in various ways for the table. The first process in their preparation, however, is the same for all recipes. When this is understood, it will be a simple matter to make up attractive dishes in which sweetbreads are used.

It is generally advisable to buy sweetbreads in pairs, as the heart and throat sweetbreads are preferable to the one that lies near the stomach. Sweetbreads spoil very quickly. Therefore, as soon as they are brought into the kitchen, put them in cold water and allow them to remain there for $\frac{1}{2}$ hour or more. Then put them to cook in boiling water for 20 minutes in order to parboil them, after which place them in cold water again. Unless they are to be used immediately, keep them in cold water, as this will prevent them from discoloring. Before using sweetbreads in the recipes that follow, remove the skin and stringy parts.

18. Broiled Sweetbreads.—Because of their tenderness, sweetbreads are especially suitable for broiling. When prepared in this way and served with sauce of some kind, they are very palatable.

In order to broil sweetbreads, first parboil them in the manner just explained. Then split each one lengthwise and broil them over a clear fire for 5 minutes or pan-broil them with a small amount of butter until both surfaces are slightly browned. Season with salt and pepper. Serve hot.

19. Creamed Sweetbreads.—If an especially dainty dish is desired for a light meal, sweetbreads may be creamed and then served over toast or in patty shells or timbale cases, the making of which is taken up later. If desired, mushrooms may be combined with sweetbreads that are served in this way. Diced cold veal or calves' brains creamed and served in this way are also delicious. Instead of creaming sweetbreads and calves' brains, however, these organs are sometimes scrambled with eggs.

To prepare creamed sweetbreads, parboil them and then separate them into small pieces with a fork or cut them into cubes. Reheat them in a cupful of white sauce, season well, and then serve them in any of the ways just mentioned. If mushrooms are to be used, cook and dice them before combining them with the sweetbreads.

20. Kidneys.—The kidneys of both lamb and veal are used for food. The cooking of them, however, must be either a quick, short process or a long, slow one. When a quick method is applied, the tissues remain tender. Additional cooking renders them tough, so that a great deal more cooking must be done to make them tender again. Whatever method is applied, kidneys must always be soaked in water for 1 hour or more so as to cleanse them, the outside covering then pared off, and the meat sliced or cut into cubes or strips. After being thus prepared, kidneys may be broiled or sautéd, or, if a long method of cookery is preferred, they may be boiled or stewed with or without vegetables.

21. Calves' Liver and Bacon.—Beef liver is sometimes used for food, but it is not so good as liver from the calf. In fact, calves' liver, especially when combined with bacon, is very appetizing. The bacon supplies the fat that the liver lacks and at the same time provides flavor.

To prepare calves' liver and bacon, cut the liver into ½-inch slices, cover these with boiling water, and let them stand for 5 minutes. Remove from the water, dip into flour, and sprinkle with salt and pepper. For each slice of liver pan-broil a slice of bacon. Remove the bacon to a hot platter, and then place the slices of liver in the bacon fat and sauté them for about 10 minutes, turning them frequently. Serve the liver and bacon together.

PREPARATION OF LEFT-OVER VEAL

22. Veal Rolls.—The portion of a veal roast that remains after it has been served hot can be combined with dressing to make veal rolls, a dish that will be a pleasing change from the usual cold sliced meat.

To make veal rolls, slice the veal and into each slice roll a spoonful of stuffing. Tie with a string, roll in flour, and sprinkle with salt and pepper. Brown the rolls in hot butter. Then pour milk, stock, or gravy over the rolls and simmer for 10 minutes. Remove the strings and serve on toast.

23. Left-Over Jellied Veal.—While jellied veal is usually made from a piece of veal bought especially for this purpose, it can be made from the left-overs of a veal roast. However, when the roast is purchased, some veal bones should be secured. Wash these bones, cover them with cold water, and to them add 1 onion, 1 bay leaf, and 1 cupful of diced vegetables, preferably celery, carrots, and turnips. Allow these to simmer for 2 hours. To this stock add the bones that remain after the roast has been served and simmer for 1 or 2 hours more. Strain the stock, skim off the fat, and season well with salt and pepper. Chop fine the left-over veal and 2 hard-cooked eggs. Put in a loaf-cake pan and pour the stock over it. When it has formed a mold, slice and serve cold.

24. Creamed Veal on Biscuits.—A very good substitute for chicken and hot biscuits is creamed veal served on biscuits. This is an especially good dish for a light meal, such as luncheon or supper. Any left-over veal may be chopped or cut up into small pieces and used for this purpose. After the veal has been thus prepared, reheat it with white sauce and season it well with paprika, salt, and pepper. Make baking-powder biscuits. To serve, split the hot biscuits, lay them open on a platter or a plate, and pour the hot creamed veal over them.

25. Scalloped Veal With Rice.—A very palatable dish can be prepared from left-over veal by combining it with rice and tomatoes. To prepare such a dish, season cooked rice with 1 teaspoonful of bacon fat to each cupful of rice. Place a layer of rice in a baking dish, and over it put a layer of chopped veal. Pour a good quantity of stewed tomatoes over the veal and season well with salt and pepper. Over the tomatoes put a layer of rice, and cover the top with buttered crumbs. Set in a hot oven and bake until the crumbs are browned and the ingredients thoroughly heated.

26. Veal Salad.—A salad is always a delightful addition to a meal and so usually finds favor. When it is made of meat, such as veal, it can be used as the main dish for luncheon or supper. As shown in the accompanying recipe, other things, such as celery, peas, and hard-cooked eggs, are usually put in a salad of this kind.

WI—C3—6

VEAL SALAD
(Sufficient to Serve Six)

2 c. cold diced veal	4 Tb. olive oil
1 c. diced celery	2 Tb. vinegar
½ c. canned peas	½ tsp. salt
3 hard-cooked eggs	⅛ tsp. pepper

Combine the veal, celery, peas, and eggs chopped fine. Mix the olive oil, vinegar, salt, and pepper to make a dressing. Marinate the ingredients with this dressing. Serve on lettuce leaves with any salad dressing desired.

MUTTON AND LAMB

COMPARISON OF MUTTON AND LAMB

27. The term **mutton** is usually applied to the flesh of a sheep that is 1 year or more old, while **lamb** is the flesh of sheep under 1 year of age. The popularity of these meats varies very much

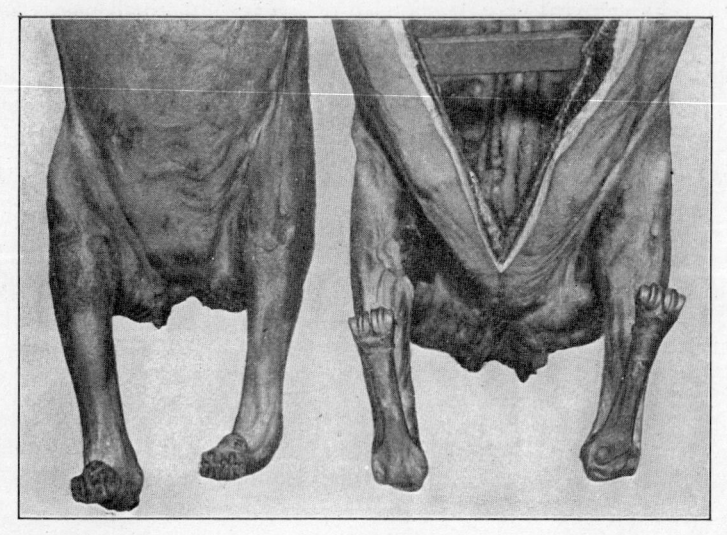

FIG. 5

with the locality. In the United States, a preference for lamb has become noticeable, but in England mutton is more popular and is more commonly used. Both of these meats, however, are very pala-

§ 11   MEAT   13

table and nutritious, so that the choice of one or the other will always be determined by the taste or market conditions.

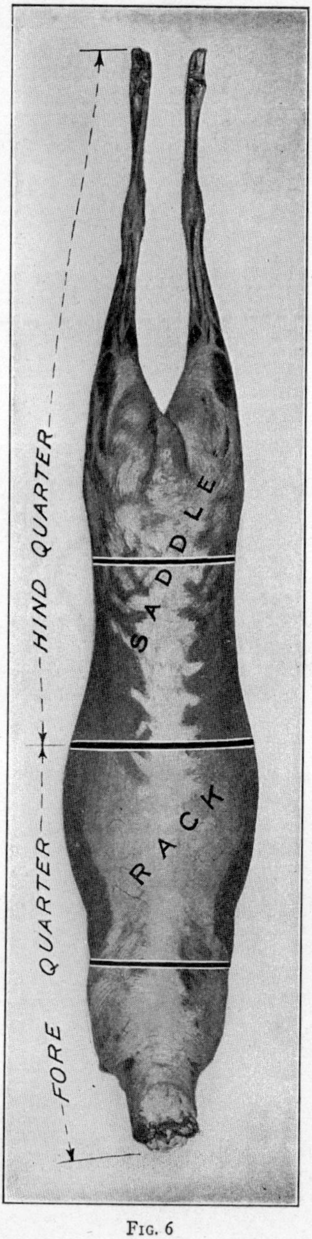

28. Lamb that is 6 weeks to 3 months old is called *spring lamb,* and usually comes into the market in January or February. The meat of sheep 1 year old is called *yearling.* Good mutton is cut from sheep that is about 3 years old. Lamb may be eaten as soon as it is killed, but mutton requires ripening for 2 or 3 weeks to be in the best condition for food. Mutton differs from lamb very much as beef differs from veal, or as the meat of any other mature animal differs from a young one of the same kind. In mutton there is a smaller percentage of water and a larger percentage of fat, protein, extractives, and flavoring substances.

There is also a difference in the appearance of these two meats. Lamb is pink and contains only small amounts of fat, while mutton is brick red and usually has considerable firm white fat. The bones of lamb are pink, while those of mutton are white. The outside of lamb is covered with a thin white skin that becomes pink in mutton. The size of the pieces of meat often aids in distinguishing between these two meats, mutton, of course, coming in larger pieces than lamb.

29. If there is any question as to whether the meat from sheep is lamb or mutton, and it canot be settled by any of the characteristics already mentioned, the front leg of the dressed animal may be examined at the first

Fig. 6

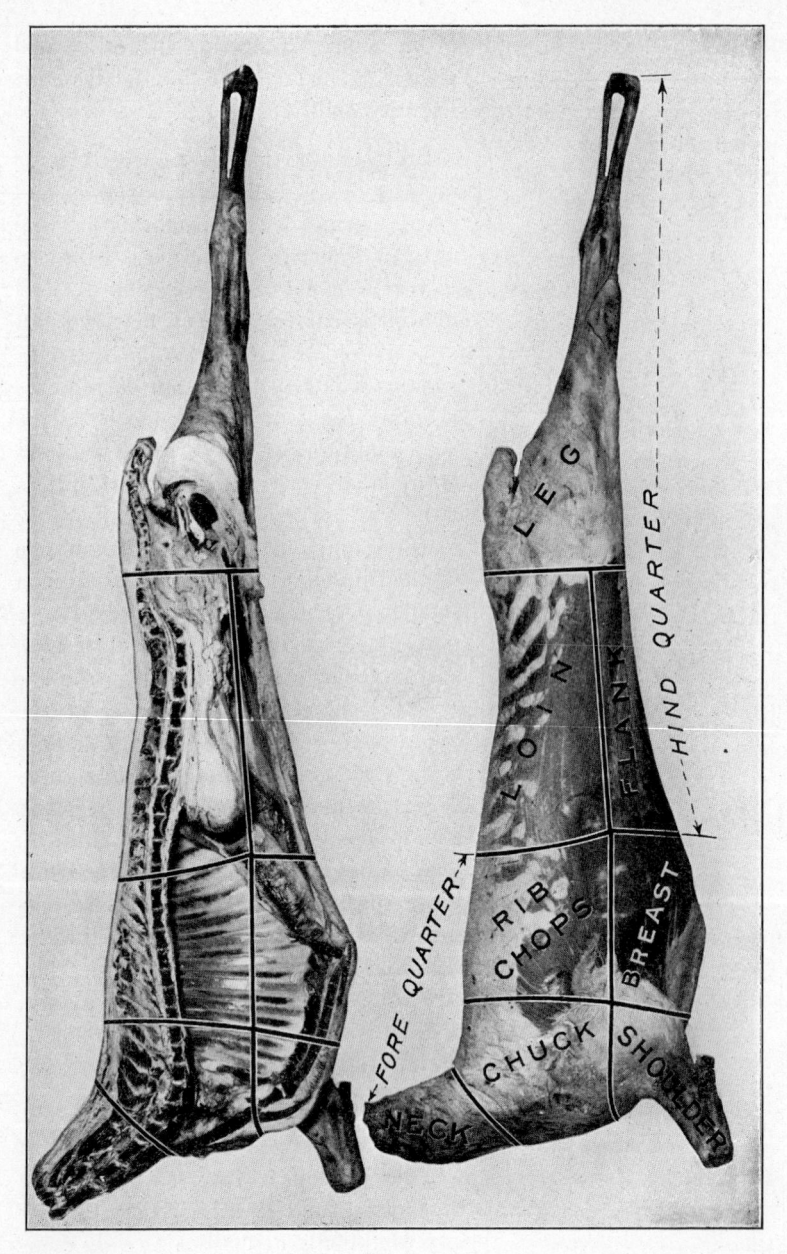

Fig. 7

joint above the foot. Fig. 5 shows this joint in both lamb and mutton. In lamb, which is shown at the left, the end of the bone can be separated from the long bone at the leg, as indicated, while in mutton this joint grows fast and looks like the illustration at the right. The joint is jagged in lamb, but smooth and round in mutton.

CUTS OF MUTTON AND LAMB

METHOD OF OBTAINING CUTS

30. Mutton and lamb are usually cut up in the same way, the dressed animal being divided into two pieces of almost equal weight. The line of division occurs between the first and second ribs, as is indicated by the heavy middle line in Fig. 6. The back half of the animal is called the *saddle* and the front half, the *rack*. In addition to being cut in this way, the animal is cut down the entire length of the backbone and is thus divided into the fore and hind quarters.

The method of cutting up the racks and saddles varies in different localities, but, as a rule, the method illustrated in Fig. 7 is the one that is used. As here shown, the rack, or fore quarter, is cut up into the neck, chuck, shoulder, rib chops, and breast; and the saddle, or hind quarter, is divided into the loin, flank, and leg.

The way in which the front and the back of a dressed sheep appear is shown in Fig. 8. The membrane, which extends from the legs down over the ribs, is the omentum, or covering of the intestines, and is known as the *caul*. This must be removed from any part that it covers before the meat is cooked. The kidneys incased in fat are also shown in the view at the left.

NAMES AND USES OF CUTS

31. Distinguishing Features of Cuts.—When the uses of the cuts of lamb and mutton are to be considered, attention must be given to the anatomy of the animal and the exercise that the different parts have received during life. This is important, because the continued action of the muscles tends to make the flesh tough, but, at the same time, it increases the amount of extractives or flavoring material. Therefore, meat taken from a part that has been subjected to much muscular action is likely to need longer cooking than that taken from portions that have not been exercised so much.

In lamb and mutton, as in beef and veal, the hind quarter is exercised less in life than the fore quarter and consequently is, on

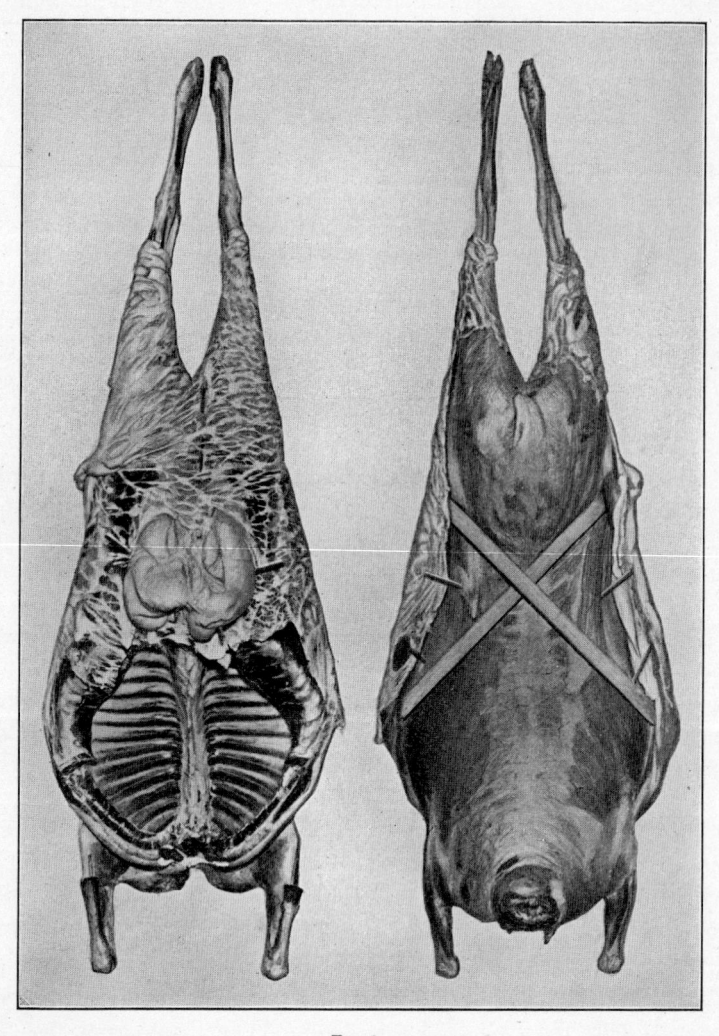

FIG. 8

the average, more tender. The cuts from this part are therefore more expensive and more suitable for roasting and broiling. The fore quarter, although having the disadvantage of containing more bone and being tougher, is more abundantly supplied with extractives and flavoring materials. Most of the pieces obtained from this portion are particularly suitable for broths, soups, stews, etc. The rib is an exception, for this is usually higher in price than the hindquarter pieces and is used for chops and roasts.

32. Table of Mutton and Lamb Cuts.—The various cuts of mutton and lamb and the uses to which they can be put are given in Table II, which may be followed as a guide whenever there is doubt as to the way in which a cut of either of these meats should be cooked.

TABLE II
NAMES AND USES OF MUTTON AND LAMB CUTS

Name of Large Cut	Name of Small Cut	Uses of Cuts
Fore quarter	Neck	Broth, stew
	Chuck	Stew, steamed
	Shoulder	Boiled, steamed, braised, roast
	Rack ribs	Chops, crown roast
	Breast	Stew, roast, braised, stuffed
Hind quarter	Loin	Seven chops, roast, boiling
	Flank	Stew
	Leg	Roast, braising, broiling
	Saddle	Roast

COOKING OF MUTTON AND LAMB

PREPARATION OF ROASTS, CHOPS, AND STEWS

33. The cookery processes applied in preparing mutton and lamb for the table do not differ materially from those applied in the preparation of other meats. However, directions for cooking mutton and lamb in the most practical ways are here given, so that the housewife may become thoroughly familiar with the procedure in preparing roasts, chops, and stews.

34. Roast Leg of Mutton or Lamb.—Of all the principal cuts of mutton or lamb, the leg contains the smallest percentage of waste. It is, therefore, especially suitable for roasting and is generally used for this purpose. In Fig. 9 are shown two views of a leg of lamb or mutton. That in (*a*) illustrates the leg with part of the loin attached, and that in (*b*), the leg trimmed and ready for cooking. In order to make the leg smaller, a slice resembling a round steak of beef is sometimes cut for broiling, as here shown. If desired, the leg may be boned and then stuffed before roasting. Since these meats are characterized by a very marked flavor, something tart or acid is generally served with them.

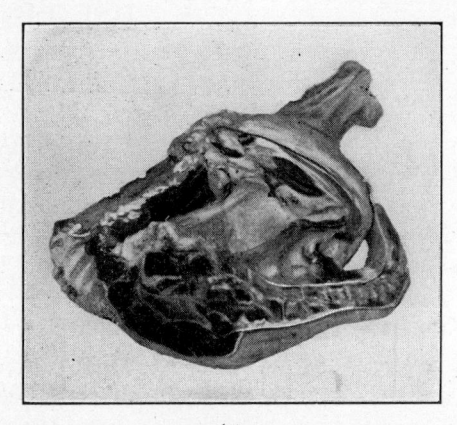

To roast a leg of lamb or mutton, remove the caul, the pink skin, and the superfluous fat. Dredge the leg with flour, salt, and pepper, set in a roasting pan, and place in a hot oven. After the meat has cooked for 15 minutes, lower the temperature, and bake for 2 hours. Baste frequently with water to which has been added a small amount of bacon or ham fat and which should be put in the pan with the meat. Serve hot with something acid, such as mint sauce, currant or mint jelly, or spiced fruit.

(*a*)

(*b*)

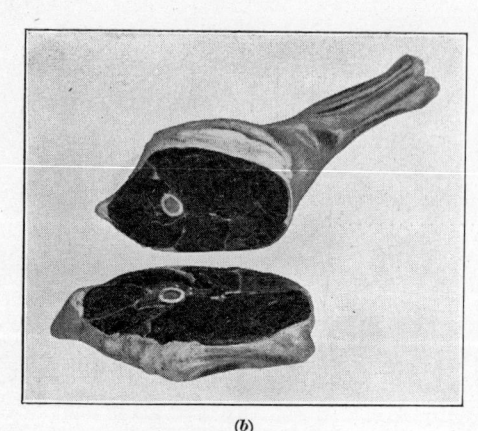

Fig. 9

A mint sauce that will be found satisfactory for this purpose is made as follows:

MINT SAUCE

2 Tb. powdered sugar $\frac{1}{4}$ c. finely chopped mint leaves,
$\frac{1}{2}$ c. vinegar   or 2 Tb. dried mint

Add the sugar to the vinegar and heat. Pour this over the mint and steep on the back of the stove for 30 minutes.

35. Roast Saddle of Mutton.—While saddle is the name applied to the hind quarters of lamb and mutton, this term, as used in the cooking of such meat, refers to the piece that consists of the two sides of the loin cut off in one piece. It may be cut with or without the flank. In either form, it is rolled and then skewered or tied into shape.

To roast such a piece, remove all superfluous fat, dredge with flour, salt, and pepper, place in a pan, and sear in a hot oven. Then reduce the heat, place a small quantity of water in the pan, and bake for $2\frac{1}{2}$ to 3 hours, basting from time to time during this cooking process. Serve with or without mint sauce, as desired.

36. Crown Roast of Lamb.—A very attractive roast is made by cutting the same number of corresponding ribs from each side of the lamb and trimming back the meat from the end of each rib. Such a roast is called a *crown roast*. Fig. 10 shows a crown roast

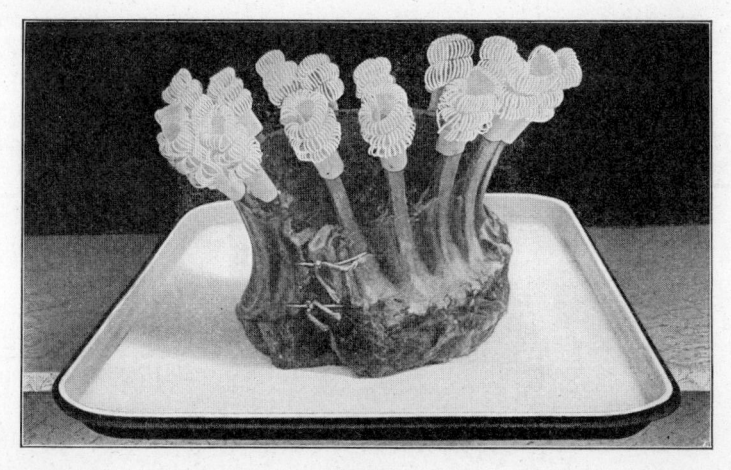

Fig. 10

with the ribs trimmed, the two pieces fastened together, and paper frills placed on the ends of the bones. Such frills are usually added by the butcher, but they may be purchased in supply stores and put on in the home.

To prepare a roast of this kind, cook in the same way as a roast leg or saddle. When it is sufficiently baked, fill the center with a cooked and seasoned vegetable. Brussels sprouts, peas, string beans, asparagus, and cauliflower are especially suitable for this purpose.

Just before serving, cover the ends of the bones with paper frills, as shown in the illustration.

37. Lamb and Mutton Chops.—Chops of mutton or lamb are obtained from two sources. They may be cut from the ribs and have one bone in each cut or they may be cut from the loin,

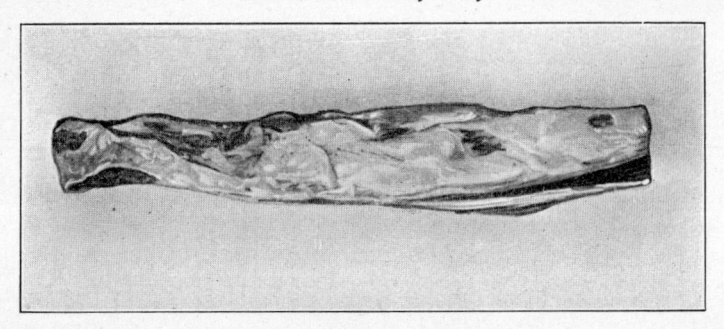

Fig. 11

when they correspond to the steaks in beef. The loins and ribs of lamb, which are sometimes used for rolled racks, but from which chops are usually cut, are shown in Fig. 11. A rib chop cut from this piece has only a small part of solid lean meat and contains one rib bone. Such a chop can be made into a French chop, as shown in Fig. 12, by trimming the meat from the bone down to the lean part, or "eye," of the chop. Just before being served, a paper frill may be placed over the bone of a chop of this kind. Chops cut from the

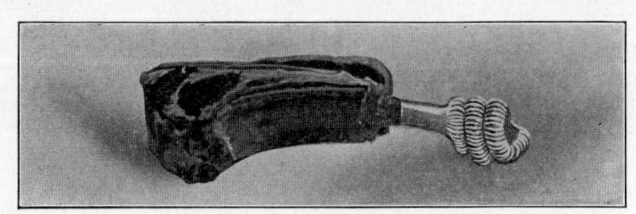

Fig. 12

loin often have a strip of bacon or salt pork rolled around the edge and fastened with a skewer, as shown in Fig. 13.

38. The most satisfactory way in which to prepare chops is either to broil them in a broiler or to pan-broil them. Apply to the cooking of them the same principles that relate to the preparation of steaks; that is, have the pan or broiler hot, sear the chops quickly on both sides, and then cook them more slowly until well done, turning them frequently. The broiling of lamb chops should require only from 8 to 10 minutes, as they are seldom more than 1 inch thick.

39. Lamb and Mutton Stews.—The cheaper cuts of lamb and mutton, such as the neck, chuck, and flank, are used for the making of stews. Mutton, however, is not so satisfactory as lamb for such dishes, as its flavor is too strong. If mutton must be used, its flavor can be improved by adding 1 or 2 tablespoonfuls of vinegar during the cooking. The chief object in the making of lamb and mutton stews is, as in the case of beef and veal stews, to draw from the meat as much as possible of the flavoring and nutritive mate-

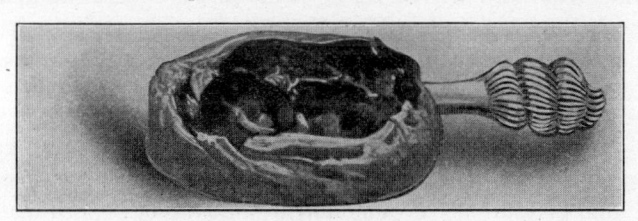

Fig. 13

rials. This can be accomplished by cutting up the meat into small pieces so as to increase the amount of surface exposed and by keeping the temperature low enough to prevent the proteins from coagulating.

With these points in mind, proceed in the making of lamb or mutton stew in the same way as for beef stew. To improve the flavor of the stew, cook with it savory herbs and spices, such as bay leaf, parsley, and cloves.

PREPARATION OF LEFT-OVER LAMB AND MUTTON

40. Turkish Lamb.—No left-over meat lends itself more readily to the preparation of made dishes than lamb. Combined with tomatoes and rice and flavored with horseradish, it makes a very appetizing dish called Turkish lamb. The accompanying recipe should be carefully followed in preparing this dish.

TURKISH LAMB
(Sufficient to Serve Six)

2 Tb. butter
1 onion, chopped
½ c. rice
1 c. water
1 c. stewed tomatoes

1½ c. diced lamb or mutton
1 Tb. horseradish
1 tsp. salt
⅛ tsp. pepper

Put the butter in a frying pan and to it add the chopped onion and the dry rice. Cook until the rice is browned. Then pour in the water and tomatoes and add the meat, horseradish, salt, and pepper. Simmer gently until the rice is completely cooked.

41. Minced Lamb on Toast.—Any lamb that remains after a meal may be minced by chopping it fine or putting it through the food chopper. If it is then heated, moistened well with water or stock, and thickened slightly, it makes an excellent preparation to serve on toast.

After mincing lean pieces of left-over lamb until they are very fine, put them in a buttered frying pan. Dredge the meat well with flour and allow it to brown slightly. Add enough water or stock to moisten well. Season with salt and pepper, cook until the flour has thickened, and then serve on toast.

42. Scalloped Lamb or Mutton.—As a scalloped dish is usually pleasing to most persons, the accompanying recipe for scalloped lamb or mutton will undoubtedly find favor. Both macaroni and tomatoes are combined with the meat in this dish, but rice could be substituted for the macaroni, if desired.

To make scalloped lamb or mutton, arrange a layer of buttered crumbs in a baking dish, and on top of them place a layer of cooked macaroni, a layer of meat, and then another layer of macaroni. Over this pour enough stewed tomato to moisten the whole well. Season each layer with salt, pepper, and butter. Over the top, place a layer of buttered crumbs. Bake in a medium-hot oven until the whole is thoroughly heated.

43. Spanish Stew.—Left-over pieces of mutton or lamb may also form the foundation of a very appetizing dish known as Spanish stew. Here tomatoes are also used, and to give the stew flavor chilli sauce is added.

SPANISH STEW
(Sufficient to Serve Six)

2 Tb. butter
1 onion, sliced
1 Tb. flour
2 c. lamb or mutton, diced
1½ c. stewed tomatoes
1 c. stock or gravy
1 Tb. chilli sauce
1 red pepper, cut fine
2 tsp. salt

Put the butter in a frying pan and brown the sliced onion in it. Add the flour and meat, and after browning them pour in the stewed tomatoes and the stock or gravy. Season with the chilli sauce, the red pepper, and the salt. Cover and let simmer until the whole is well thickened and blended.

44. Individual Lamb Pies.—Individual pies are always welcome, but when they are made of lamb or mutton they are especially attractive. The proportions required for pies of this kind are given in the accompanying recipe.

INDIVIDUAL LAMB PIES

2 c. diced lamb or mutton   ½ c. peas, cooked or canned
¼ c. diced carrots   1 c. gravy or thickened stock

Cut into small pieces any left-over lamb or mutton. Cook the carrots until they are soft, add them, together with the peas, to the meat, and pour the gravy or thickened stock over all. Simmer gently for a few minutes. Line patty pans with a thin layer of baking-powder biscuit dough, fill with the mixture, and cover the top with another thin layer of the dough. Bake in a quick oven until the dough is baked.

PORK

GENERAL CHARACTERISTICS OF PORK

45. Pork is the flesh of slaughtered swine used as food. It is believed to be more indigestible than other meats, but if it is obtained from a young and properly fed animal, it is not only digestible, but highly appetizing, and, when eaten occasionally, it is very wholesome.

The age of the animal from which pork is cut can be determined by the thickness of the skin; the older the animal, the thicker the skin. To be of the best kind, pork should have pink, not red, flesh composed of fine-grained tissues, and its fat, which, in a well-fattened animal, equals about one-eighth of the entire weight, should be white and firm. Although all cuts of pork contain some fat, the proportion should not be too great, or the pieces will not contain as much lean as they should. However, the large amount of fat contained in pork makes its food value higher than that of other meats, unless they are excessively fat, and consequently difficult of digestion.

46. One of the chief advantages of pork is that about nine-tenths of the entire dressed animal may be preserved by curing and smoking. Originally, these processes required a period of 2 to 3 months for their completion, but they have gradually been shortened until now only a few days are required for the work. Pork cured and smoked by the new methods, however, does not possess such excellent flavor and such good keeping qualities as that so treated by the longer process. Any one who has the right storage facilities to care for the meat properly will find it much more economical to purchase a whole carcass or a part of one and then salt, smoke, or pickle the various pieces that can be treated in this way than to purchase this meat cut by cut as it is needed or desired.

CUTS OF PORK

47. Names of Pork Cuts.—The butcher usually buys a whole carcass of pork. He first divides it into halves by splitting it through the spine, and then cuts it up into smaller pieces according to the divisions shown in Fig. 14, which illustrates the outside and the inside of a dressed hog. As will be observed, the method of cutting up a hog differs greatly from the cutting of the animals already studied. After the head is removed, each side is divided into the shoulder, clear back fat, ribs, loin, middle cut, belly, ham, and two hocks.

48. Uses of Pork Cuts.—Hogs are usually fattened before they are slaughtered, and as a result there is a layer of fat under the skin which is trimmed off and used in the making of lard. The best quality of lard, however, is made from the fat that surrounds the kidneys. This is called *leaf lard,* because the pieces of fat are similar in shape to leaves. Such lard has a higher melting point and is more flaky than that made from fat covering the muscles.

49. The head of pork does not contain a great deal of meat, but, as the quality of this meat is very good, it is valuable for a number of special dishes, such as headcheese and scrapple.

The hocks contain considerable gelatine, so they are used for dishes that solidify, or become firm, after they are made.

50. A shoulder of pork cut roughly from the carcass is shown in Fig. 15. This piece provides both roasts and steaks, or, when

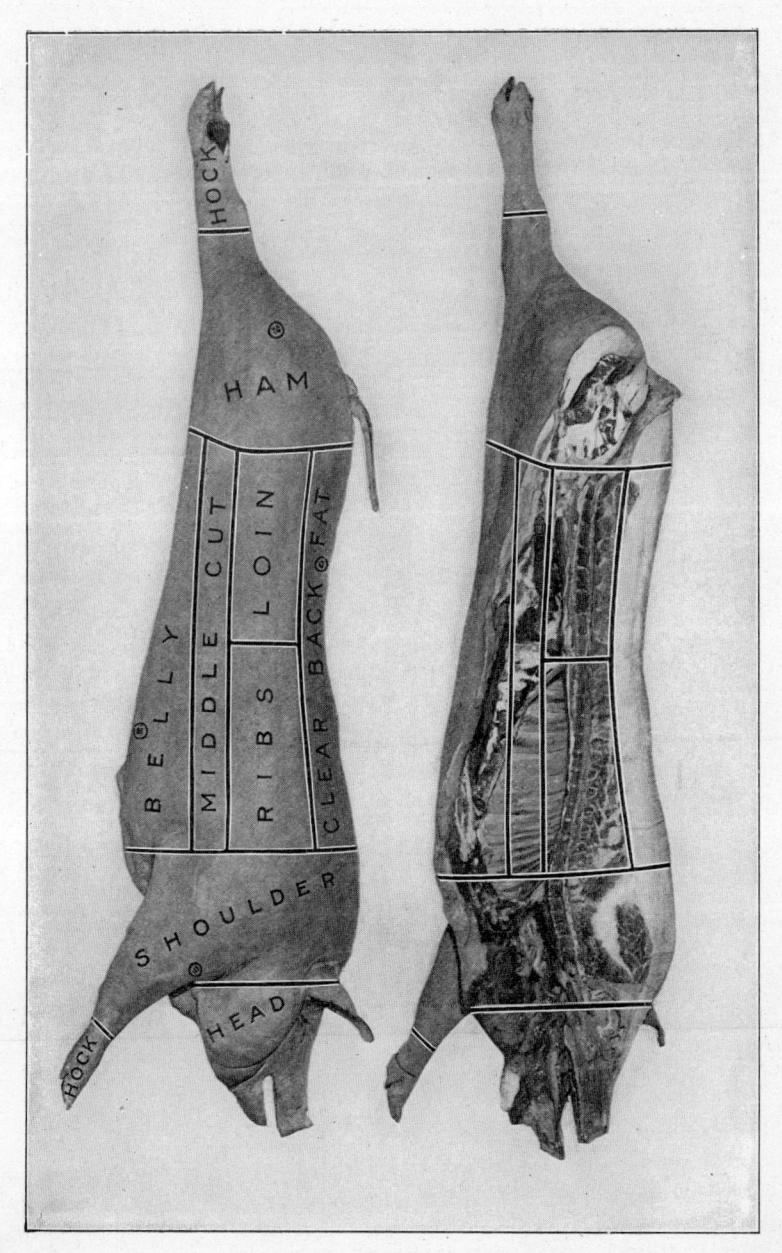

Fig. 14

Fig. 15

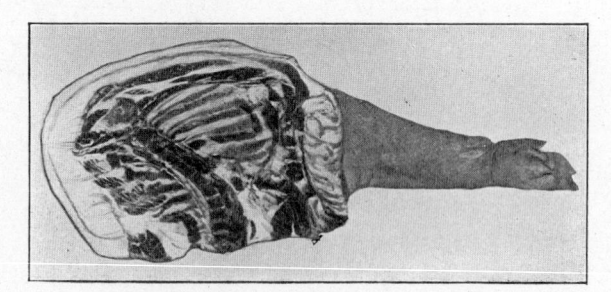

Fig. 16

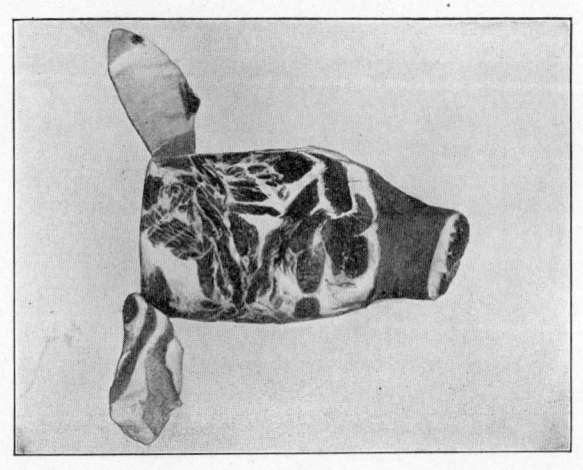

Fig. 17

§ 11 MEAT 27

trimmed, it may be cured or smoked. The front leg, which is usually cut to include the lower part of the shoulder, is shown in Fig. 16. The ribs inside this cut, when cut from underneath, are

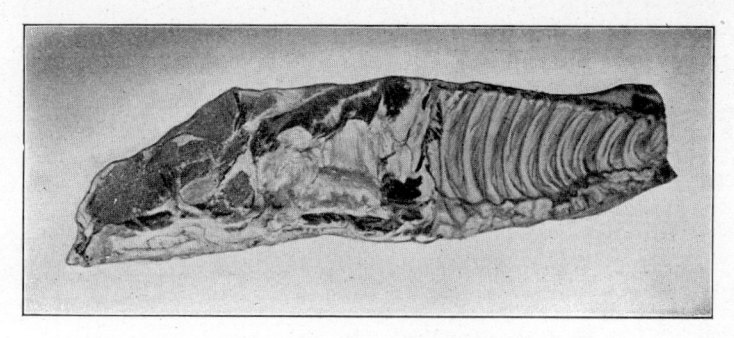

FIG. 18

sold as spareribs. This piece, as shown in Fig. 17, is generally trimmed to make what is known as shoulder ham.

51. The ribs and the loin cut in one piece are shown in Fig. 18. From this piece are obtained the most desirable chops and roasts. When a roast is desired, the rib bones are removed from the rib cut, which then resembles the piece shown in Fig. 19. Directly under the backbone in these cuts is the tenderest piece of pork to be had. When this is removed in one piece, it is, as in beef, called the

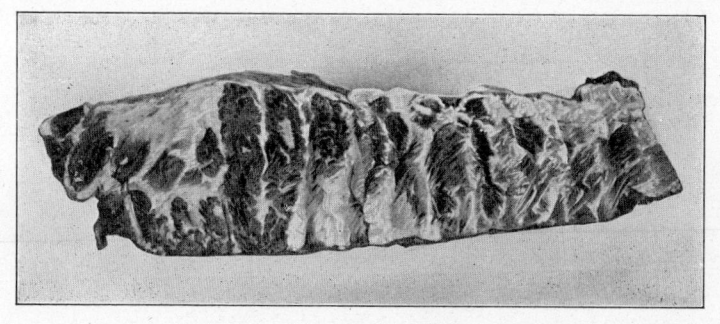

FIG. 19

tenderloin. Very often, however, it is left in to be cut up with the rest of the loin.

52. The middle cut is commonly used for bacon, while the belly is most suitable for salt pork. These two cuts consist of large quan-

WI—C3—9

tities of fat and only narrow layers of lean. They are especially valuable for enriching and flavoring foods, such as beans, that are neither rich in fat nor highly flavored.

53. The hind leg, or untrimmed ham, just as it is cut from the carcass, is shown in Fig. 20. When this piece is trimmed and ready

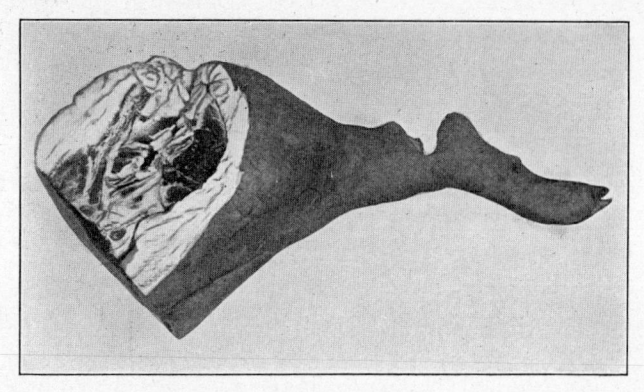

Fig. 20

for curing or for roasting, it appears as shown in Fig. 21. As will be noticed, the outside skin, or rind, is not removed from either the shoulder or the ham.

54. Table of Pork Cuts.—As is done in explaining the meats that have been considered previously, there is here presented a table,

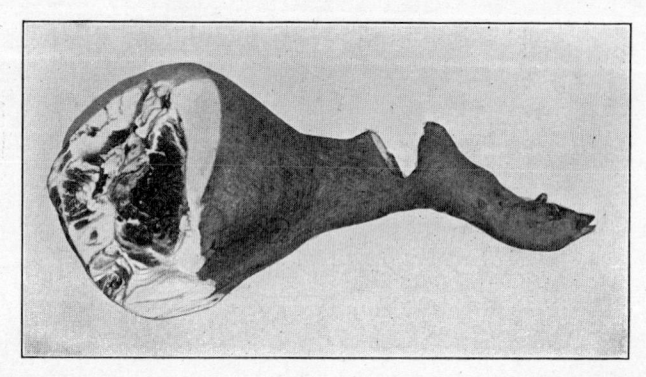

Fig. 21

designated as Table III, that gives the names of the pork cuts and the uses to which they may be put. This table will assist the housewife materially in learning the names and uses of the various cuts of pork.

TABLE III
NAMES AND USES OF PORK CUTS

Names of Cuts	Uses of Cuts
Head	Headcheese, boiling, baking
Shoulder	Steaks, roasting, curing, smoking
Spareribs	Roasting, boiling
Belly	Salt pork, curing
Middle cut	Bacon, curing, smoking
Ribs	Chops, roasting
Loin	Chops, roasting
Ham	Roasting, curing, smoking
Back fat	Lard
Hock	Boiling, making jelly
Internal organs and trimmings	Sausage

COOKING OF PORK

FRESH PORK AND ITS PREPARATION

55. Roast Pork.—In the preparation of pork for the table, and a roast in particular, several points must be taken into consideration. Unlike beef, which is often served rare, pork must be well done in order to be satisfactory. Rare pork to most persons is repulsive. Also, as a large part of the surface of a pork roast, especially one cut from the shoulder, loin, or ribs, is covered with a layer of fat, pork does not have to be seared to prevent the loss of juice, nor does it have to be put into such a hot oven as that required for beef. In fact, if the temperature of the oven is very high, the outside will finish cooking before the heat has had a chance to penetrate sufficiently to cook the center. While this makes no difference with meat that does not need to be thoroughly cooked, it is a decided disadvantage in the case of pork.

56. When a shoulder of pork is to be roasted, it makes a very satisfactory dish if it is boned and stuffed before roasting. To bone such a piece, run a long, narrow knife all around the bone and cut it loose; then pick up the bone by one end and shake it until it will pull out. Fill the opening thus formed with bread or cracker stuffing.

If an especially inviting roast of pork is desired, a *crown roast* should be selected, for this is just as attractive as a crown roast of lamb. It is made by cutting corresponding pieces from each side of the rib piece, trimming the bones clean as far back as the lean part of the chops, and fastening the pieces together. A garnish of fried apple rings is very attractive for such a roast.

57. To cook a roast of any of these varieties, wipe the meat thoroughly, dredge it with flour, salt, and pepper, and place it on a rack in a dripping pan. Bake about 3 hours, depending on the size of the roast, and baste every 15 minutes with fat from the bottom of the dripping pan.

After the roast is removed from the roasting pan, make a gravy as for any other roast. Serve with apple sauce, baked apples, cranberry sauce, chilli sauce, pickles, or some other acid dish. Such an accompaniment aids considerably in the digestion of pork, for it cuts the large amount of fat that this meat contains and that so often retards the digestion, and hastens the fat through the stomach.

58. Roast Pig.—In some households, roasted pig is the favorite meat for the Thanksgiving or the Christmas dinner. There is sufficient reason for its popularity, for when properly prepared and attractively garnished, roasted pig offers a pleasing change from the meat usually served on such days.

To be suitable for roasting, a pig should be not more than 1 month or 6 weeks old and should not weigh more than 7 or 8 pounds after it is cleaned. The butcher should prepare it for cooking by scalding off the hair, washing the pig thoroughly, inside and out, and withdrawing the entrails of the animal through an incision made in the under part of the body.

59. When the pig is received in the home, wash it thoroughly, within and without, wipe it dry, and fill it with stuffing. To make a stuffing suitable for this purpose, season 2 quarts of fine bread crumbs with 4 tablespoonfuls of chopped onion, 2 teaspoonfuls of salt, 1 teaspoonful of pepper, and $\frac{1}{2}$ cupful of melted butter. Mix thoroughly and add 3 beaten eggs. If the stuffing needs moisture, add water or milk. Stuff the pig firmly with this stuffing, using every effort to restore its original shape. Then sew up the opening and truss the animal; that is, draw the hind legs forwards and bend the front legs backwards under the body, and skewer and tie them into place.

With the animal in this shape, wipe it off with a damp cloth, dredge it with flour, and place it in a dripping pan, adding 1 cupful of boiling water in which 1 teaspoonful of salt has been dissolved. Roast in a moderate oven for at least 1½ hours, or 20 minutes for each pound of pig. Baste frequently, first with butter and water and later with drippings. When the skin begins to brown slightly, rub over it a clean piece of cloth dipped in melted butter. Repeat this operation every 10 minutes until the meat is well done. Then remove the pig to a hot platter and garnish with parsley, lettuce, celery, or fried or baked apples. If a more ornamental garnishing is desired, place a lemon in the mouth and use cranberries for the eyes. In carving, cut the head off, split through the spine lengthwise, remove the legs, and cut the ribs so as to form chops.

60. Sautéd or Broiled Pork.—Slices cut from the ribs and loin of pork are called chops, and those obtained from the shoulder and hind legs are called steaks. These, together with the tenderloin, the small piece of lean, tender meat lying under the bones of the loin and seldom weighing more than a pound, are especially suitable for sautéing or broiling. When they are to be prepared by these processes, sauté or broil them as any other meat, remembering, however, that pork must be well done. Because of this fact, a more moderate temperature must be employed than that used for beefsteak.

61. Pork Chops in Tomato Sauce.—A slight change from the usual way of preparing pork chops can be had by cooking them with tomatoes. The combination of these two foods produces a dish having a very agreeable flavor.

First brown the chops in their own fat in a frying pan, turning them frequently so that the surfaces will become evenly browned. When they have cooked for 15 minutes, pour enough strained stewed tomatoes over them to cover them well, and season with salt and pepper. Cover the pan tight, and allow them to simmer until the tomatoes become quite thick. Place the chops on a hot platter, pour the tomato sauce over them, and serve hot.

62. Sautéd Tenderloin of Pork.—Since the tenderloin of pork is a very tender piece of meat, it needs no accompaniment to make it a delicious dish, but sometimes a change of preparation is welcomed in order to give variety to the diet. The accompanying directions should therefore be followed when something different from broiled tenderloin is desired.

Cut the tenderloin into lengthwise slices and brown these slices in melted butter, turning them several times. Then remove to a cooler part of the stove, and let them cook slowly in the butter for 15 minutes, taking care to have them closely covered and turning them once or twice so that they will cook evenly. At the end of this time, pour enough milk or cream in the pan to cover the meat well and cook for 15 minutes longer. With a skimmer, remove the meat, which should be very tender by this time, from the pan, and put it where it will keep hot. Make a gravy of the drippings that remain in the pan by thickening it with 1 tablespoonful of flour, stirring it until it is thick and smooth and seasoning it to taste with salt and pepper. Pour the gravy over the meat and serve hot.

63. Pork Sausage.—The trimmings and some of the internal organs of pork are generally utilized to make sausage by chopping them very fine and then highly seasoning the chopped meat. Pork in this form may be bought fresh or smoked and loose or in casings. It usually contains considerable fat and therefore shrinks upon being cooked, for the fat is melted by the heat and runs out of the sausage.

To cook pork sausages put up in casings, place the required number in a hot frying pan with a small quantity of hot water. Cover the pan with a lid and allow the sausages to cook. When they have swelled up and the skins, or casings, look as if they would burst, remove the cover and thoroughly prick each one with a sharp fork, so as to allow the fat and the water to run out. Then allow the water to evaporate and sauté the sausages in their own fat, turning them frequently until they are well browned.

To cook loose pork sausage, shape it into thin, flat cakes. Grease a frying pan slightly, in order to keep the cakes from sticking to the surface, place the cakes in the pan, and allow them to cook in the fat that fries out, turning them occasionally until both sides are well browned.

CURED PORK AND ITS PREPARATION

64. Under the heading of cured pork may be included many of the cuts of pork, for a large part of a pork carcass can be preserved by curing. However, this term is usually restricted to include salt pork, bacon, and ham. As has already been learned, salt pork is obtained from the belly; bacon, from the middle cut; and ham, from the two hind legs of pork.

65. Salt Pork.—As the cut used for salt pork is almost entirely fat, this piece is seldom used alone for the table. Occasionally, it is broiled to be served with some special food, such as fried apples, but for the most part it is used for *larding;* that is, slices of it are laid across the surface of meat and fish that are lacking in fat and that therefore cook better and have a more agreeable flavor when fat in some form is added. Pork of this kind is usually bought by the pound and then sliced by the housewife as it is needed for cooking purposes.

66. Bacon.—The middle cut of pork, upon being cured by smoking, is regarded as bacon. It is sometimes used for larding

Fig. 22

purposes, but as it contains more lean than salt pork, has a very pleasing flavor, and is the most easily digested fat known, it is much used for food. A piece that contains the usual proportion of fat and lean is shown in Fig. 22. The strip of fat that occurs between the rind, or outer coat, and the first layer of lean is the firmest and the best for larding. The fat that fries out of bacon is excellent for use in the cooking and seasoning of other foods, such as vegetables and meats. When bacon is cooked for the table, its flavor will be improved if it is broiled rather than fried in its own fat. The rind of bacon should, as a rule, be trimmed off, but it should never be wasted, for it may be used to grease a pancake griddle or any pan in which food is to be cooked, provided the bacon flavor will not be objectionable.

In purchasing bacon, it is usually more economical to buy the whole side, or the entire middle cut, but if smaller quantities are desired, any amount, either in one piece or in slices, may be bought. The commercially cut bacon, which is very thin and becomes very crisp in its preparation, may be bought with the rind retained or removed. In both of these forms, it is often put up in jars or packed neatly in flat pasteboard boxes. While such bacon is undoubtedly the most popular kind, it should be remembered that the more preparation that is put on such a food before it enters the home, the more expensive it becomes. Very satisfactory results can be obtained from bacon bought in the piece if care is used in cutting it. To secure very thin, even slices, a knife having a thin blade that is kept sharp and in good condition should always be used.

67. Bacon and Eggs.—There are many combinations in which bacon is one of the foods, but no more palatable one can be found than bacon and eggs. This is generally a breakfast dish; still there is no reason why it cannot be used at times for luncheon or supper to give variety.

To prepare this combination of foods, first pan-broil the desired number of slices of bacon in a hot frying pan until they are crisp and then remove them to a warm platter. Into the fat that has fried out of the bacon, put the required number of eggs, which have first been broken into a saucer. Fry them until they reach the desired degree of hardness, and then remove to the platter containing the bacon. Serve by placing a slice or two of bacon on the plate with each egg.

68. Bacon Combined With Other Foods.—Many other foods may be fried in the same way as eggs and served with bacon. For instance, sliced apples or sliced tomatoes fried in bacon fat until they become tender, but not mushy, are delicious when served with crisp pieces of bacon. Also, cold cereals, such as cream of wheat, oatmeal, corn-meal mush, etc., may be sliced and fried until crisp and then served with bacon.

69. Ham.—The hind leg of pork, when cured and smoked, is usually known as ham. Fig. 23 shows a ham from which the rind has not been removed. In such a ham, the proportion of fat and lean is about right, but when ham is bought with the rind removed, much of the fat is also taken off. The best hams weigh from 8 to

15 pounds, and have a thin skin, solid fat, and a small, short tapering leg or shank.

Several ways of cooking ham are in practice. Very often slices resembling slices of round steak are cut from the whole ham and then fried or broiled. If a larger quantity is desired, the entire ham or a thick cut may be purchased. This is boiled or baked and then served hot or cold. It is a good idea to purchase an entire ham and keep it in supply, cutting off slices as they are desired. In such an event, the ham should be kept carefully wrapped and should be hung in a cool, dry place. In cutting a ham, begin at the large end, as in Fig. 23, and cut off slices until the opposite end becomes too

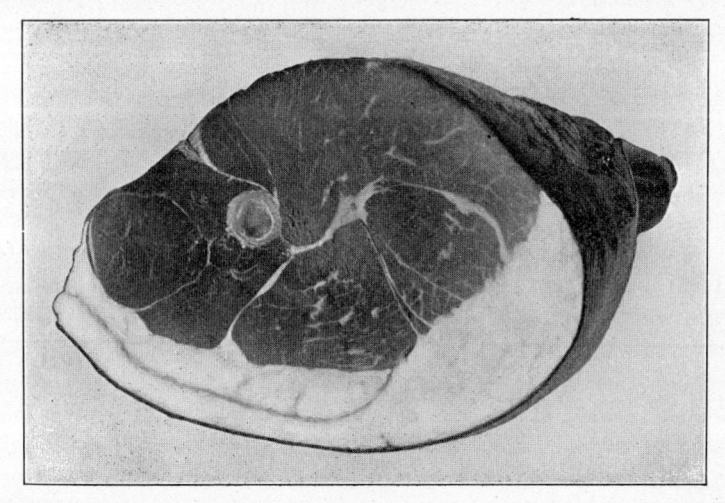

Fig. 23

small to make good slices. The piece that remains may be cooked with vegetables, may be boiled and served either hot or cold, or, if it is only a small piece, may be used for making soup.

70. Broiled Ham.—The methods of broiling and pan broiling are very satisfactory when applied to ham that is cut in slices. Ham is pan-broiled in the same way as other meats. To broil ham, place slices 1 inch thick on the hot broiler rack and sear quickly on both sides. Then reduce the temperature and broil for 15 to 18 minutes, turning the ham every few minutes until done. Remove to a hot platter. Add a little water to the drippings in the broiler pan, pour this over the meat, and serve at once.

71. Ham Baked in Milk.—A change from the usual ways of preparing slices of ham can be had by baking them in milk. A point to remember in carrying out this method is that the meat must bake slowly in order to be tender when it is done.

Secure a 2-inch slice of ham, place it in a dripping pan, and completely cover it with milk. Put in a moderate oven and cook for 2 or more hours. When the ham is done, its surface should be brown and the milk should be almost entirely evaporated. If the liquid added in the beginning is not sufficient, more may be added during the baking.

72. Boiled Ham.—Sometimes it is desired to cook an entire ham, particularly when a large number of persons are to be served. The usual way to prepare a whole ham is to boil it. When it is sufficiently cooked, it may be served hot or kept until it is cold and then served in slices. Nothing is more appetizing for a light meal, as luncheon or supper, or for picnic lunches than cold sliced ham. Then, too, boiled ham is very delicious when it is fried until the edges are crisp.

To prepare boiled ham, first soak the ham in cold water for several hours and then remove it and scrub it. Place it in a large kettle with the fat side down and cover well with cold water. Put over a slow fire and allow to come to the boiling point very slowly. Boil for 15 minutes and skim off the scum that has risen. Simmer slowly for about 5 hours, or at least 25 minutes for each pound of ham. Take from the kettle and remove the skin about two-thirds of the way back. It will be found that the skin will peel off easily when the ham is cooked enough. Garnish in any desirable way and serve hot or cold.

73. Baked Ham.—Another very appetizing way in which to cook an entire ham is to bake it. This involves both cooking in water on the top of the stove and baking in the oven. While this recipe, as well as those preceding, specifies ham, it should be remembered that shoulder may be cooked in the same ways.

For baked ham, proceed in the way just explained for boiled ham, but boil only 12 minutes for each pound. Take the ham from the kettle and allow it to cool enough to permit it to be handled. Remove the skin. Then place the ham in a roasting pan and pour over it 1 cupful of water. Bake 12 minutes for each pound and baste frequently while baking. Serve hot or cold.

PREPARATION OF LEFT-OFF PORK

74. Cold Pork With Fried Apples.—A combination that most persons find agreeable and that enables the housewife to use up left-over pork, is cold pork and fried apples. To prepare this dish, remove the cores from sour apples and cut the apples into ½-inch slices. Put these in a frying pan containing hot bacon fat and fry until soft and well browned. Slice cold pork thin and place in the center of a platter. Arrange the apples around the pork in a border.

75. Scalloped Pork and Cabbage.—If not enough pork remains to serve alone, it can be combined with cabbage to make a most appetizing scalloped dish. The accompanying recipe shows just how to prepare such a dish.

SCALLOPED PORK AND CABBAGE
(Sufficient to Serve Six)

2 c. small thin slices of pork   1½ c. thin white sauce
1½ c. cooked chopped cabbage   ¼ c. buttered crumbs

Arrange the pork and cabbage in layers in a baking dish, having a layer of cabbage on top. Pour the white sauce over all and sprinkle the crumbs on top. Bake until the sauce boils and the crumbs are brown.

76. Mock Chicken Salad.—The similarity in appearance of pork to chicken makes it possible to prepare a salad of cold pork that is a very good substitute for chicken salad. A salad of this kind can be used as the main dish in such a meal as luncheon or supper.

MOCK CHICKEN SALAD
(Sufficient to Serve Six)

4 Tb. vinegar   1½ c. diced celery
2 c. diced pork   Salad dressing

Heat the vinegar and pour it over the diced pork. Set aside to chill. When ready to serve, add the diced celery and mix well. Pour the salad dressing over all and serve on crisp lettuce leaves.

SERVING AND CARVING OF MEAT

77. The manner of carving and serving meat in the home depends to some extent on the kind of meat that is to be served. A way that is favored by some is to carve the meat before it is placed on the table and then serve it according to the style of service used. However, the preferable way is to place the platter containing the meat on the table, together with the plates, in front of the person who is to do the carving and serving.

The carver should use considerable care in cutting and serving the meat so that the platter and the surrounding tablecloth will not become unsightly. To make each portion as attractive as possible, it should be cut off evenly and then placed on the plate with the best side up. Furthermore, the carving should be done in an economical way in order that whatever remains after the first serving may be served later in the same meal, and what is not eaten at the first meal may be utilized to advantage for another. To obtain the best results in carving, a good carving knife should be secured and it should always be kept well sharpened.

78. With the general directions clear in mind, the methods of carving and serving particular kinds of meat may be taken up. Chops, of course, require no carving. By means of a large fork, one should be placed on each person's plate. Steaks and roasts, however, need proper cutting in order that equally good pieces may be served to each person dining. To carve a steak properly, cut it across from side to side so that each piece will contain a portion of the tender part, as well as a share of the tougher part. When cut, the pieces should be strips that are about as wide as the steak is thick. It is often advisable to remove the bone from some steaks before placing them on the table.

79. Roasts require somewhat more attention than steaks. Before they are placed on the table, any cord used for tying should be cut and removed and all skewers inserted to hold the meat in shape should be pulled out. To carve a roast of any kind, run the fork into the meat deeply enough to hold it firmly and then cut the meat into thin slices across the grain. In the case of a roast leg that contains the bone, begin to carve the meat from the large end, cutting each slice down to the bone and then off so that the bone is left clean. Place round of beef and rolled roasts on the platter so that the tissue side, and not the skin side, is up, and then cut the slices off in a horizontal direction. To carve a rib roast properly, cut it parallel with the ribs and separate the pieces from the backbone.

SAUSAGES AND MEAT PREPARATIONS

80. In addition to the fresh, raw meats that the housewife can procure for her family, there are on the market numerous varieties of raw, smoked, cooked, and partly cooked meats, which are generally included under the term **sausages**. These meats are usually highly seasoned, so they keep better than do fresh meats. They should not be overlooked by the housewife, for they help to simplify her labor and at the same time serve to give variety to the family diet. Still, it should be remembered that when meats are made ready for use before they are put on the market, the cost of the labor involved in their manufacture is added to the price charged for them. For this reason, the housewife must be prepared to pay more for meats of this kind than she would pay if she could prepare them at home. However, she need not be concerned regarding their safety, for the government's inspection and regulations prevent any adulteration of them.

81. Among the numerous varieties of these meats, many of them are typical of certain localities, while others have a national or an international reputation. They also vary in the kind of meat used to make them. Some of them are made from beef, as *frankfurters* and certain kinds of *bologna,* while others are made from pork and include the smoked and unsmoked sausages. *Liverwurst* is made from the livers of certain animals, and may be purchased loose or in skins.

Some of these sausages are used so often in certain combinations of foods that they are usually thought of in connection with the foods that it is customary for them to accompany. Frankfurters and sauerkraut, pork sausage and mashed potatoes, liverwurst and fried corn-meal mush are well-known combinations of this kind.

82. Closely allied to these sausages, although not one of them, is a meat preparation much used in some localities and known as *scrapple,* or *ponhasse.* This is prepared by cooking the head of pork, removing the meat from the bones, and chopping it very fine. The pieces of meat are then returned to the broth in which the head was cooked and enough corn meal to thicken the liquid is stirred in. After the whole has boiled sufficiently, it is turned into molds and allowed to harden. When it is cold and hard, it can be cut into slices, which are sautéd in hot fat.

83. Besides scrapple, numerous other meat preparations, such as *meat loaves* of various kinds and *pickled pig's feet,* can usually be obtained in the market. While the thrifty housewife does not make a habit of purchasing meats of this kind regularly, there are times when they are a great convenience and also afford an opportunity to vary the diet.

PREPARATION OF FOODS BY DEEP-FAT FRYING

PRINCIPLES OF DEEP-FAT FRYING

84. Up to this point, all frying of foods has been done by sautéing them; that is, frying them quickly in a small amount of fat. The other method of frying, which involves cooking food quickly in deep fat at a temperature of 350 to 400 degrees Fahrenheit, is used so frequently in the preparation of many excellent meat dishes, particularly in the use of left-overs, that specific directions for it are here given, together with several recipes that afford practice in its use. No difficulty will be experienced in applying this method to these recipes or to other recipes if the underlying principles of deep-fat frying are thoroughly understood and the proper utensils for this work are secured.

85. In the first place, it should be remembered that if foods prepared in this way are properly done, they are not so indigestible as they are oftentimes supposed to be, but that incorrect preparation makes for indigestibility in the finished product. For instance, allowing the food to soak up quantities of fat during the frying is neither economical nor conducive to a digestible dish. To avoid such a condition, it is necessary that the mixture to be fried be made of the proper materials and be prepared in the right way. One of the chief requirements is that the surface of the mixture be properly coated with a protein material, such as egg or egg and milk, before it is put into the fat or that the mixture contain the correct proportion of egg so that its outside surface will accomplish the same purpose. The reason for this requirement is that the protein material is quickly coagulated by the hot fat and thus prevents the entrance of fat into the inside material of the fried food.

Care must be taken also in the selection of the fat that is used for deep-fat frying. This may be in the form of an oil or a solid fat and may be either a vegetable or an animal fat. However, a vegetable fat is usually preferred, as less smoke results from it and less flavor of the fat remains in the food after it is cooked.

86. The utensils required for deep-fat frying are shown in Fig. 24. They consist of a wire basket and a pan into which the basket will fit. As will be observed, the pan in which the fat is put has an upright metal piece on the side opposite the handle. Over this fits a piece of wire with which the basket is equipped and which is attached to the side opposite the handle of the basket. This arrangement makes it possible to drain the fat from whatever food has been fried without having to hold the basket over the pan.

Fig. 24

APPLICATION OF DEEP-FAT FRYING

87. With the principles of deep-fat frying well in mind, the actual work of frying foods by this method may be taken up. Numerous foods and preparations may be subjected to this form of cookery, but attention is given at this time to only croquettes and timbale cases. *Croquettes* are small balls or patties usually made of some finely minced food and fried until brown. *Timbale cases* are shells in which various creamed foods are served. As these two preparations are representative of the various dishes that can be cooked by frying in deep fat, the directions given for these, if carefully mastered, may be applied to many other foods.

88. Frying of Croquettes.—After the mixture that is to be fried has been prepared, and while the croquettes are being shaped, have the fat heating in the deep pan, as in Fig. 24. Before the food is immersed, test the temperature of the fat in the manner shown in Fig. 25, to make sure that it is hot enough. To do this, put a ½-inch cube of bread in the hot fat and keep it there for 40 seconds. If at the end of this time it is a golden brown, it may be known that the fat is sufficiently hot for any mixture. Be careful to regulate the heat so as to keep the fat as near this temperature as possible, for it should be remembered that each time a cold food is immersed in hot fat, the temperature is lowered. Usually, a few minutes' frying is necessary to assure this regulation of the temperature.

Fig. 25

As soon as the correct temperature is reached, put several of the croquettes in the basket and set the basket in the pan of hot fat so that the croquettes are entirely covered. Fry until a good brown color is secured. Then lift the basket out of the fat and allow it to drain until all the fat possible has dripped from it. Finally remove the croquettes from the basket and place them on any kind of paper that will absorb the excessive fat. Serve at once or keep hot until ready to serve.

89. Veal Croquettes.—Veal that remains from a roast after it has been served once can be utilized in no better way than in the making of croquettes; or, if desired, veal may be cooked especially for this purpose. When such croquettes are served with a sauce of any desirable kind, such as white sauce or tomato sauce, or with left-over gravy, no more appetizing dish can be found.

VEAL CROQUETTES
(Sufficient to Serve Six)

2 c. cold ground veal   Salt and pepper
1 c. thick white sauce 1 egg
2 Tb. chopped onion   Fine crumbs
1 Tb. chopped parsley

Mix the ground veal with the white sauce, add the onion and parsley, and salt and pepper to taste. Shape into oblong croquettes. Roll first in the beaten egg, which, if necessary, may be increased by the addition of a little milk, and then in the crumbs. Fry in deep fat until a golden brown. Serve with or without sauce.

90. Sweetbread Croquettes.—An extremely palatable dish can be made by frying in deep fat sweetbreads cut any desirable shape and size. These are usually served with a vegetable, and often a sauce of some kind is served over both.

To prepare the sweetbreads, parboil them according to the directions given in Art. **17.** Cut them into the kind of pieces desired, sprinkle the pieces with salt and pepper, and dip them into beaten egg and then into crumbs. Fry in deep fat and serve with a vegetable or a sauce or both.

91. Rice-and-Meat Patties.—Sometimes not enough meat remains after a meal to make a tasty dish by itself. In such a case, it should be combined with some other food, especially a starchy one, so as to extend its flavor and produce a dish that approaches nearer a balanced ration than meat alone does. A small amount of any kind of meat combined with rice and the mixture then formed into patties, or croquettes, provides both an appetizing and a nutritious dish.

RICE-AND-MEAT PATTIES
(Sufficient to Serve Six)

1 c. finely chopped left-over meat   1 tsp. celery salt
1 c. cold steamed rice   Salt and pepper
½ c. thick white sauce   1 egg
1 Tb. chopped onion   Fine crumbs

Mix the meat and rice, stir into them the white sauce, onion, and celery salt, and salt and pepper to taste. Shape into croquettes, or patties; roll first in the egg and then in the crumbs. Fry in deep fat until golden brown and serve with any desirable sauce.

92. Timbale Cases.—Such foods as creamed sweetbreads, creamed sweetbreads and mushrooms, and other delicate foods that are served in small quantities can be made very attractive by serving them in timbale cases. These are made out of a batter by means of a timbale iron and fried in deep fat until brown. In serving them, place them either on a small plate or on the dinner plate with the rest of the dinner. To make them especially attractive, dip the edge into egg white and then into very finely chopped parsley. Fig. 26 shows creamed sweetbreads served in a timbale case.

FIG. 26

93. To prepare timbale cases, a *timbale iron,* such as is shown in Fig. 27, is required. Such an iron consists of a fluted piece of metal that is either solid or hollow and that has attached to it a handle long enough to keep the hand sufficiently far away from the hot fat.

The batter required for timbale cases and the directions for combining them are as follows:

TIMBALE-CASE BATTER
(Sufficient to Make Twenty)

1 egg	1 tsp. sugar
$\frac{1}{2}$ c. milk	$\frac{3}{4}$ c. flour
$\frac{1}{2}$ tsp. salt	

FIG. 27

Beat the egg with a fork just enough to break it up thoroughly. Add the milk, salt, and sugar. Stir in the flour with as little beating as possible. After preparing this mixture, allow it to stand for $\frac{1}{2}$ hour, so that any air it contains in the form of bubbles may escape and thus prevent the formation of holes and bubbles in the finished timbale cases.

When about to use the batter, pour it into a cup or some other small utensil that is just large enough to admit the iron easily. The iron must be nearly covered with batter, but no large amount of it will be needed if a small utensil is used. Dip the iron into the hot fat, as shown in Fig. 27, lift it, and allow it to drip. Then place it in the batter in the way shown in Fig. 28, being careful not to permit the batter to come quite to the top of the iron, and remove it at once. Place it immediately into the hot fat, as in Fig. 29, allowing the fat to come higher on the iron than the batter does. This precaution will prevent the formation of a ridge of bubbles around the top of the timbale case. Fry in the deep fat until the case is nicely browned, as shown in Fig. 26. Remove the iron from the fat, and allow it to drip. Then carefully remove the timbale case from the iron with a fork and place it on paper that will absorb the fat. Fill with the desired mixture and serve. If the first few timbale cases are not a success, do not be discouraged, but continue the process and profit by the mistakes that are made.

FIG. 28

FIG. 29

MEAT
(PART 2)

EXAMINATION QUESTIONS

(1) (*a*) What is veal? (*b*) From animals of what age is the best veal obtained?

(2) Compare veal and beef as to characteristics.

(3) What cuts of veal are most suitable for: (*a*) roasts? (*b*) cutlets? (*c*) soup and stews? (*d*) chops?

(4) (*a*) What organs of veal are used for foods? (*b*) What are sweetbreads?

(5) (*a*) Why is veal more indigestible than beef? (*b*) What important point must be remembered concerning the cooking of veal?

(6) (*a*) What substance in veal is utilized in the preparation of jellied veal? (*b*) Explain how this dish is prepared.

(7) (*a*) At what age is sheep sold as lamb? (*b*) How do lamb and mutton differ as to food substances?

(8) Compare the flesh of lamb and mutton as to appearance.

(9) As they apply to lamb and mutton, explain the terms: (*a*) rack; (*b*) saddle.

(10) Explain why some cuts of lamb and mutton are tough and others tender.

(11) What is: (*a*) a crown roast of lamb? (*b*) a French chop?

(12) (*a*) Describe pork of the best kind. (*b*) Why is the food value of pork higher than that of other meats?

(13) (*a*) Name the cuts of pork. (*b*) What is meant by leaf lard?

(14) What important points must be taken into consideration in the cooking of pork?

(15) (*a*) Name some of the accompaniments that are usually served with pork. (*b*) What is the purpose of these accompaniments?

(16) (*a*) For what purpose is salt pork generally used? (*b*) What is bacon? (*c*) To what uses is bacon put?

(17) (*a*) Give the general directions for the carving and serving of meat. (*b*) Explain how to carve and serve a steak.

(18) (*a*) What is meant by deep-fat frying? (*b*) Why must a food that is to be fried in deep fat contain or be coated with a protein material?

(19) (*a*) What utensils are necessary for deep-fat frying? (*b*) Explain the procedure in frying croquettes in deep fat.

(20) (*a*) For what purpose are timbale cases used? (*b*) Explain how to make a batter for timbale cases.

ADDITIONAL WORK

Select a cut of beef that you consider most desirable from an economical standpoint. Buy a quantity that may be used to the greatest advantage for your family. Prepare it in any way you desire.

State the number of pounds purchased, the price of the meat, the number of meals in which it was served, and the number of persons (tell how many adults and how many children) served at each meal. Estimate the cost of each portion by dividing the cost of the whole by the number of persons served.

Make up an original dish in which left-over meat is used and submit the recipe to us.

§ 11

POULTRY AND GAME

POULTRY

POULTRY AS A FOOD

1. **Poultry** is the term used to designate birds that have been domesticated, or brought under the control of man, for two purposes, namely, the eggs they produce and the flesh food they supply. All the common species of domestic fowls—chickens, ducks, geese, turkeys, guinea fowls, and pigeons—are known as poultry. However, none of these species is included under this term unless it is raised for at least one of the two purposes mentioned. As the term is to be understood in this Section, poultry includes all domestic fowls that are killed in order that their flesh may be cooked and used as food for human beings. Of course, many wild birds are killed for the flesh food they furnish, but they are classed under the term *game*.

2. Poultry is probably never a necessity in the ordinary dietary, and when prices are high it is a decided luxury. Still it does aid materially in relieving the monotony of the usual protein foods, and it supplies that "something out of the ordinary" for special occasions. Then, too, it is often valuable in the diet of an invalid or some person with a poor appetite. Poultry is, of course, used more in some homes than in others; yet there is scarcely a home in which it is not served some time or another. A knowledge of this food and its preparation and serving will therefore prove to be a valuable asset to any housewife.

3. To arrive at a knowledge of the use of poultry as a food, the housewife must necessarily become familiar with its selection and purchase. Then she must give attention to both its preparation for cooking and its actual cooking, and, finally, to its serving. In all these matters she will do well to adhere to the practice of economy, for, at best, poultry is usually an expensive food. Before entering into these matters in detail, however, it will be well to look into them in a general way.

4. In the selection of poultry, the housewife should realize that poultry breeders have so developed certain breeds, even of the same species, that they are better for table use than others. The flesh of any breed of poultry may be improved by feeding the birds good food and giving them proper care; and it is by applying these principles that the breeders are enabled to better the quality of this food. Other things also influence the quality of poultry flesh as food, as, for example, the way in which the poultry is prepared for market and the care it receives in transportation and storage. Unless these are as they should be, they have a detrimental effect on poultry, because such food is decidedly perishable.

It is possible to exercise economy in the purchase of poultry, but before the housewife can do this she must be able to judge the age of each kind she may desire. On the age depends to a great extent the method of cookery to be followed in preparing the poultry for the table. Likewise, she must know the marks of cold-storage poultry, as well as those of poultry that is freshly killed; and she must be familiar with the first marks of deterioration, or decay, that result from storing the food too long or improperly.

Economy may also be practiced in preparing poultry for cooking. To bring this about, however, the housewife should realize that the best method of preparing any kind of poultry for cooking is always the most economical. It means, too, that she should understand thoroughly the methods of drawing and cutting, so that she may either do this work herself or direct it.

The way in which poultry is cooked has a bearing on the cost of this food, too. For example, a young, tender bird prepared by a wrong method not only is a good dish spoiled, but is a waste of expensive material. Likewise, an older bird, which has more flavor but tougher tissues, is almost impossible as food if it is not properly prepared. Both kinds make appetizing dishes and do not result in waste if correct methods of cooking are followed in their preparation.

Even the way in which poultry is served has a bearing on the cost of this food. For this reason, it is necessary to know how to carve, as well as how to utilize any of this food that may be left over, if the housewife is to get the most out of her investment.

SELECTION OF POULTRY

GENERAL INFORMATION

5. The selection of any kind of poultry to be used as food is a matter that should not be left to the butcher. Rather, it should be done by some one who understands the purpose for which the poultry is to be used, and, in the home, this is a duty that usually falls to the housewife. There are a number of general facts about poultry, and a knowledge of them will assist the housewife greatly in performing her tasks.

6. Classification of Poultry.—Poultry breeders and dealers divide the domestic fowls into three classes. In the first class are included those which have combs, such as chickens, turkeys, and guinea fowls. Quails and pheasants belong to this class also, but they are very seldom domesticated. The birds in this class are distinguished by two kinds of tissue—light meat on the breast and dark meat on the other parts of the body. In the second class are included those fowls which swim, such as ducks and geese. These are characterized by web feet and long thick bills, and their meat is more nearly the same color over the entire body. The third class is comprised of birds that belong to the family of doves. Pigeons, which are called *squabs* when used as food, are the only domesticated birds of this class. They stand between the other two classes with respect to their flesh, which has some difference in color between the breast and other muscles, but not so much as chicken and other fowls of the first class.

7. Influence of Feeding and Care on Quality. — To some extent, the breed affects the quality of poultry as food; still this is a far less important matter than a number of things that the purchaser is better able to judge. Among the factors that greatly influence the quality are the feeding and care that the birds receive up to the time of slaughter. These affect not only the flavor and the tenderness of the tissue, as well as the quantity of tissue in proportion to bone, but also the healthfulness of the birds themselves. To keep the birds in good health and to build up sufficient flesh to make them plump, with as much meat as possible on the bones and a fair amount of fat as well, the food they get must be clean and of the right kind. Likewise, the housing conditions must be such that the birds are kept dry and sufficiently warm. The living space, also, must be adequate for the number that are raised. Domestic fowls are not discriminating as to their food, and when they are forced to live in dirt and filth they will eat more or less of it and thus injure the quality of their flesh. Poultry that comes into the market looking drawn and thin, with blue-looking flesh and no fat, shows evidence of having had poor living conditions and inadequate feeding. Such poultry will be found to have a less satisfactory flavor than that which has received proper care.

8. Effect of Sex on Quality.—When birds of any kind are young, sex has very little to do with the quality of the flesh. But as they grow older the flesh of males develops a stronger flavor than that of females of the same age and also becomes tougher. However, when birds, with the exception of mature ones, are dressed, it would take an expert to determine the sex. The mature male is less plump than the female, and it is more likely to be scrawny. Likewise, its spurs are larger and its bones are large in proportion to the amount of flesh on them.

Very often the reproductive organs of young males are removed, and the birds are then called *capons*. As the capon grows to maturity, it develops more of the qualities of the hen. Its body becomes plump instead of angular, the quality of its flesh is much better than that of the cock, and the quantity of flesh in proportion to bone is much greater. In fact, the weight of a capon's edible flesh is much greater than that of either a hen or a cock. In the market, a dressed capon can usually be told by the long tail and wing feathers that are left on, as well as by a ring of feathers around the neck. Female birds that are spayed are called *poulards*. Spaying, or removing the reproductive organs, of female birds, however, makes so little improvement that it is seldom done.

9. Preparation of Poultry for Market.—The manner in which poultry is prepared for market has a great bearing on its quality as food. In some cases, the preparation falls to the producer, and often, when birds are raised in quantities, they are sold alive and dressed by the butcher. However, poultry that is to be shipped long distances and in large quantities or stored for long periods of time is usually prepared at a slaughtering place. This process of slaughtering and shipping requires great care, for if attention is not given to details, the poultry will be in a state of deterioration when it reaches the consumer and therefore unfit for food.

In order to avoid the deterioration of poultry that is slaughtered some distance from the place of its consumption, each bird is well fed up to within 24 hours before it is killed. Then it is starved so that its alimentary tract will be as empty as possible at the time of killing. Such birds are killed by cutting the large blood vessel running up to the head. When properly done, this method of killing allows almost all the blood to be drained from the body and the keeping qualities are much improved. At practically the same time, the brain is pierced by the knife thrust, and as soon as the bleeding commences the fowl becomes paralyzed. As the tissues relax, the feathers may be pulled easily from the skin without immersing the bird in hot water. This method of plucking, known as *dry plucking,* is preferable when the skin must be kept intact and the poultry kept for any length of time. The head and feet are left on and the entrails are not removed. The poultry is then chilled to the freezing point, but not below it, after which the birds are packed ten in a box and shipped to the market in refrigerator cars or placed in cold storage. Unless the poultry is to be cooked immediately after slaughter, such measures are absolutely necessary, as its flesh is perishable and will not remain in good condition for a long period of time.

10. Cold-Storage Poultry.—Poultry that has been properly raised, killed, transported, and stored is very likely to come into the market in such condition that it cannot be readily distinguished from freshly killed birds. When exposed to warmer temperatures, however, storage poultry spoils much more quickly than does fresh poultry. For this reason, if there is any evidence that poultry has been in storage, it should be cooked as soon as possible after purchase.

There are really two kinds of cold-storage poultry: that which is kept at a temperature just above freezing and delivered within a few weeks after slaughtering, and that which is frozen and kept in storage a much longer time. When properly cared for, either one is preferable to freshly killed poultry that is of poor quality or has had a chance to spoil. Poultry that has been frozen must be thawed carefully. It should be first placed in a refrigerator and allowed to thaw to that temperature before it is placed in a warmer one. It should never be thawed by putting it into warm water. Thawing it in this way really helps it to decompose.

A sure indication of cold-storage poultry is the pinched look it possesses, a condition brought about by packing the birds tightly against one another. Storage poultry usually has the head and feet left on and its entrails are not removed. Indeed, it has been determined by experiment that poultry will keep better if these precautions are observed. The removal of the entrails seems to affect the internal cavity of the bird so that it does not keep well, and as a matter of safety it should be cooked quickly after this has been done in the home.

SELECTION OF CHICKEN

11. To be able to select chicken properly, the housewife must be familiar with the terms that are applied to chickens to designate their age or the cookery process for which they are most suitable. *Chicken* is a general name for all varieties of this kind of poultry, but in its specific use it means a common domestic fowl that is less than 1 year old. *Fowl* is also a general term; but in its restricted use in cookery it refers to the full-grown domestic hen or cock over 1 year of age, as distinguished from the chicken or pullet. A *broiler* is chicken from 2 to 4 months old which, because of its tenderness, is suitable for broiling. A *frying chicken* is at least 6 months old, and a *roasting chicken* is between 6 months and 1 year old. With these terms understood, it can readily be seen that if fried chicken is desired a 2-year-old fowl would not be a wise purchase.

The quality of the bird is the next consideration in the selection of chicken. A number of things have a bearing on the quality. Among these, as has already been pointed out, are the feeding and care that the bird has received during its growth, the way in which it has been prepared for market, and so on. All of these things may be determined by careful observation before making a purchase. However, if the bird is drawn, and especially if the head and feet are removed, there is less chance to determine these things accurately,

POULTRY AND GAME

12. General Marks of Good Quality.—A chicken older than a broiler that has been plucked should not be scrawny nor drawn looking like that shown in Fig. 1, nor should the flesh have a blue tinge that shows through the skin. Rather, it should be

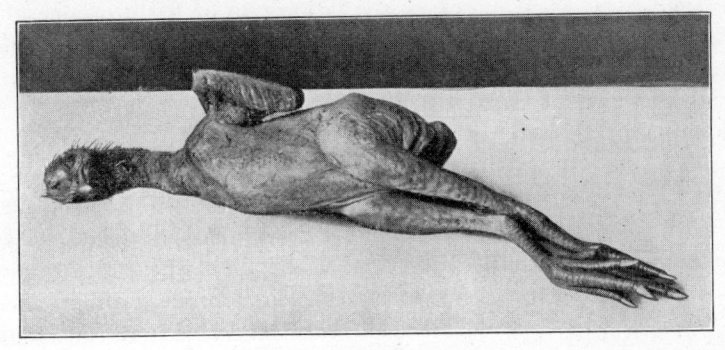

Fig. 1

plump and well rounded like the one shown in Fig. 2. There should be a sufficient amount of fat to give a rich, yellow color. It should be plucked clean, and the skin should be clear and of an even color over the entire bird. Tender, easily broken skin indicates a young bird; tougher skin indicates an older one. The skin should be

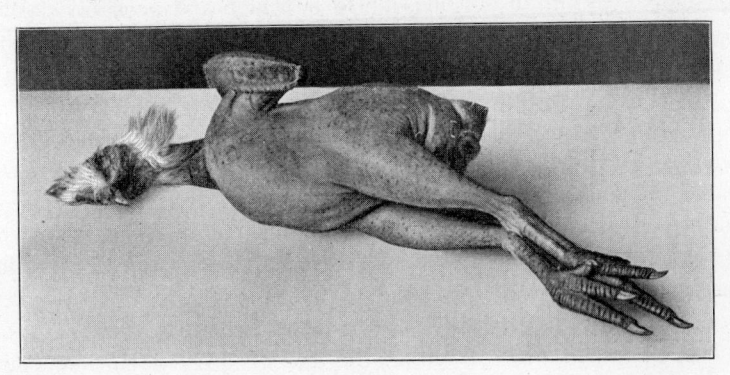

Fig. 2

whole and unbroken; likewise, when pressed with the fingers, it should be neither flabby nor stiff, but pliable.

13. The increase of age in a chicken is to some extent an advantage, because with age there is an increase in flavor. Thus, a year-old chicken will have more flavor than a broiler. However, after more than a year, the flavor increases to such an extent that it becomes strong and disagreeable. With the advance of age there is also a loss of tenderness in the flesh, and this after 1½ or 2 years becomes so extreme as to render the bird almost unfit for use. As the age of a chicken increases, the proportion of flesh to bone also increases up to the complete maturity of the bird. Hence, one large bird is a more economical purchase than two small ones that equal its weight, because the proportion of bone to flesh is less in the large bird than in the small ones.

14. Determining the Age of Chicken.—An excellent way in which to determine the age of a chicken that has been dressed consists in feeling of the breast bone at the point where it protrudes below the neck. In a very young chicken, a broiler, for instance, the point of this bone will feel like cartilage, which is firm, elastic tissue, and may be very easily bent. If the bird is about a year old, the bone will be brittle, and in a very old one it will be hard and will not bend.

15. If the head has been left on, the condition of the beak is a means of determining age. In a young chicken, it will be smooth and unmarred; in an old one, it will be rough and probably darker in color. If the feet have been left on, they too will serve to indicate the age. The feet of a young chicken are smooth and soft; whereas, those of an old bird are rough, hard, and scaly. The claws of a young one are short and sharp; but as the bird grows older they grow stronger and become blunt and marred with use. The spur, which is a projection just above the foot on the back of each leg, is small in the young chicken, and increases in size as the age increases. However, the spurs are more pronounced in males than in females.

16. Another way of telling the age of dressed chicken is to observe the skin. After plucking, young birds usually have some pin feathers left in the skin. *Pin feathers* are small unformed feathers that do not pull out with the larger ones. Older birds are usually free from pin feathers, but have occasional long hairs remaining in the skin after the feathers have been plucked. These do not pull out readily and must be singed off when the chicken is being prepared for cooking.

17. Determining the Freshness of Chicken.—There are a number of points that indicate whether or not a chicken is fresh. In a freshly killed chicken, the feet will be soft and pliable and moist to the touch; also, the head will be unshrunken and the eyes full and bright. The flesh of such a chicken will give a little when pressed, but no part of the flesh should be softer than another. As actual decomposition sets in, the skin begins to discolor. The first marks of discoloration occur underneath the legs and wings, at the points where they are attached to the body. Any dark or greenish color indicates decomposition, as does also any slimy feeling of the skin. The odor given off by the chicken is also an indication of freshness. Any offensive odor, of course, means that the flesh has become unfit for food.

18. Live Chickens.—Occasionally chickens are brought to the market and sold alive. This means, of course, that the birds are subjected to a certain amount of fright and needless cruelty and that the work of slaughtering falls to the purchaser. The cost, however, is decreased a few cents on the pound. Such birds must be chosen first of all by weight and then by the marks that indicate age, which have already been given.

SELECTION OF POULTRY OTHER THAN CHICKEN

19. The determination of quality, especially freshness, is much the same for other kinds of poultry as it is for chicken. In fact, the same points apply in most cases, but each kind seems to have a few distinguishing features, which are here pointed out.

20. Selection of Turkeys.—Turkeys rank next to chickens in popularity as food. They are native to America and are perhaps better known here than in foreign countries. Turkey is a much more seasonal food than chicken, it being best in the fall. Cold-storage turkey that has been killed at that time, provided it is properly stored and cared for, is better than fresh turkey marketed out of season.

21. The age of a turkey can be fairly accurately told by the appearance of its feet. Very young turkeys have black feet, and as they mature the feet gradually grow pink, so that at more than 1 year old the feet will be found to be pink. However, as the bird grows still older, the color again changes, and a 3-year-old turkey will have dull-gray or blackish looking feet. The legs, too, serve to indicate the age of turkeys. Those of a young turkey are smooth, but as the birds grow older they gradually become rough and scaly. A young turkey will have spurs that are only slightly developed, whereas an old turkey will have long, sharp ones.

22. Turkeys are seldom marketed when they are very young. But in spite of the fact that this is occasionally done, the mature birds are more generally marketed. Turkeys often reach a large size, weighing as much as 20 to 25 pounds. A mature turkey has proportionately a larger amount of flesh and a smaller amount of bone than chicken; hence, even at a higher price per pound, turkey is fully as economical as chicken.

23. Selection of Ducks.—Ducks probably come next to turkeys in popularity for table use. Young ducks are sold in the market during the summer and are called *spring duck*. The mature ducks may be purchased at any time during the year, but they are best in the winter months.

The flexibility of the windpipe is an excellent test for the age of ducks. In the young bird, the windpipe may be easily moved; whereas, in the old one, it is stationary and quite hard. The meat of ducks is dark over the entire bird, and the greatest amount is found on the breast. Its flavor is quite typical, and differs very much from turkey and chicken. However, there is a comparatively small amount of meat even on a good-sized duck, and it does not carve to very good advantage; in fact, more persons can be served from a chicken or a turkey of the same weight. Young ducks are rather difficult to clean, as a layer of fine down, which is not easily removed, covers the skin.

24. Selection of Geese.—Geese are much more commonly used for food in foreign countries than in America. Their age may be told in the same way as that of ducks, namely, by feeling of the windpipe. The flesh is dark throughout and rather strongly flavored. The fat is used quite extensively for cooking purposes, and even as a butter substitute in some countries. Because of this fact, geese are generally fattened before they are slaughtered, and often half the weight of the bird is fat. The livers of fattened geese reach enormous proportions and are considered a delicacy. They are used for *pâté de fois gras*. Usually, this is put up in jars and brings a very high price.

25. Selection of Pigeons.—Pigeons are raised primarily for their use as *squabs*. These are young birds about 4 weeks old, and their meat is tender and agreeable to the taste. The meat of the mature pigeon becomes quite tough and unpalatable. The breast is the only part of the bird that has meat on it in any quantity, and this meat is slightly lighter in color than that which comes from the remainder of the body. Midsummer is the best season for squabs, but they can be purchased at other times of the year. The cost of squabs is too high to allow them to be used extensively as a food in the ordinary household.

26. Selection of Guinea Fowls.—Guinea fowls are coming into common use as food. The young birds are preferable to the

TABLE I
GUIDE TO THE SELECTION OF POULTRY

Market Name	Weight Pounds	Age	Season
Squab broiler	¾ to 1¼	6 to 8 wk.	April to July
Broiler	1½ to 2	2 to 4 mo.	May to Sept.
Frying chicken	2½ to 3	6 mo.	June to Oct.
Roasting chicken	3 to 6	6 mo. to 1 yr.	All year
Fowl	4 to 5	Over 1 yr.	All year
Capon	6 to 10	6 mo. to 1 yr.	Nov. to July
Turkey broiler	1½ to 4	6 to 8 wk.	June to Sept.
Roasting turkey	8 to 25	6 mo. to 3 yr.	Oct. to Jan.
Spring duck	1½ to 2½	2 to 6 mo.	May to Dec.
Roasting duck	4 to 6	6 mo. to 1 yr.	Best in winter
Green goose	1½ to 2½	2 to 6 mo.	May to Dec.
Roasting goose	4 to 8	6 mo. to 1 yr.	Oct. to Mar.
Squab	½ to ¾	4 wk.	June to Sept.
Guinea hen broiler	1 to 2	2 to 4 mo.	Aug. to Nov.
Guinea fowl	3 to 5	6 mo. to 1 yr.	Oct. to Mar.

older ones. They are ready for the market in early autumn, while the old birds may be procured at any time. The breast meat of guinea fowls is almost as light as that of chicken, but all the meat of this bird has a gamy taste, which is absent in the chicken. If this particular flavor is much desired, it may be developed to even a greater degree by allowing the bird to hang after killing until the meat begins to "turn," that is, become "high." Such meat, however, is not usually desirable in the ordinary menu.

27. Selection of Pheasant, Partridge, and Quail. Pheasant, partridge, and quail are usually considered game birds, but certain varieties are being extensively domesticated and bred for market. Such birds are small and are used more in the nature of a delicacy than as a common article of food.

28. Table of Poultry and Game.—In Table I are given the market names of the various kinds of poultry and game birds, as well as the corresponding age, the weight, and the season of the year when they are most desirable. This table will serve as a guide in selecting poultry that is to be used as food.

COMPOSITION OF POULTRY

29. The composition of poultry is very similar to that of meats. In fact, poultry is composed of protein, fat, water, mineral salts, and extractives that do not differ materially from those found in meats. The protein, which usually varies from 15 to 20 per cent., is a much more constant factor than the fat, which varies from 8 to 40 per cent. This variation, of course, makes the total food value high in some kinds of poultry and low in others. For instance, in a young broiler that has not been fattened, the food value is extremely low; whereas, in a mature well-fattened bird, such as a goose, which increases very markedly in fatty tissue after reaching maturity, it is extremely high. A factor that detracts considerably from the edible portion of poultry is the waste material, or refuse. This consists of the bones, cartilage, head, feet, and entrails, or inedible internal organs. The greater the proportion of such waste material, the more the total nutritive value of the flesh is reduced. It is claimed that birds that have light-colored flesh do not become so fat as those which have dark flesh. This, of course, makes their nutritive value less, because the fat of poultry is what serves to supply a large part of the nutrition. There is no particular difference, as is commonly supposed, between the red and white meat of poultry. The difference in color is due to a difference in the blood supply, but this does not affect the composition to any extent.

PREPARATION OF POULTRY FOR COOKING

PREPARATION OF CHICKEN

30. As has been implied, poultry must be properly prepared before it is ready for cooking; likewise, the method of cookery determines how it must be prepared. For example, if it is to be roasted, it must be drawn; if it is to be stewed, it must be drawn and cut into suitable pieces; and so on. The various steps that must be taken to make poultry suitable for cooking are therefore considered here in detail.

31. Dressing a Chicken.—Although, as has been shown, the housewife does not have to dress the chicken that she is to cook—that is, kill and pluck it—there may be times when she will be called on to perform this task or at least direct it. A common way of killing chicken in the home is simply to grasp it firmly by the legs, lay it on a block, and then chop the head off with a sharp hatchet or a cleaver. If this plan is followed, the beheaded chicken must be held firmly until the blood has drained away and the reflex action that sets in has ceased. Otherwise, there is danger of becoming splashed with blood.

32. After a chicken has been killed, the first step in its preparation, no matter how it is to be cooked, consists in removing the feathers, or *plucking* it, as this operation is called. Plucking can be done dry by simply pulling out the feathers. However, a bird can be plucked more readily if it is first immersed in water at the boiling point for a few minutes. Such water has a tendency to loosen the feathers so that they can be pulled from the skin easily. Unless the chicken is to be used at once, though, dry plucking is preferable to the other method. Care should be taken not to tear or mar the skin in plucking, and the operation is best performed by pulling out the feathers a few at a time, with a quick jerk. In a young chicken, small feathers, commonly called pin feathers, are apt to remain in the skin after plucking. These may be pulled out by pinching each with the point of a knife pressed against the thumb and then giving a quick jerk.

33. Whether live poultry is dressed by a local butcher or in the home, the length of time it should be kept after killing demands attention. Such poultry should either be cooked before rigor mortis, or the stiffening of the muscles, has had time to begin, or be

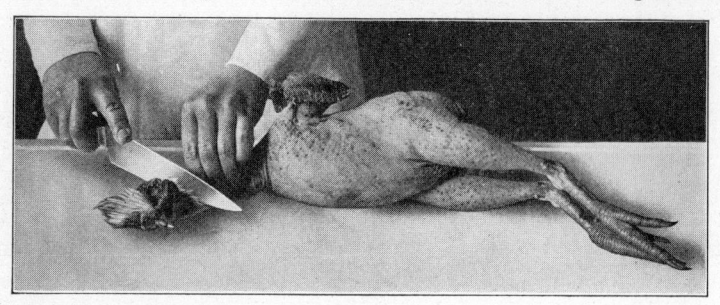

Fig. 3

allowed to remain in a cool place long enough for this to pass off and the muscles to become tender again. Naturally, if this softening, or ripening, process, as it is sometimes called, goes on too long, decomposition will set in, with the usual harmful effects if the meat is used as food.

34. Singeing a Chicken.—On all chickens except very young ones, whether they are home dressed or not, hairs will be found on the skin; and, as has been mentioned, the older the bird the more hair will it have. The next step in preparing a chicken for cooking, therefore, is to singe it, or burn off these hairs. However, before singeing, provided the head has not been removed, cut it off just where the neck begins, using a kitchen cleaver or a butcher knife, as in Fig. 3. To singe a dressed chicken, grasp it by the head or the neck and the feet and then revolve it over a gas flame, as shown in Fig. 4, or a burning piece of paper for a few seconds or just long enough to burn off the hairs without scorching the skin. After singeing, wash the skin thor-

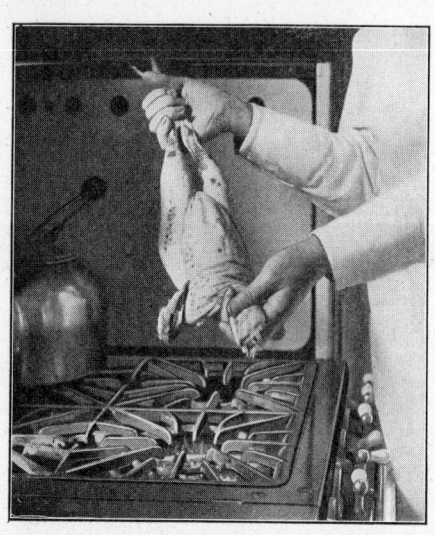

Fig. 4

§ 12　　POULTRY AND GAME　　15

oughly with a cloth and warm water, as shown in Fig. 5. Then it will be ready for drawing and cutting up.

35. Drawing a Chicken.—By drawing a chicken is meant the taking out of the entrails and removing all parts that are not edible. Although this work will be done by some butchers, the better plan is to do it at home, for, as has been stated, chicken or any other poultry must be cooked very soon after the entrails are removed. Chicken that is to be roasted is always prepared in this way, as the cavity that remains may be filled with stuffing. Drawing is also necessary when chicken is to be cooked in any other way, as by stewing or frying, but in addition it must be cut up. The procedure in drawing a chicken is simple, but some practice is required before deftness will result.

FIG. 5

36. In order to draw a chicken, carefully cut a lengthwise slit

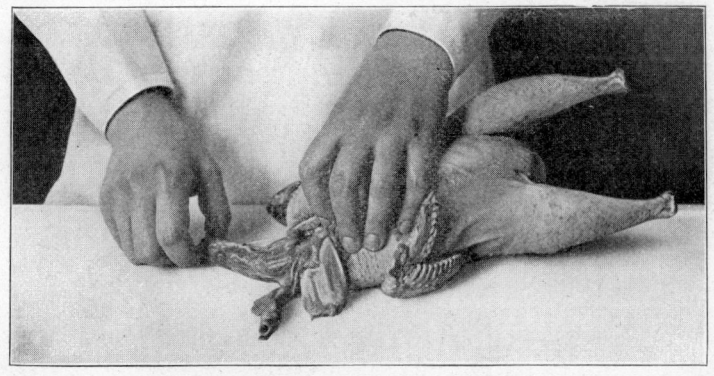

FIG. 6

through the skin on the neck, and slip the fingers down around the *crop,* which is a small sack that holds the food eaten by the chicken.

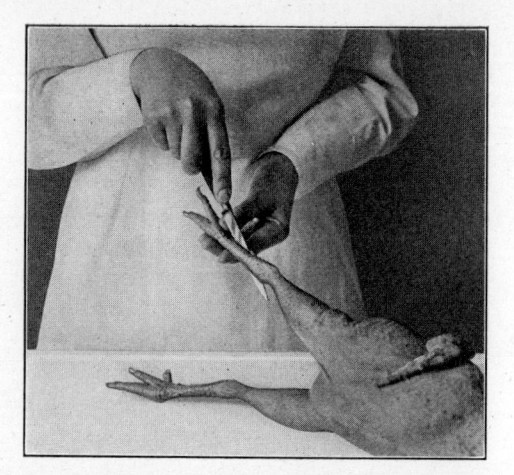

Fig. 7

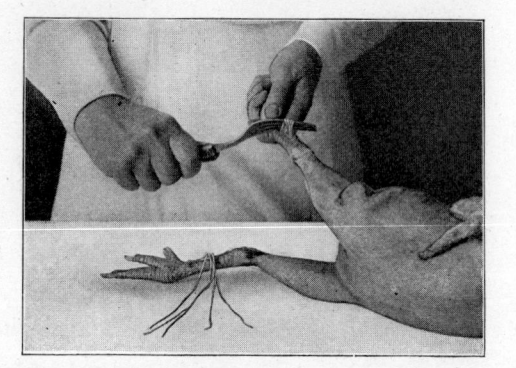

Fig. 8

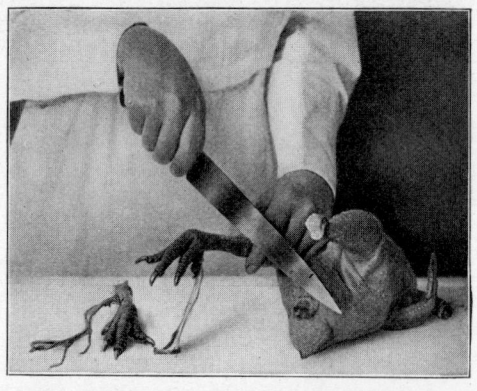

Fig. 9

16

Then pull the crop out, and with it the windpipe, as in Fig. 6, taking pains not to tear the skin nor to break the crop.

Next, remove the tendons, or thick white cords, from the legs, so as to improve the meat. These may be easily removed, especially from a chicken that is freshly killed; that is, one in which the flesh is still moist. Simply cut through the skin, just above the foot, as in Fig. 7, being careful not to cut the tendons that lie just beneath the skin; then slip a skewer or some other small, dull implement, as a fork, under the tendons, pull down toward the foot until they loosen at the second joint, and pull them out. This operation is clearly shown in Fig. 8. With the tendons removed, the feet may be cut off. To do this, cut through the skin where the two bones join, as shown in Fig. 9. As the joint separates, cut through the remaining tendons and skin on the back of the legs.

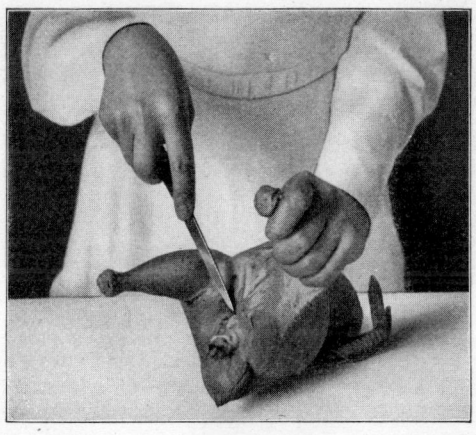

FIG. 10

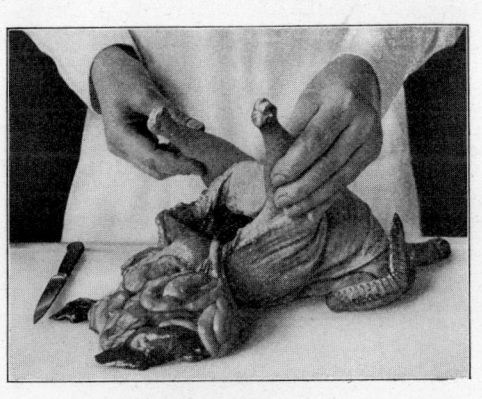

37. Proceed, next, to cut a crosswise slit through the skin between the legs at a point above the vent, as in Fig. 10, so that the entrails may be removed. This slit should be just large enough to admit the hand and no larger. Insert the fingers of one hand in this slit and gently move them around the mass of the internal organs, keeping them close to the framework of the bird. This will loosen the entrails at the points where they are attached

FIG. 11

to the body. Then, inserting the hand, slip the fingers around the mass at the top, near the neck, and with one pull remove the entire internal contents, as Fig. 11 shows. The lungs, or lights, as they are sometimes called, do not come out with this mass. They will be found covered with a membrane and tightly fastened inside the breast bone, and must be removed by pulling them out with the tips of the fingers. After the entrails are removed, pour clean cold water into the cavity, rinse it well several times, and pour the water out.

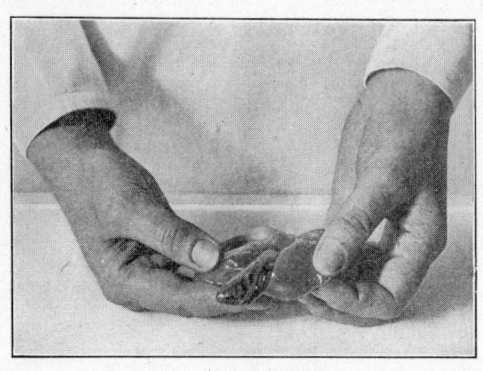

Fig. 12

38. Among the contents drawn from the chicken will be found the heart, the liver, and the gizzard. These are called the *giblets*. They are the only edible internal organs, and must be separated from the rest. To do this, squeeze the blood from the heart, and then cut the large vessels off close to the top of it. Then cut the liver away. In handling this part of the giblets extreme care must be taken, for tightly attached to it, as Fig. 12 shows, is the *gall bladder,* which is a tiny sack filled with green fluid, called bile. If this sack breaks, anything that its contents touches will become very bitter and therefore unfit to eat. The gall bag should be cut out of the liver above the place where it is attached, so as to be certain that it does not break nor lose any of the bile. Next, remove the gizzard, which consists of a fleshy part surrounding a sack con-

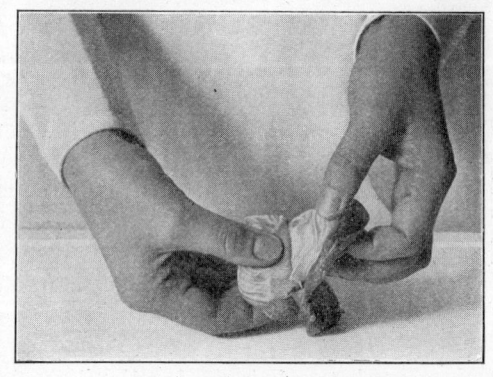

Fig. 13

§ 12   POULTRY AND GAME   19

taining partly digested food eaten by the chicken. First trim off any surplus fat, and carefully cut through the fleshy part just to the surface of the inside sack. Then pull the outside fleshy part away from the sack without breaking it, as in Fig. 13, an operation that can be done if the work is performed carefully. After removing the giblets and preparing them as explained, wash them well, so that they may be used with the rest of the chicken. As a final step, cut out the *oil sack*, which lies just above the tail, proceeding in the manner illustrated in Fig. 14.

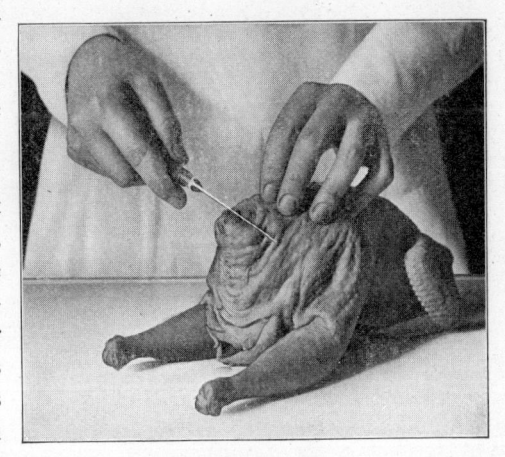

FIG. 14

39. Cutting Up a Chicken.—When chicken that has been drawn is to be fried, stewed, fricasseed, or cooked in some similar way, it must be cut into suitable pieces. In order to do this properly, it is necessary to learn to locate the joints and to be able to cut squarely between the two bones where they are attached to each other. To sever the legs from the body of the chicken, first cut through the skin underneath each leg where it is attached to the body, as in Fig. 15, bend the leg back far enough to break the joint, and then cut through it, severing the entire leg in one piece. When the legs are cut off, cut each one apart at the joint between the thigh and the lower

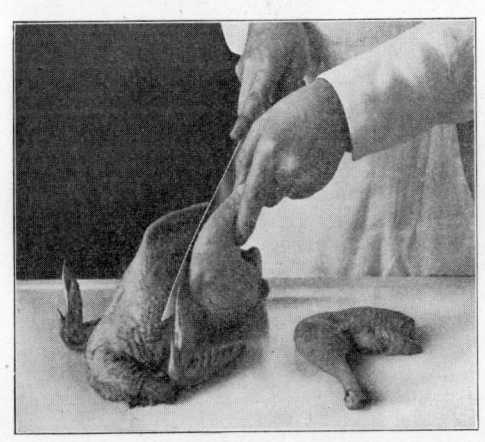

FIG. 15

Fig. 16

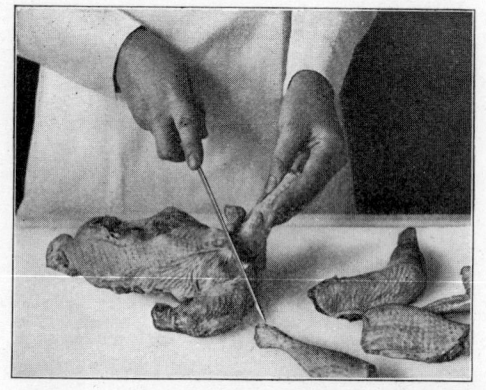

Fig. 17

Fig. 18

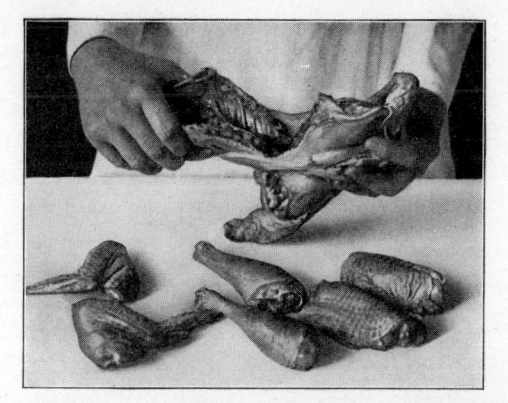

Fig. 19

Fig. 20

Fig. 21

part, as in Fig. 16, making two pieces. To sever the wings from the body, cut through the skin where the wing is attached, as in Fig. 17, and bend it back until the joint breaks. Then cut it off where the ends of the bones are attached to the joint. When both legs and both wings are removed, proceed to cut the body apart. As shown in Fig. 18, place the chicken, neck down, on a table, and cut down through the ribs parallel with the breast and the back, until the knife strikes a hard bone that it cannot cut. Then firmly grasp the breast with one hand and the back with the other and break the joints that attach these parts by pulling the back and the breast away from each other, as in Fig. 19. Cut through the joints, as in Fig. 20, so that the back, ribs, and neck will be in one piece and the breast in another.

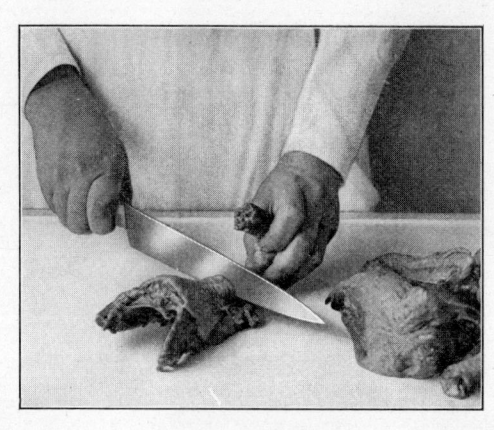

Fig. 22

Fig. 23

If desired, the breast may be divided into two pieces by cutting it in the manner shown in Fig. 21; also, as the back will break at the end of the ribs, it may be cut into two pieces there. Finally, cut the neck from the top piece of the back, as in Fig. 22.

The pieces of chicken thus procured may be rinsed clean with cold water, but they should never be allowed to stand in water, because this will draw out some of the extractives, or flavoring material, soluble albumin, and mineral salts.

40. Preparing Chicken Feet.—Many persons consider that chicken feet are not worth while for food. This, however, is a mistaken idea, for they will add to the flavor of soup stock or they may be cooked with the giblets to make stock for gravy. Chicken feet do not contain much meat, but what little there is has an excellent flavor and should be removed for use when creamed chicken or any dish made with left-over chicken is to be cooked.

To prepare chicken feet for use as food, scrub the feet well and pour boiling water over them. After a minute or two, remove them from the water and rub them with a clean cloth to peel off the scaly skin, as shown in Fig. 23. Finally remove the nails by bending them back.

41. Utilizing the Wing Tips.—The last joint, or tip, of chicken wings has no value as food, but, like the feet, it will help to add flavor to any stock that is made. This small piece of wing may be removed and then cooked with the feet and giblets.

PREPARATION OF POULTRY OTHER THAN CHICKEN

42. Preparation of Turkey.—The preparation of a plucked turkey for cooking is almost identically the same as that of a plucked chicken. Begin the preparation by singeing it; that is, hold it over a flame and turn it so that all the hairs on the skin will be burned off. Then look the skin over carefully, remove any pin feathers that may not have been removed in plucking, and wash it thoroughly. Next, cut off the head, leaving as much of the neck as possible. Draw the tendons from the legs as in preparing chicken; the ease with which this can be done will depend greatly on the length of time the turkey has been killed. Then cut off the legs at the first joint above the foot.

Having prepared the external part of the turkey, proceed to draw it. First, remove the crop by cutting a slit lengthwise in the neck over the crop, catching it with the fingers, and pulling it out. Next, cut a slit between the legs, below the breast bone, and draw out the internal organs. Clean and retain the giblets. Remove the lungs, wash out the cavity in the turkey, and cut off the oil bag on the back, just above the tail.

Turkey prepared in this way is ready to stuff and roast. It is never cut into pieces in the ordinary household until it has been cooked and is ready to serve. Directions for carving are therefore given later.

43. Preparation of Duck and Goose.—The preparation of duck and goose for cooking does not differ materially from that of turkey or chicken. Like turkey, duck or goose is generally roasted and not cut up until it is ready to serve. It will be well to note that young ducks are covered with small feathers, or down, which is very difficult to remove. However, the down may be removed by pulling it out with a small knife pressed against the thumb. When the down is removed, proceed with the preparation. Singe, wash, remove the head and feet, draw, wash the inside of the bird, and remove the oil sack. Goose may be prepared for cooking in the same way.

44. Preparation of Small Birds.—Squabs, partridge, pheasant, and other small birds are usually cooked by broiling. To prepare such a bird for cooking, singe, remove any small feathers that may remain, wash, remove the head and feet, and draw, following the directions given for drawing chicken. When it is thus cleaned, lay the bird open. To do this, begin at the neck and cut down the back along the spine. If desired, however, the bird may be cut down the back before drawing and the entrails removed through the cut down the back. Finally, wash the inside and wipe it dry, when the bird will be ready for broiling.

COOKING OF POULTRY

COOKERY METHODS

45. With poultry, as in the case of meats of any kind, it is the composition that determines the method of cookery; and, as the structure and composition of the tissue of poultry do not differ materially from those of meats, the application of the various cooking methods is practically the same. Young and tender birds that have comparatively little flesh, such as young chickens, squabs, and guinea fowl, are usually prepared by such rapid methods as frying and broiling. Medium-sized poultry, including chickens, turkeys, guinea fowl, ducks, and geese, require more cooking, and this, of course, must be done at a lower temperature; therefore, such poultry is generally roasted. Old poultry, particularly old chicken, or fowl, which is apt to be tough, requires still more cooking, and for this reason is stewed, braized, or fricasseed. The recipes for the cooking of various kinds of poultry here given will serve to make clear the cookery method to employ, as well as how to carry it out to advantage.

PREPARATION BY BROILING

46. The method of broiling in the case of poultry of all kinds does not differ in any way from the same method applied to cuts of meat. Since broiling is a rapid method of cookery and heat is applied at a high temperature, it is necessary that the poultry chosen for broiling be young and tender and have a comparatively small amount of meat on the bones.

Broiled poultry is not an economical dish, neither is it one in which the greatest possible amount of flavor is obtained, since, as in the case of the meat of animals used for food, the flavor develops with the age of the birds. However, broiled poultry has value in the diet of invalids and persons with poor appetite and digestion, for if it is properly done it is appetizing and easily digested.

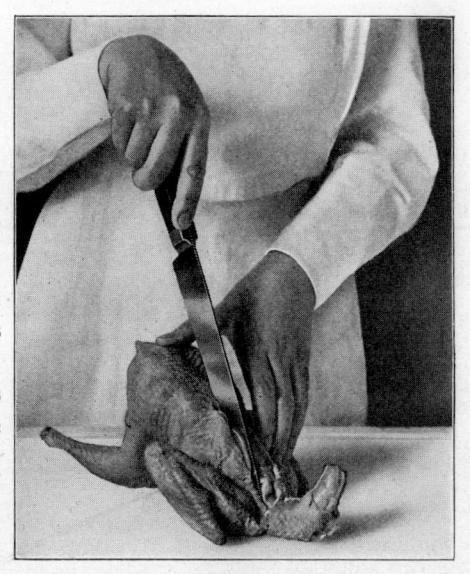

FIG. 24

47. Broiled Poultry.—Poultry that is to be broiled must first be dressed, drawn, and cleaned. Then, as has been mentioned for the preparation of small birds, lay the bird open by cutting down along the spine, beginning at the neck, as shown in Fig. 24.

This will permit the bird to be spread apart, as in Fig. 25. When it is thus made ready, washed, and wiped dry, heat the broiler and grease it. Then place the bird on the broiler in the manner shown in Fig. 26 and expose it to severe heat. Sear quickly on one side, and turn and sear on the other side. Then reduce the heat to a lower temperature and broil more slowly, turning often. To prevent burning, the parts that stand up close to the flame may be covered with strips of bacon fastened on with skewers; also, to get the best results, the side of the bird on which the flesh is thick should be exposed to the heat for a greater length of time than the other side. If there is any danger of the high places burning in the broiler, the bird may be removed and the cooking continued in a hot oven. Broiled poultry should be well done when served. This means, then, particularly in the case of chickens, that the broiling process should be carried on for about 20 minutes. When the bird is properly cooked, remove it from the broiler, place it on a hot platter, dot it with butter, sprinkle with salt and pepper, garnish, and serve.

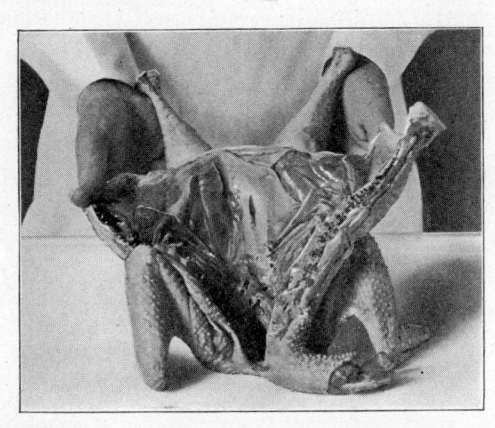

Fig. 25

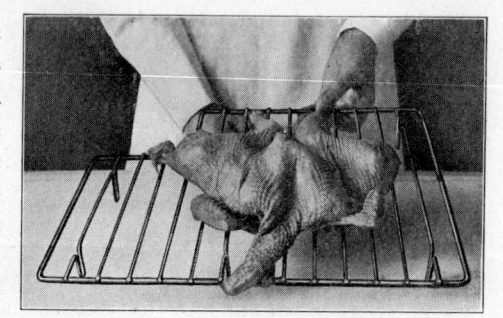

Fig. 26

PREPARATION BY FRYING

48. As has been mentioned, birds slightly older and larger than those used for broiling should be fried, because frying is a slower method and gives the flesh a more thorough cooking. However, most of the dishes commonly known as fried poultry are not fried, but sautéd in shallow fat. The same principles employed in sautéing any food are applied in the cooking of poultry by this method; that is, the surface is seared as quickly as possible and the cooking is finished at a lower temperature. Often in this cooking process, the pieces to be sautéd are dipped into batter or rolled in flour to assist in keeping the juices in the meat.

49. Fried Chicken.—To many persons, fried chicken—or, rather, sautéd chicken, as it should be called—is very appetizing. Chicken may be fried whole, but usually it is cut up, and when this is done it serves to better advantage. Likewise, the method of preparation is one that adds flavor to young chicken, which would be somewhat flavorless if prepared in almost any other way.

Frying is not a difficult cookery process. To prepare chickens, which should be young ones, for this method of preparation, draw, clean, and cut them up in the manner previously explained. When they are ready, wash the pieces and roll them in a pan of flour, covering the entire surface of each piece. Then, in a frying pan, melt fat, which may be chicken fat, bacon fat, part butter, lard, or any other frying fat that will give an agreeable flavor. When the fat is thoroughly hot, place in it the pieces of floured chicken and sprinkle them with salt and pepper. As soon as the pieces have browned on one side, turn them over and brown on the other side. Then reduce the heat, cover the frying pan with a tight-fitting lid, and continue to fry more slowly. If, after 25 or 30 minutes, the meat can be easily pierced with a fork, it is ready to serve; if this cannot be done, add a small quantity of hot water, replace the cover, and simmer until the meat can be pierced readily. To serve fried chicken, place the pieces on a platter and garnish the dish with parsley so as to add to its appearance.

50. Gravy for Fried Chicken.—If desired, brown gravy may be made and served with fried chicken. After the chicken has been removed from the frying pan, provided an excessive amount of fat remains, pour off some of it. Sprinkle the fat that remains with dry flour, 1 tablespoonful to each cupful of liquid that is to be used, which may be milk, cream, water, or any mixture of the three. Stir the flour into the hot fat. Heat the liquid and add this hot liquid to the fat and flour in the frying pan. Stir rapidly so that no lumps will form, and, if necessary, season with more salt and pepper to suit the taste.

Gravy may also be made in this manner: Stir cold liquid slowly into the flour in the proportion of 1 tablespoonful of flour to 1 cupful of liquid, which may be milk, cream, water, or any mixture of the three. Add the cold liquid and flour to the frying pan containing a small amount of fat in which the chicken was fried. Stir rapidly until the gravy has thickened and there are no lumps.

Very often the giblets, that is, the liver, heart, and gizzard of chicken, are used in making gravy. For example, the giblets may be cooked in water until they are tender and then sautéd in butter to serve, and when this is done the water in which they were cooked may be used for making gravy. Again, if it is not desired to eat them in this way, they may be chopped fine and added to gravy made from the fat that remains from frying.

51. Maryland Fried Chicken.—Maryland fried chicken is a popular dish with many persons. As a rule, corn fritters are used as a garnish and served with the chicken, and strips of crisp bacon are placed over the top of it. Often, too, potato croquettes are served on the same platter, a combination that makes almost an entire meal.

To prepare Maryland fried chicken, draw, clean, and cut up young chickens. Then wash the pieces and dry them with a soft cloth. Sprinkle the pieces with salt and pepper, and dip each into fine cracker crumbs or corn meal, then into beaten egg, and again into the crumbs or the corn meal. Next, melt in a frying pan chicken or bacon fat, part butter, lard, or any other fat for frying. When it is hot, place the pieces of chicken in it. Fry them until they are brown on one side; then turn and brown them on the other side. Lower the temperature and continue to fry slowly until the meat may be easily pierced with a fork. When the chicken is done, pour 2 cupfuls of white sauce on a hot platter and place the chicken in it. Then garnish and serve.

52. Fried Chicken With Paprika Sauce.—Chickens that are a trifle older than those used for plain fried chicken may be prepared to make what is known as fried chicken with paprika sauce. If in preparing this dish the chicken does not appear to be tender after frying, it may be made so by simmering it in the sauce.

To prepare this chicken dish, which is tempting to many, draw, clean, and cut up a chicken as for frying. Then melt fat in a frying pan, place the pieces in the hot fat, sprinkle them with salt and pepper, and brown on both sides quickly. When both sides are brown, continue to fry the pieces until they are tender. Then sprinkle all with 2 level tablespoonfuls of flour, add 2 cupfuls of milk or thin cream, and allow this to thicken. Then sprinkle with paprika until the sauce is pink. Let the chicken simmer slowly until the sauce penetrates the meat a little. Serve on a platter with a garnish.

PREPARATION BY ROASTING

53. Roasting is the cookery process that is commonly employed for preparing chickens that are of good size, as well as turkeys, ducks, and geese. It is also followed at times for cooking guinea fowl, partridges, pheasants, and similar small birds. As a rule, birds prepared in this way are filled with stuffing, which may be made in so many ways that roasted stuffed poultry makes a delightful change in the regular routine of meals.

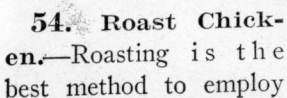

54. Roast Chicken.—Roasting is the best method to employ for the preparation of old chicken unless, of course, it is extremely old and tough. Then stewing is about the only method that is satisfactory. Chicken for roasting should weigh no less than 3 pounds. Chicken prepared according to the following directions makes a dish that is very appetizing.

To prepare chicken for roasting, clean and draw it in the manner previously given. When it is made clean, rub salt and pepper on the inside of the cavity, and stuff the cavity of the chicken, as shown in Fig. 27, with any desirable stuffing. Directions for preparing stuffing are given later. Also, fill with stuffing the space from which the crop was removed, inserting it through the slit in the neck.

Thread a large darning needle with white cord and sew up the slit in the neck, as well as the one between the legs, as in Fig. 28, so that the stuffing will not fall out. Also, force the neck inside of the skin, and tie the skin with a piece of string, as in Fig. 29. Then, as Fig. 29 also shows, truss the chicken by forcing the tip of each wing back of the first wing joint, making a triangle; also, tie the ends of the legs together and pull them down, tying them fast to the tail, as in Fig. 30. Trussing in this manner will give the chicken a much better appearance for serving than if it were not so fastened; but, of course, before it is placed on the table, the strings must be cut and removed. After stuffing and trussing, put the chicken on its back in a roasting pan, sprinkle it with flour, and place it in a very hot oven. Sear the skin quickly. Then reduce the temperature slightly and pour a cupful of water into the roasting pan. Baste the chicken every 10 or 15 minutes with this water, until it is well browned and the breast and legs may be easily pierced with a fork. Remove to a platter and serve. If gravy is desired, it may be made in the roasting pan in the same way as for fried chicken. The giblets may be cut into pieces and added or they may be left out and served after first cooking and then browning them.

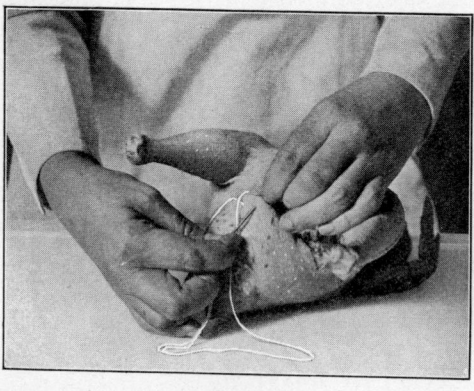

Fig. 28

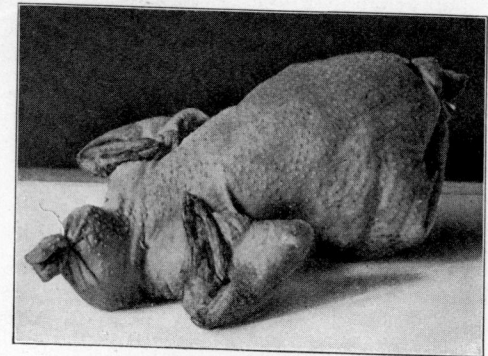

Fig. 29

§ 12 POULTRY AND GAME

55. Roast Turkey.—In America, roast turkey is usually considered as a holiday dish, being served most frequently in the homes on Thanksgiving day. However, at times when the price is moderate, it is not an extravagance to serve roast turkey for other occasions. Roasting is practically the only way in which turkey is prepared in the usual household, and it is by far the best method of preparation. Occasionally, however, a very tough turkey is steamed before roasting in order to make it sufficiently tender.

The preparation of roast turkey does not differ materially from the method given for the preparation of roast chicken. After the turkey is cleaned, drawn, and prepared according to the directions previously given, rub the inside of the cavity with salt and pepper. Then stuff with any desirable stuffing, filling the cavity and also the space under the skin of the neck where the crop was removed. Then sew up the opening, draw the skin over the neck and tie it, and truss the turkey by forcing the tip of each wing back of the first wing joint in a triangular shape and tying both ends of the legs to the tail. When thus made ready, place the turkey in the roasting pan so that the

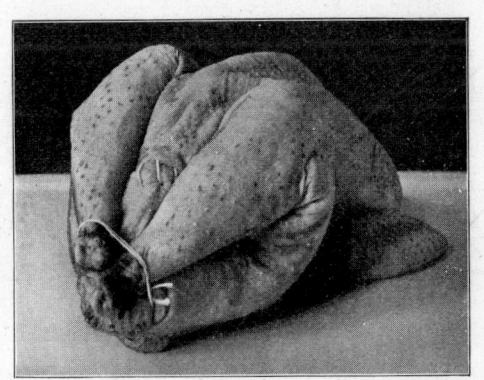

FIG. 30

back rests on the pan and the legs are on top. Then dredge with flour, sprinkle with salt and pepper, and place in a hot oven. When its surface is well browned, reduce the heat and baste every 15 minutes until the turkey is cooked. This will usually require about 3 hours, depending, of course, on the size of the bird. For basting, melt 4 tablespoonfuls of butter or bacon fat in $\frac{1}{2}$ cupful of boiling water. Pour this into the roasting pan. Add water when this evaporates, and keep a sufficient amount for basting. Turn the turkey several times during the roasting, so that the sides and back, as well as the breast, will be browned. When the turkey can be easily pierced with a fork, remove it from the roasting pan, cut the strings and pull them out, place on a platter, garnish, and serve. Gravy to be served with roast turkey may be made in the manner mentioned for making gravy to be served with fried chicken.

56. Roast Duck.—While young duck is often broiled, the usual method of preparing this kind of poultry is by roasting; in fact, roasting is an excellent way in which to cook duck that is between the broiling age and full maturity.

57. Duck is roasted in practically the same way as chicken or turkey. In the case of a *young duck,* or *spring duck,* however, stuffing is not used. After it is drawn and cleaned, truss it by folding back the wings and tying the ends of the legs to the tail, so as to give it a good appearance when served. Season with salt and pepper and dredge with flour, and, over the breast, to prevent it from burning, place strips of bacon or salt pork. When thus made ready, put the duck in a roasting pan, pour in $\frac{1}{2}$ cupful of water, and cook it in a hot oven until it is very tender, basting it about every 15 minutes during the roasting. About 15 minutes before the roasting is done, remove the strips of bacon or pork, so as to permit the breast underneath them to brown. Serve on a platter with a garnish. Make gravy if desired.

58. In the case of an *old duck,* proceed as for roasting chicken or turkey; that is, draw, clean, stuff, and truss it. In addition, place strips of bacon or salt pork over its breast. Place it in a roasting pan, pour $\frac{1}{2}$ cupful of water into the pan, and put it in a hot oven. During the roasting baste the duck every 15 minutes; also, as in roasting a young duck, remove the bacon or salt pork in plenty of time to permit the part underneath to brown. When the surface is well browned and the meat may be easily pierced with a fork, place the duck on a platter, remove the strings used to sew it up, garnish, and serve. Make gravy if desired.

59. Roast Goose.—Specific directions for roasting goose are not given, because the methods differ in no way from those already given for roasting duck. Very young goose, or green goose, is usually roasted without being stuffed, just as young duck. Older goose, however, is stuffed, trussed, and roasted just as old duck. A very old goose may be placed in a roasting pan and steamed until it is partly tender before roasting. Apples in some form or other are commonly served with goose. For example, rings of fried apple may be used as a garnish, or apple sauce or stewed or baked apples may be served as an accompaniment. Make gravy if desired.

60. Roast Small Birds.—Such small birds as guinea fowl, partridge, pheasant, quail, etc. may be roasted if desired, but on account of being so small they are seldom filled with stuffing. To roast such poultry, first clean, draw, and truss them. Then lard them with strips of bacon or salt pork, and place in a roasting pan in a very hot oven. During the roasting, turn them so as to brown all sides; also, baste every 15 minutes during the roasting with the water that has been poured into the roasting pan. Continue the roasting until the flesh is very soft and the joints can be easily pulled apart. Serve with a garnish. Make gravy if desired.

61. Stuffing for Roast Poultry.—As has been mentioned, stuffing, or dressing, of some kind is generally used when poultry is roasted. Therefore, so that the housewife may be prepared to vary the stuffing she uses from time to time, recipes for several kinds are here given. Very often, instead of using the giblets for gravy, they are cooked in water and then chopped and added to the stuffing. Giblets are not included in the recipes here given, but they may be added if desired. The quantities stated in these recipes are usually sufficient for a bird of average size; however, for a smaller or a larger bird the ingredients may be decreased or increased accordingly.

BREAD STUFFING

4 c. dry bread crumbs
$\frac{1}{2}$ c. butter
1 small onion
1 beaten egg
1 tsp. salt

1 tsp. celery salt, or $\frac{1}{2}$ tsp. celery seed
$\frac{1}{4}$ tsp. powdered sage (if desired)
$\frac{1}{4}$ tsp. pepper

Pour a sufficient amount of hot water over the bread crumbs to moisten them well. Melt the butter and allow it to brown slightly. Add the onion, chopped fine, to the butter and pour this over the bread crumbs. Add the beaten egg, salt, celery salt, and other seasonings, mix thoroughly, and stuff into the bird.

CRACKER STUFFING

3 c. cracker crumbs
1 small onion (if desired)
$\frac{1}{3}$ c. butter

$\frac{1}{2}$ tsp. salt
$\frac{1}{4}$ tsp. powdered sage (if desired)
$\frac{1}{4}$ tsp. pepper

Moisten the cracker crumbs with hot milk or water until they are quite soft. Brown the chopped onion with the butter and pour over the crackers. Add the seasonings, mix thoroughly, and stuff into the bird.

Oyster Stuffing

3 c. dry bread crumbs ¼ tsp. pepper
¼ c. butter 1 c. oysters
1 tsp. salt ½ c. chopped celery

Moisten the bread crumbs with a sufficient amount of hot water to make them quite soft. Brown the butter slightly and add it, with the seasonings, to the bread. Mix with this the oysters and chopped celery. Stuff into the bird.

Chestnut Stuffing

1 pt. blanched chestnuts 1 tsp. salt
1 pt. bread crumbs ¼ tsp. pepper
¼ c. butter 2 Tb. chopped parsley

Blanch the chestnuts in boiling water to remove the dark skin that covers them. Cook them until they are quite soft, and then chop them or mash them. Moisten the bread crumbs with hot water and add the chestnuts. Brown the butter slightly and pour it over the mixture. Add the seasonings and chopped parsley and stuff.

Green-Pepper Stuffing

1 qt. dried bread crumbs ¼ c. finely chopped green pepper
1 c. stewed tomatoes 2 Tb. chopped parsley
¼ c. melted butter 1 tsp. salt
2 Tb. bacon fat ¼ tsp. pepper
1 small onion, chopped

Moisten the bread crumbs with the stewed tomatoes and add a sufficient amount of hot water to make the crumbs quite soft. Melt the butter and bacon fat, add the onion, green pepper, and the seasonings, and pour over the crumbs. Mix thoroughly and stuff.

Rice Stuffing

2 c. steamed rice 1 tsp. salt
2 c. bread crumbs ¼ tsp. pepper
1 c. stewed tomatoes ¼ c. butter
¼ c. chopped pimiento 4 small strips bacon, diced and
2 Tb. chopped parsley fried brown
1 small onion, chopped

Mix the steamed rice with the bread crumbs. Add the stewed tomatoes, pimiento, chopped parsley, chopped onion, salt, pepper, melted butter, bacon and bacon fat, and a sufficient amount of hot water to moisten the whole well. Mix thoroughly and stuff.

Peanut Stuffing for Roast Duck

1 pt. cracker crumbs	¼ tsp. pepper
1 c. shelled peanuts, finely chopped	Dash of Cayenne pepper
	¼ c. butter
½ tsp. salt	Hot milk

Mix the crumbs and the chopped peanuts. Add the salt, pepper, and Cayenne pepper, and pour over them the melted butter and a sufficient amount of hot milk to soften the whole. Stuff into the duck.

Liver Stuffing for Roast Duck

1 duck liver	½ tsp. salt
¼ c. butter	¼ tsp. pepper
1 small onion, chopped	1 Tb. chopped parsley
2 c. dry bread crumbs	1 egg

Chop the liver and sauté in the butter to which has been added the chopped onion. Pour over the bread crumbs. Then add the salt, pepper, finely chopped parsley, and the beaten egg. Pour over all a sufficient amount of water to moisten well. Stuff into the duck.

BONED CHICKEN

62. To offer variety in the serving of chicken, as well as to present an easily carved bird, the process known as *boning* is often resorted to. Boning, as will be readily understood, consists in removing the flesh from the bones before the bird is cooked. Boned chicken may be prepared by roasting or broiling. In either case, the cookery process is the same as that already given for poultry that is not boned. If it is to be roasted, the cavity that results from the removal of the bones and internal organs should be filled with stuffing or forcemeat, so that the bird will appear as if nothing had been removed. If it is to be broiled, stuffing is not necessary. Cooked boned chicken may be served either hot or cold. Of course, other kinds of poultry may be boned if desired, and if the directions here given for boning chicken are thoroughly learned no difficulty will be encountered in performing this operation on any kind. Boning is not a wasteful process as might be supposed, because after the flesh is removed from the bones, they may be used in the making of soup.

63. Before proceeding to bone a chicken, singe it, pull out the pin feathers, cut off the head, remove the tendons from the legs,

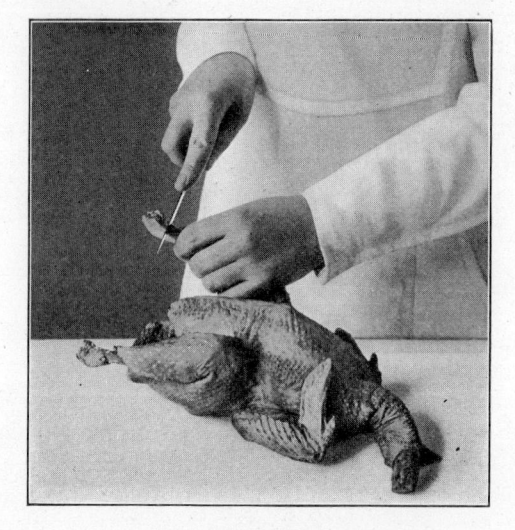

Fig. 31

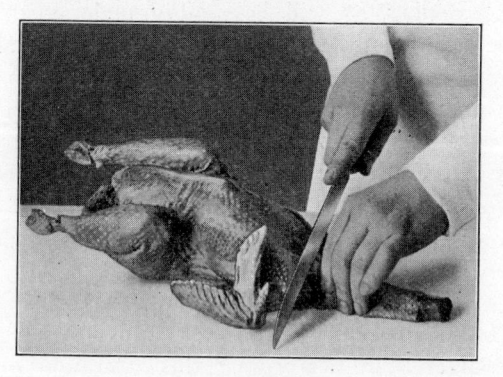

Fig. 32

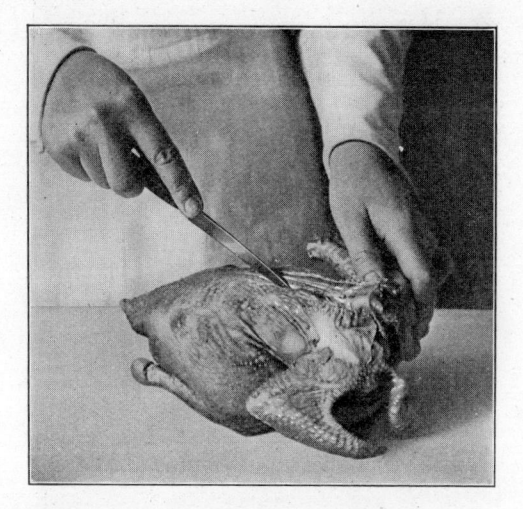

Fig. 33

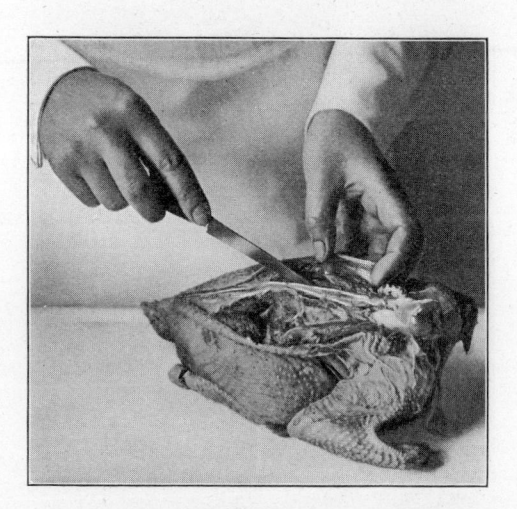

Fig. 34

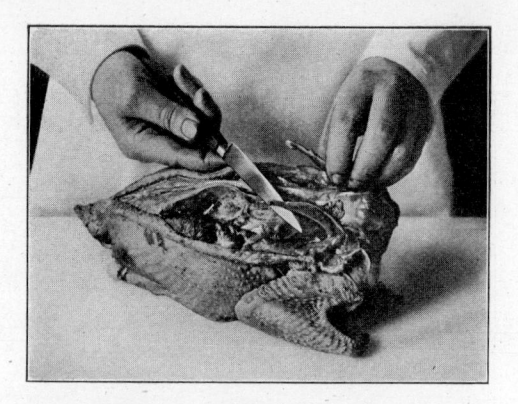

Fig. 35

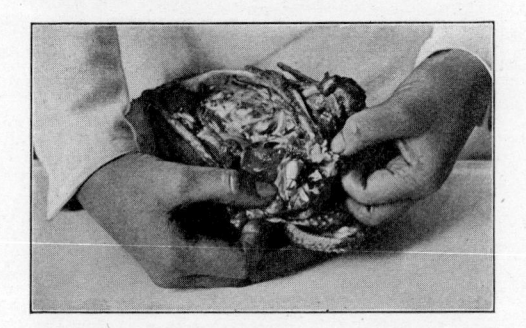

Fig. 36

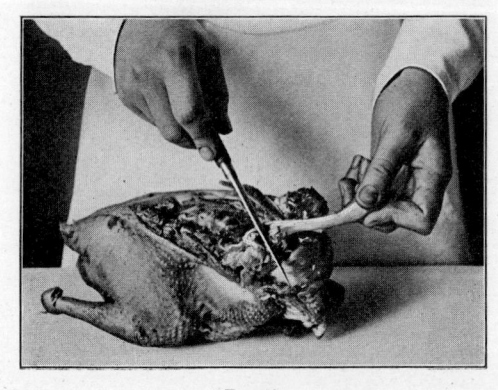

Fig. 37

and take out the crop through the neck. The bird may be drawn or not before boning it, but in any event care must be taken not to break any part of the skin. With these matters attended to, wash the skin well and wipe it carefully. First, cut off the legs at the first joint, and, with the point of a sharp knife, as shown in Fig. 31, loosen the skin and muscles just above the joint by cutting around the bone. Cut the neck off close to the body, as in Fig. 32. Then, starting at the neck, cut the skin clear down the back to the tail, as in Fig. 33. Begin on one side, and scrape the flesh, with the skin attached to it, from the back bone, as in Fig. 34. When the shoulder blade is reached, push the flesh from it with the fingers, as in Fig. 35, until the wing joint is reached. Disjoint the wing where it is attached to the body, as in Fig. 36, and loosen the skin from the wing bone down to the second joint. Disjoint the bone here and remove it up to this place, as Fig. 37 illustrates. The remaining bone is left in the tip of the wing to give it shape. When the bone from one wing is removed, turn the chicken around and remove the bone from the other wing. Next, start at the back, separating the flesh from the ribs, as in Fig. 38, taking care not to penetrate into the side cavity of the chicken, provided it has not been drawn. Push the flesh down to the thigh, as in Fig. 39, disjoint the bone here, and remove it down to the second joint, as in

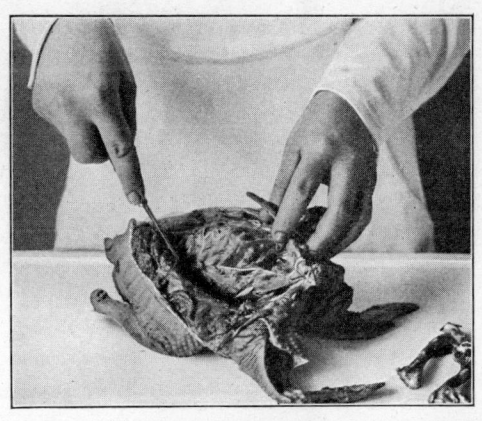

Fig. 38

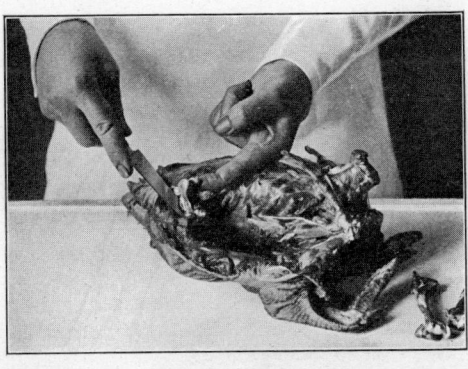

Fig. 39

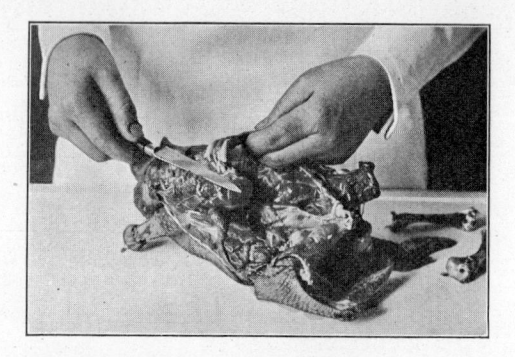

Fig. 40

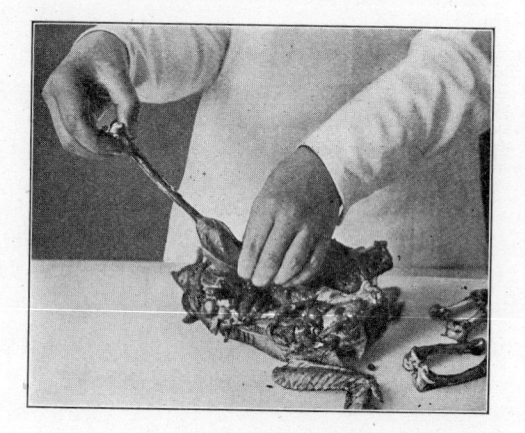

Fig. 41

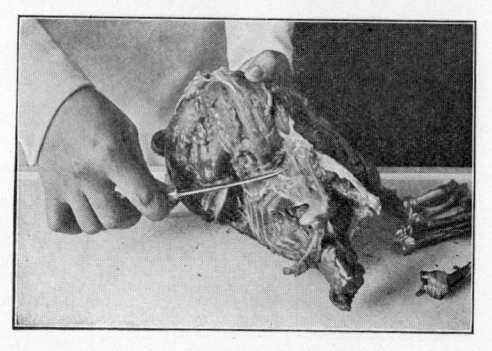

Fig. 42

Fig. 43

Fig. 44

Fig. 45

Fig. 40. Disjoint the bone at the other joint, and remove the skin and meat from the bone by turning them inside out, as in Fig. 41. If the bone has been properly loosened at the first joint of the leg, there will be no trouble in slipping it out. When this is done, turn the meat and skin back again, so that they will be right side out. Then proceed in the same way with the other leg. Next, free the flesh from the collar bone down to the breast bone on both sides, proceeding as in Fig. 42. When the ridge of the breast bone is reached, care must be taken not to break the skin that lies very close to the bone. The fingers should be used to separate the flesh at this place. When the sides and front have been thus taken care of, free the skin and the flesh from the bones over the rump. After this is done, the skeleton and internal organs of the undrawn bird may be removed, leaving the flesh intact. The skeleton of a chicken will appear as in Fig. 43.

If the boned chicken is to be roasted, the entire chicken, including the spaces from which the wing and leg bones were removed, may be filled with highly seasoned stuffing. When this is done, shape the chicken as much as possible to resemble its original shape and sew up the back. The chicken will then be ready to roast. If the boned chicken is to be broiled, shape it on the broiler as shown in Fig. 44 and broil. When broiled, boned chicken should appear as in Fig. 45.

PREPARATION BY STEWING AND OTHER COOKING METHODS

64. Chicken Stew With Dumplings or Noodles.—Perhaps the most common way of preparing chicken is to stew it. When chicken is so cooked, such an addition as dumplings or noodles is generally made because of the excellent food combination that results. For stewing, an old chicken with a great deal of flavor should be used in preference to a young one, which will have less flavor.

In order to prepare chicken by stewing, clean, draw, and cut up the bird according to directions previously given. Place the pieces in a large kettle and cover them well with boiling water. Bring all quickly to the boiling point and add 2 teaspoonfuls of salt. Then remove the scum, lower the temperature, and continue to cook at the simmering point. Keep the pieces well covered with water; also, keep the stew pot covered during the cooking. When the chicken has become tender enough to permit the pieces to be easily pierced with a fork, remove them to a deep platter or a vegetable dish. Dumplings or noodles may be cooked in the chicken broth, as the water in which the chicken was stewed is called, or they may be boiled or steamed separately. If they are cooked separately, thicken the broth with flour and serve it over the chicken with the noodles or dumplings.

65. Fricassee of Chicken.—For chicken that is tough, fricasseeing is an excellent cooking method to employ. Indeed, since it is a long method of cookery, a rather old, comparatively tough fowl lends itself best to fricasseeing. Fricassee of chicken also is a dish that requires a great deal of flavor to be drawn from the meat, and this, of course, cannot be done if a young chicken is used.

To prepare fricassee of chicken, clean and cut the bird into pieces according to the directions previously given. Put these into a saucepan, cover with boiling water, add 2 teaspoonfuls of salt, bring to the boiling point quickly, skim, and reduce the temperature so that the meat will simmer slowly until it is tender. Next, remove the pieces of chicken from the water in which they were cooked, roll them in flour, and sauté them in butter or chicken fat until they are nicely browned. If more than 2 or $2\frac{1}{2}$ cupfuls of broth remains, boil it until the quantity is reduced to this amount. Then moisten 2 or 3 tablespoonfuls of flour with a little cold water, add this to the stock, and cook until it thickens. If desired, the broth may be reduced more and thin cream may be added to make up the necessary quantity. Arrange the pieces of chicken on a deep platter, pour the sauce over them, season with salt and pepper if necessary, and serve. To enhance the appearance of this dish, the platter may be garnished with small three-cornered pieces of toast, tiny carrots, or carrots and green peas.

66. Chicken Pie.—A good change from the usual ways of serving chicken may be brought about by means of chicken pie. Such a dish is simple to prepare, and for it may be used young or old chicken.

To prepare chicken pie, dress, clean, and cut up a chicken in the usual manner. Put it into a saucepan, add a small onion and a sprig of parsley, cover with boiling water, and cook slowly until the meat is tender. When the meat is cooked, add 2 teaspoonfuls of salt and $\frac{1}{4}$ teaspoonful of pepper, and when it is perfectly tender remove it from the stock. Thicken the stock with 1 tablespoonful of flour to each cupful of liquid. Next, arrange the chicken in a baking dish. It may be left on the bones or cut into large pieces and the bones removed. To it add small carrots and onions that have been previously cooked until tender and pour the thickened stock over all. Cover this with baking-powder biscuit dough made according to the directions given in *Hot Breads* and rolled ¼ inch thick. Make some holes through the dough with the point of a sharp knife to let the steam escape, and bake in a moderate oven until the dough is well risen and a brown crust is formed. Then remove from the oven and serve.

67. Chicken Curry.—Chicken combined with rice is usually an agreeable food combination, but when flavored with curry powder, as in the recipe here given, it is a highly flavored dish that appeals to the taste of many persons.

CHICKEN CURRY

1 3-lb. chicken	1 Tb. curry powder
2 Tb. butter	2 tsp. salt
2 onions	2 c. steamed rice

Clean, dress, and cut up the chicken as for stewing. Put the butter in a hot frying pan, add the onions, sliced thin, then the pieces of chicken, and cook for 10 minutes. Parboil the liver, gizzard, and heart, cut them into pieces and add them to the chicken in the frying pan. Sprinkle the curry powder and the salt over the whole. Add boiling water or the stock in which the giblets were cooked, and simmer until the chicken is tender. Remove the meat from the frying pan and place it on a deep platter. Surround it with a border of steamed rice. Thicken the stock in the frying pan slightly with flour and pour the gravy over the chicken. Serve hot.

68. Chicken en Casserole.—Food prepared in casseroles always seems to meet with the approval of even the most discriminating persons; and chicken prepared in this way with vegetables is no exception to the rule. For such a dish should be selected a chicken of medium size that is neither very old nor very young. Any flavor that the bird contains is retained, so a strong flavor is not desirable.

In preparing chicken en casserole, first clean, dress, and cut it up in the manner directed for stewed chicken. Place the pieces in a casserole dish, together with 1 cupful of small carrots or larger carrots cut into strips. Fry a finely chopped onion with several strips of bacon, and cut these more finely while frying until the whole is well browned. Then add them to the meat in the casserole dish. Also, add 1 cupful of potato balls or 1 cupful of diced potatoes. Season well with salt and pepper, add 2 tablespoonfuls of flour, and over the whole pour sufficient hot water to cover. Cover the casserole dish, place it in a moderate oven, and cook slowly until the chicken is tender. Serve from the dish.

69. Jellied Chicken.—The housewife who desires to serve an unusual chicken dish will find that there is much in favor of jellied chicken. Aside from its food value, jellied chicken has merit in that it appeals to the eye, especially if the mold used in its preparation has a pleasing shape.

JELLIED CHICKEN

1 3- or 4-lb. chicken	1 hard-cooked egg
2 tsp. salt	1 pimiento
Several slices of onion	Several sprigs of parsley

Clean, dress, and cut up the chicken. Put it into a saucepan and cover with boiling water. Season with the salt and add the slices of onion. Cook slowly until the meat will fall from the bones. Remove the chicken from the saucepan, take the meat from the bones, and chop it into small pieces. Reduce the stock to about $1\frac{1}{2}$ cupfuls, strain it, and skim off the fat. With this done, place slices of the hard-cooked egg in the bottom of a wet mold. Chop the pimiento and sprigs of parsley and mix them with the chopped meat. Put the mixture on top of the sliced egg, and pour the stock over the whole. Keep in a cool place until it is set. If the stock is not reduced and more jelly is desired, unflavored gelatine may be dissolved and added to coagulate the liquid. To serve jellied chicken, remove from the mold, turn upside down, so that the eggs are on top and act as a garnish, and then cut in thin slices.

70. Chicken Bechamel.—Still another chicken dish that may be used to break the monotony of meals is chicken bechamel, the word bechamel being the name of a sauce invented by Béchamel, who was steward to Louis XIV, a king of France.

CHICKEN BECHAMEL

1 good-sized chicken	$\frac{1}{4}$ c. chopped pimiento
2 tsp. salt	3 Tb. flour
$\frac{1}{4}$ tsp. pepper	1 c. thin cream
1 c. small mushrooms	

Clean, dress, and cut up the chicken. Place the pieces into a saucepan, and cover with boiling water. Add the salt and the pepper, and allow to come to the boiling point. Remove the scum and simmer the chicken slowly until it is tender. Remove the chicken from the liquid, take the meat from the bones, and cut it into small pieces. Add to these the mushrooms and chopped pimiento. Reduce the stock to 1 cupful and thicken it with the flour added to the thin cream. Cook until the sauce is thickened. Then add to it the chopped chicken with the other ingredients. Heat all thoroughly and serve on toast points or in timbale cases, the making of which is explained in *Meat,* Part 2.

71. Cooking of Giblets.—As has been pointed out, the giblets—that is, the liver, heart, and gizzard of all kinds of fowl—are used in gravy making and as an ingredient for stuffing. When poultry is stewed, as in making stewed chicken, it is not uncommon to cook the giblets with the pieces of chicken. The gizzard and heart especially require long, slow cooking to make them tender enough to be eaten. Therefore, when poultry is broiled, fried, or roasted, some other cookery method must be resorted to, as these processes are too rigid for the preparation of giblets. In such cases, the best plan is to cook them in water until they are tender and then sauté them in butter. When cooked in this way, they may be served with the poultry, for to many persons they are very palatable.

DISHES FROM LEFT-OVER POULTRY

72. Left-over poultry of any kind is too valuable to be wasted, but even if this were not so there are so many practical ways in which such left-overs may be used to advantage that it would be the height of extravagance not to utilize them. The bones that remain from roast fowl after carving are especially good for soup making, as they will yield quite a quantity of flavor when they are thoroughly cooked. If sufficient meat remains on the carcass to permit of slicing, such meat may be served cold. However, if merely small pieces are left or if fried or broiled poultry remains, it will be advisable to make some other use of these left-overs. It is often possible for the ingenious housewife to add other foods to them so as to increase the quantity and thus make them serve more. For example, a small quantity of pork or veal may be satisfactorily used with chicken, as may also pieces of hard-cooked eggs, celery, mushrooms, etc. In fact, salads may be made by combining such ingredients and salad dressings. To show the use of left-overs still further, there are here given a number of recipes that may well be used.

73. Chicken Salad.—A common way in which to utilize left-over chicken is in chicken salad. Such salad may be served to advantage for luncheons and other light meals.

Chicken Salad

2 c. cold diced chicken   Salad dressing
1 c. chopped celery   2 hard-cooked eggs
1 small onion, chopped

Mix the meat with the chopped celery and onion. Marinate with well-seasoned vinegar or a little lemon juice. French dressing may be used for this if oil is desired. Just before serving pour off any excess liquid. Add any desired salad dressing. Heap the salad on lettuce leaves and garnish with slices of the hard-cooked eggs.

74. Chicken à la King.—Chicken à la king is not necessarily a left-over dish, for it may be made from either left-over chicken or, if desired, chicken cooked especially for it. It makes an excellent dish to prepare in a chafing dish, but it may be conveniently prepared in a saucepan on the fire and served in any desirable way.

Chicken à la King

3 Tb. fat (butter or bacon fat   1 tsp. salt
   or part of each) $\frac{1}{2}$ c. mushrooms
2 Tb. flour $\frac{1}{4}$ c. canned pimiento
$\frac{3}{4}$ c. chicken stock $1\frac{1}{2}$ c. cold chicken
1 c. milk or thin cream   2 eggs

Melt the fat in a saucepan, add the flour, and stir until well mixed. Heat the stock and the milk or cream, pour this into the mixture, stir rapidly, and bring to boiling point. Add the salt and the mushrooms, pimientoes, and cold chicken cut into pieces $\frac{1}{2}$ to 1 inch long, allow the mixture to come to the boiling point again, and add the slightly beaten eggs. Remove from the fire at once to prevent the egg from curdling. Serve over pieces of fresh toast and sprinkle with paprika.

75. Chicken Croquettes.—Left-over chicken may be used to advantage for croquettes made according to the following recipe. When the ingredients listed are combined with chicken, an especially agreeable food will be the result. If there is not sufficient cold chicken to meet the requirements, a small quantity of cold veal or pork may be chopped with the chicken.

Chicken Croquettes

3 Tb. fat
¼ c. flour
1 tsp. salt
⅛ tsp. pepper
¼ tsp. paprika
1 c. chicken stock or cream

2 c. cold chicken, chopped
¼ c. mushrooms, chopped
1 tsp. parsley, chopped
1 egg
Fine bread crumbs

Melt the fat in a saucepan, add the flour, and stir until well blended. Add the salt, pepper, and paprika. Heat the stock or cream and add to the mixture in the saucepan. Stir constantly until the sauce is completely thickened. Then add the chopped chicken, mushrooms, and parsley. When cold, shape into oblong croquettes, roll in the egg, slightly beaten, and then in fine crumbs. Fry in deep fat until brown. Serve with a garnish or some vegetable, such as peas, diced carrots, or small pieces of cauliflower, as well as with left-over chicken gravy or well-seasoned white sauce.

76. Turkey Hash.—Possibly the simplest way in which to utilize left-over turkey meat is to make it up into hash. Such a dish may be used for almost any meal, and when made according to the recipe here given it will suit the taste of nearly every person.

Turkey Hash

2 Tb. butter
½ c. coarse rye-bread crumbs
1 small onion, sliced
2 c. finely chopped cold turkey

½ c. finely chopped raw potato
½ tsp. salt
⅛ tsp. pepper
1 pt. milk

Melt the butter in a saucepan. When brown, add to it the rye-bread crumbs and mix well. Then add the sliced onion, chopped turkey, potato, salt, and pepper. Cook for a short time on top of the stove, stirring frequently to prevent burning. Pour the milk over the whole, and place the pan in the oven or on the back of the stove. Cook slowly until the milk is reduced and the hash is sufficiently dry to serve. Serve on buttered toast.

77. Chicken With Rice.—Left-over chicken may be readily combined with rice to make a nutritious dish. To prepare chicken with rice, add to left-over gravy any left-over cold chicken cut into small pieces. If there is not enough gravy to cover the meat, add sufficient white sauce; if no gravy remains, use white sauce entirely.

Heat the chicken in the gravy or the sauce to the boiling point. Then heap a mound of fresh steamed or boiled rice in the center of a deep platter or a vegetable dish and pour the chicken and sauce over it. Serve hot.

78. Baked Poultry With Rice.—A casserole or a baking dish serves as a good utensil in which to prepare a left-over dish of any kind of poultry, because it permits vegetables to be added and cooked thoroughly. Baked poultry with rice is a dish that may be prepared in such a utensil.

Line a casserole or a baking dish with a thick layer of fresh steamed or boiled rice. Fill the center with chopped cold poultry, which may be chicken, turkey, duck, or goose. Add peas, chopped carrots, potato, and a few slices of onion in any desirable proportion. Over this pour sufficient left-over gravy or white sauce to cover well. First, steam thoroughly; then cover the utensil and bake slowly until the vegetables are cooked and the entire mixture is well heated. Serve from the casserole or baking dish.

SERVING AND CARVING POULTRY

79. Poultry of any kind should always be served on a platter or in a dish that has been heated in the oven or by running hot water over it. After placing the cooked bird on the platter or the dish from which it is to be served, it should be taken to the dining room and placed before the person who is to serve. If it is roasted, it will require carving. If not, the pieces may be served as they are desired by the individuals at the table. Poultry having both dark and white meat is usually served according to the taste of each individual at the table. If no preference is stated, however, a small portion of each kind of meat is generally served.

80. The carving of broiled or roast chicken, turkey, duck, or goose may be done in the kitchen, but having the whole bird brought to the table and carved there adds considerably to a meal. Carving is usually done by the head of the family, but in a family in which there are boys each one should be taught to carve properly, so that he may do the carving in the absence of another person.

For carving, the bird should be placed on the platter so that it rests on its back; also, a well-sharpened carving knife and a fork should be placed at the right of the platter and the person who is to

Fig. 46

serve. To carve a bird, begin as shown in Fig. 46; that is, thrust the fork firmly into the side or breast of the fowl and cut through

Fig. 47

the skin where the leg joins the body, breaking the thigh joint.

§ 12　　　POULTRY AND GAME　　　51

Cut through this joint, severing the second joint and leg in one piece. Then, if desired, cut the leg apart at the second joint. As

Fig. 48

the portions are thus cut, they may be placed on a separate platter that is brought to the table heated. Next, in the same manner, cut

Fig. 49

off the other leg and separate it at the second joint. With the legs cut off, remove each wing at the joint where it is attached to the body, proceeding as shown in Fig. 47. Then slice the meat from the breast by cutting down from the ridge of the breast bone toward the wing, as in Fig. 48. After this meat has been sliced off, there still remains some meat around the thigh and on the back. This should be sliced off or removed with the point of the knife, as in Fig. 49, so that the entire skeleton will be clean, as in Fig. 50. If the entire bird is not to be served, as much as is necessary may be cut and the remainder left on the bones. With each serving of meat a spoonful of dressing should be taken from the inside of the bird, provided it is stuffed, and, together with some gravy, served on the plate.

FIG. 50

GAME

GENERAL DESCRIPTION

81. Game, which includes the meat of deer, bear, rabbit, squirrel, wild duck, wild goose, partridge, pheasant, and some less common animals, such as possum, is not a particularly common food. However, it is sufficiently common to warrant a few directions concerning its use. Game can be purchased or caught only during certain seasons, designated by the laws of various states. Such laws are quite stringent and have been made for the protection of each particular species.

82. The meat of wild animals and birds is usually strong in flavor. Just why this is so, however, is not definitely known. Undoubtedly some of the strong flavor is due to the particular food on which the animal or the bird feeds, and much of this flavor is due to extractives contained in the flesh.

When game birds and animals have considerable fat surrounding the tissues, the greater part of it is often rejected because of its extremely high flavor. By proper cooking, however, much of this flavor, if it happens to be a disagreeable one, can be driven off.

The general composition of the flesh of various kinds of game does not differ greatly from that of similar domestic animals or birds. For instance, the flesh of bear is similar in its composition to that of fat beef, as bear is one of the wild animals that is very fat. Venison, or the meat obtained from deer, contains much less fat, and its composition resembles closely that of very lean beef. Rabbits and most of the wild birds are quite lean; in fact, they are so lean that it is necessary in the preparation of them to supply sufficient fat to make them more appetizing.

RECIPES FOR GAME

83. Only a few recipes for the preparation of game are here given, because, in the case of wild birds, the cookery methods do not differ materially from those given for poultry, and, in the case of such animals as bears, the directions for preparing steaks and other cuts are identical with the cooking of similar cuts of beef. Rabbit and squirrel are perhaps the most common game used as food in the home; therefore, directions for cleaning and cooking them receive the most consideration.

84. Preparing a Rabbit for Cooking.—In order to prepare a rabbit for cooking, it must first be skinned and drawn, after which it may be cut up or left whole, depending on the cookery method that is to be followed.

To skin a rabbit, first chop off the feet at the first joint; then remove the head at the first joint below the skull and slit the skin of the stomach from a point between the forelegs to the hind legs. With this done, remove the entrails carefully, proceeding in much the same manner as in removing the entrails of a chicken. Then slit the skin from the opening in the stomach around the back to the opposite side. Catch hold on the back and pull the skin first from the hind legs and then from the forelegs. If the rabbit is to be stewed, wash it thoroughly and separate it into pieces at the joints.

If it is to be roasted or braized, it may be left whole. A rabbit that is left whole presents a better appearance when it is trussed. To truss a rabbit, force the hind legs toward the head and fasten them in place by passing a skewer through the leg on one side, through the body, and into the leg on the other side. Then skewer the front legs back under the body in the same way. In such a case, the head may be left on or removed, as desired.

85. Roast Rabbit.—Roasting is the cookery process often used to prepare rabbit. To cook it in this way, first skin and clean the animal and stuff it. Any of the stuffings previously given may be used for this purpose. Then skewer the legs in position, place strips of bacon across the back, put in a roasting pan, and dredge with salt and pepper. Also, add $\frac{1}{2}$ cupful of hot water to which has been added a little butter or bacon fat. Roast in a quick oven, and baste every 15 minutes during the roasting. A few minutes before the rabbit is tender enough to be pierced with a fork, remove the strips of bacon so that the flesh underneath may brown. Then remove from the pan and serve.

86. Sautéd Rabbit.—If it is desired to prepare a rabbit by sautéing, skin and clean it, cut it into pieces, and dry all the pieces with a soft cloth. Then melt bacon fat in a frying pan, and when it is hot place the pieces of rabbit in it and allow them to brown. Add several sprigs of parsley and two small onions, sliced, season with salt and pepper, add a slice or two of bacon, and pour water over the whole until it is nearly covered. Place a cover on the frying pan and simmer slowly. Add water when it is necessary. When the meat is tender, remove it from the frying pan. Then thicken the fluid that remains with a small amount of flour so as to make a gravy. Serve hot.

87. Rabbit Pie.—Rabbit made into pie is also a desirable way in which to serve rabbit. To prepare such a dish, skin and clean one or more rabbits and cut them up into as small pieces as possible, removing the largest bones. Put these pieces into a baking dish, and over them place bacon cut into small strips. Sprinkle all with chopped parsley, salt, and pepper, and add a few slices of onion, as well as some strips of carrot and potato, if desired. Pour a sufficient amount of boiling water over the whole and allow to simmer slowly until the meat is partly cooked. Then place in the oven and cook until the meat is tender. Next, dredge the contents of the baking dish with flour and cover with a ¼-inch layer of baking-powder biscuit dough. Make several slits through the dough to allow the steam to escape. Bake until the dough becomes a well-browned crust. Serve hot in the baking dish.

88. Broiled Squirrel.—For cooking, squirrel is cleaned in practically the same way as rabbit. Squirrel may be made ready to eat by stewing, but as it is so small a creature, broiling is the usual method of preparation. To broil a squirrel, first remove the skin and clean it. Then break the bones along the spine, so that the squirrel can be spread out flat. When thus made ready, place it on a well-greased hot broiler and sear it quickly on one side; then turn it and sear the other side. Next, sprinkle it with salt and pepper, place strips of bacon across the back, and allow it to broil slowly until it is well browned. Squirrel may be served in the same way as rabbit.

89. Cuts of Venison.—The meat obtained from deer, called *venison*, as has been mentioned, may be cut up to form cuts similar to those obtained from beef, such as steaks and roasts. Although such meat is a rarity, it will be well to be familiar with a few of the methods of cooking it. These, however, do not differ materially from the methods of cooking other meats.

90. Broiled Venison.—To prepare venison for broiling, cut a steak from 1 to 1½ inches thick. Place this on a well-greased broiler and broil until well done. Serve on a hot platter. Garnish the broiled venison with parsley and pour over it sauce made as follows:

SAUCE FOR BROILED VENISON

2 Tb. butter
2 Tb. flour
½ tsp. salt
¼ tsp. ground cinnamon
4 Tb. currant jelly
2 tsp. lemon juice
¼ c. port wine
6 finely chopped Maraschino cherries

Melt the butter in a saucepan, add the flour, salt, ground cinnamon, currant jelly, lemon juice, and the port wine, which should be heated with 1 cupful of water. Cook until the flour has thickened, remove from the fire, and add the cherries.

91. Roast Fillet of Venison.—If a fillet of venison is to be roasted, proceed by larding it with strips of salt pork. Then place it in a pan with one small onion, sliced, a bay leaf, and a small quantity of parsley, 1 teaspoonful of salt, and ¼ teaspoonful of pepper. Dilute ¼ cupful of vinegar with ¾ cupful of water and add a teaspoonful of Worcestershire sauce. Pour this over the fillet and place it in a hot oven. Cook until the liquid has evaporated sufficiently to allow the venison to brown. Turn, so as to brown on both sides, and when quite tender and well browned, serve on a hot platter.

92. Roast Leg of Venison.—If a leg of venison is to be roasted, first remove the skin, wipe the meat with a damp cloth, and cover it with a paste made of flour and water. Then put it into a roasting pan and roast in a very hot oven. Baste with hot water every 15 minutes for about 1½ hours. At the end of this time, remove the paste, spread the surface with butter, sprinkle with salt and pepper, and continue to roast for 1 to 1¼ hours longer. Baste every 15 minutes, basting during the last hour with hot water in which has been melted a small quantity of butter. Then remove the venison from the pan and serve it on a hot platter with any desired sauce.

POULTRY AND GAME

EXAMINATION QUESTIONS

(1) Of what value is poultry in the diet?

(2) What effect do the feeding and care of poultry have upon it as food?

(3) Mention briefly the proper preparation of poultry killed for market.

(4) (*a*) What are the most important things to consider when poultry is to be selected? (*b*) Give the points that indicate good quality of poultry.

(5) How would you determine the age of a chicken?

(6) How would you determine the freshness of a chicken?

(7) (*a*) What are the marks of cold-storage poultry? (*b*) Should cold-storage poultry be drawn or undrawn? Tell why.

(8) How should frozen poultry be thawed?

(9) Tell briefly how turkey should be selected.

(10) At what age and season is turkey best?

(11) Discuss the selection of: (*a*) ducks; (*b*) geese.

(12) (*a*) How does the composition of poultry compare with that of meat? (*b*) What kind of chicken has a high food value?

(13) (*a*) How should a chicken be dressed? (*b*) What care should be given to the skin in plucking?

(14) Give briefly the steps in drawing a chicken.

(15) Give briefly the steps in cutting up a chicken.

(16) How is poultry prepared for: (*a*) roasting? (*b*) frying? (*c*) broiling? (*d*) stewing?

(17) (*a*) Describe trussing. (*b*) Why is trussing done?

(18) Give briefly the steps in boning a chicken.

(19) Tell briefly how to serve and carve a roasted bird.

(20) Discuss game in a general way.

ADDITIONAL WORK

Select a fowl by applying the tests given for selection in the lesson. Prepare it by what seems to you to be the most economical method. Tell how many persons are served and the use made of the left-overs. Compute the cost per serving by dividing the cost of the fowl by the number of servings it made.

At another time, select a chicken for frying by applying the tests given in the lesson. Compute the cost per serving by dividing the cost of the chicken by the number of servings it made.

Compare the cost per serving of the fried chicken with that of the fowl, to find which is the more economical. In each case, collect the bones after the chicken is eaten and weigh them to determine which has the greater proportion of bone to meat, the fowl or the frying chicken. Whether you have raised the poultry yourself or have purchased it in the market, use the market price in computing your costs. Weigh the birds carefully before drawing them.

§ 12

FISH AND SHELL FISH

FISH

FISH IN THE DIET

1. **Fish** provides another class of high-protein or tissue-building food. As this term is generally understood, it includes both vertebrate fish—that is, fish having a backbone, such as salmon, cod, shad, etc.—and many other water animals, such as lobsters, crabs, shrimp, oysters, and clams. A distinction, however, is generally made between these two groups, those having bones being regarded properly as *fish* and those partly or entirely encased in shells, as *shell fish*. It is according to this distinction that this class of foods is considered in this Section. Because all the varieties of both fish and shell fish are in many respects similar, the term *sea food* is often applied to them, but, as a rule, this term is restricted to designate salt-water products as distinguished from fresh-water fish.

2. Fish can usually be purchased at a lower price than meat, and for this reason possesses an economic advantage over it. Besides the price, the substitution of fish for meat makes for economy in a number of ways to which consideration is not usually given. These will become clearly evident when it is remembered that nearly all land animals that furnish meat live on many agricultural products that might be used for human food. Then, too, other foods fed to animals, although not actually human foods, require in their raising the use of soil that might otherwise be utilized for the raising of food for human beings. This is not true in the case of fish. They consume the vegetation that grows in lakes, streams, and the ocean, as well as various kinds of insects, small fish, etc., which cannot be used as human food and which do not require the use of the soil.

In addition, much of the food that animals, which are warm-blooded, take into their bodies is required to maintain a constant temperature above that of their surroundings, so that not all of what they eat is used in building up the tissues of their bodies. With fish, however, it is different. As they are cold-blooded and actually receive heat from their surroundings, they do not require food for bodily warmth. Practically all that they take into the body is built up into a supply of flesh that may be used as food for human beings.

3. With fish, as with other foods, some varieties are sought more than others, the popularity of certain kinds depending on the individual taste or the preference of the people in a particular locality. Such popularity, however, is often a disadvantage to the purchaser, because a large demand for certain varieties has a tendency to cause a rise in price. The increased price does not indicate that the fish is of more value to the consumer than some other fish that may be cheaper because it is less popular, although quite as valuable from a food standpoint. The preference for particular kinds of fish and the persistent disregard of others that are edible is for the most part due to prejudice. In certain localities, one kind of fish may be extremely popular while in others the same fish may not be used for food at all. Such prejudice should be overcome, for, as a matter of fact, practically every fish taken from pure water is fit to eat, in the sense that it furnishes food and is not injurious to health.

In addition, any edible fish should be eaten in the locality where it is caught. The transportation of this food is a rather difficult matter, and, besides, it adds to the cost. It is therefore an excellent plan to make use of the kind of fish that is most plentiful, as such practice will insure both better quality and a lower market price.

4. As is well known, fish is an extremely perishable food. Therefore, when it is caught in quantities too great to be used at one time, it is preserved in various ways. The preservation methods that have proved to be the most satisfactory are canning, salting and drying, smoking, and preserving in various kinds of brine and pickle. As such methods are usually carried out in the locality where the fish is caught, many varieties of fish can be conveniently stored for long periods of time and so distributed as to meet the requirements of the consumer. This plan enables persons far removed from the source of supply to procure fish frequently.

COMPOSITION AND FOOD VALUE OF FISH

COMPOSITION OF FISH

5. Comparison of Fish With Meat.—In general, the composition of fish is similar to that of meat, for both of them are high-protein foods. However, some varieties of fish contain large quantities of fat and others contain very little of this substance, so the food value of the different kinds varies greatly. As in the case of meat, fish is lacking in carbohydrate. Because of the close similarity between these two foods, fish is a very desirable substitute for meat. In fact, fish is in some respects a better food than meat, but it cannot be used so continuously as meat without becoming monotonous; that is to say, a person will grow tired of fish much more quickly than of most meats. The similarity between the composition of fish and that of meat has much to do with regulating the price of these protein foods, which, as has already been learned, are the highest priced foods on the market.

6. Protein in Fish.—In fish, as well as in shell fish, a very large proportion of the food substances present is protein. This proportion varies with the quantity of water, bone, and refuse that the particular food contains, and with the physical structure of the food. In fresh fish, the percentage of this material varies from 6 to 17 per cent. The structure of fish is very similar to that of meat, as the flesh is composed of tiny hollow fibers containing extractives, in which are dissolved mineral salts and various other materials. The quantity of extractives found in these foods, however, is less than that found in meat. Fish extracts of any kind, such as clam juice, oyster juice, etc., are similar in their composition to any of the extractives of meat, differing only in the kind and proportions. In addition to the muscle fibers of fish, which are, of course, composed of protein, fish contains a small quantity of albumin, just as meat does. It is the protein material in fish, as well as in shell fish, that is responsible for its very rapid decomposition.

The application of heat has the same effect on the protein of fish as it has on that of meat, fowl, and other animal tissues. Consequently, the same principles of cookery apply to both the retention and the extraction of flavor.

WI—C3—14

7. Fat in Fish.—The percentage of fat in fish varies from less than 1 per cent. in some cases to a trifle more than 14 per cent. in others, but this high percentage is rare, as the average fish probably does not exceed from 3 to 6 or 7 per cent. of fat. This variation affects the total food value proportionately. The varieties of fish that contain the most fat deteriorate most rapidly and withstand transportation the least well, so that when these are secured in large quantities they are usually canned or preserved in some manner. Fish containing a large amount of fat, such as salmon, turbot, eel, herring, halibut, mackerel, mullet, butterfish, and lake trout, have a more moist quality than those which are without fat, such as cod. Therefore, as it is difficult to cook fish that is lacking in fat and keep it from becoming dry, a fat fish makes a more palatable food than a lean fish. The fat of fish is very strongly flavored; consequently, any that cooks out of fish in its preparation is not suitable for use in the cooking of other foods.

8. Carbohydrate in Fish.—Like meat, fish does not contain carbohydrate in any appreciable quantity. In fact, the small amount that is found in the tissue, and that compares to the glycogen found in animal tissues, is not present in sufficient quantities to merit consideration.

9. Mineral Matter in Fish.—In fish, mineral matter is quite as prevalent as in meat. Through a notion that fish contains large proportions of phosphorus, and because this mineral is also present in the brain, the idea that fish is a brain food has become widespread. It has been determined, however, that this belief has no foundation.

FOOD VALUE OF FISH

10. Factors Determining Food Value.—The total food value of fish, as has been shown, is high or low, varying with the food substances it contains. Therefore, since, weight for weight, the food value of fat is much higher than that of protein, it follows that the fish containing the most fat has the highest food value. Fat and protein, as is well known, do not serve the same function in the body, but each has its purpose and is valuable and necessary in the diet. Some varieties of fish contain fat that is strong in flavor, and from these the fat should be removed before cooking, especially if the flavor is disagreeable. This procedure of course reduces the total food value of the fish, but it should be done if it increases the palatability.

11. Relative Nutritive Value of Fish and Meat.—When fish and meat are compared, it will be observed that some kinds of fish have a higher food value than meat, particularly if the fish contains much fat and the meat is lean. When the average of each of

TABLE I
COMPARISON OF COMPOSITION AND FOOD VALUE OF FISH AND MEAT

Edible Portion	Protein Per Cent.	Fat Per Cent.	Total Food Value per Pound Calories	Food Value per Pound Due to Protein Calories
Fish:				
Bass, black	20.6	1.7	443	373
Bluefish	19.4	1.2	401	352
Carp	17.4	2.6	421	315
Catfish	14.4	20.6	1,102	262
Halibut steak	18.6	5.2	550	337
Lake trout	17.8	1.0	363	323
Red snapper	19.2	1.0	389	348
Salmon (canned)	21.8	12.1	888	396
Whitefish	22.9	6.5	680	415
Meat:				
Beef, round, medium fat	20.3	13.6	895	368
Chicken, broilers	21.5	2.5	492	390
Fowl	19.3	16.3	1,016	350
Lamb, leg	19.2	16.5	870	348
Pork chops	16.6	30.1	1,455	301

these foods is compared, however, meat will be found to have a higher food value than fish. To show how fish compares with meat and fowl, the composition and food value of several varieties of each food are given in Table I, which is taken from a United States government bulletin.

12. A study of this table will show that on the whole the percentage of protein in the various kinds of fish is as much as that in meat, while in a few instances, it is greater. This proves that so far as the quantity of protein is concerned, these two foods are equally valuable in their tissue-forming and tissue-building qualities. It will be seen also that the percentage of fat in fish varies greatly, some varieties containing more than meat, but most of them containing less. Furthermore, the total food value per pound, in calories, is for the most part greater in meat than in fish, whereas the food value per pound due to protein is equivalent in most cases, but higher in some of the fish than in the meat.

13. It must also be remembered that the drying or preserving of fish does not in any way decrease its food value. In fact, pound for pound, dried fish, both smoked and salt, contains more nutritive value than fresh fish, because the water, which decreases the food value of fresh fish, is driven off in drying. However, when prepared for eating, dried fish in all probability has more food value than fresh fish, because water or moisture of some sort must be supplied in its preparation.

14. The method of preparing dried or preserved fish, as well as fresh fish, has much to do with the food value obtained from it. Just as nutritive value is lost in the cooking of meat by certain methods, so it may be lost in the preparation of fish if the proper methods are not applied. To obtain as much food value from fish as possible, the various points that are involved in its cookery must be thoroughly understood. Certain facts concerning the buying of fish must also be kept in mind. For instance, in canned fish, almost all the bones, skin, and other inedible parts, except the tails, heads, and fins of very small fish, have been removed before packing, indicating that practically all the material purchased is edible. In the case of fresh fish, a large percentage of what is bought must be wasted in preparation and in eating, the percentage of waste varying from 5 to 45 per cent.

15. Digestibility of Fish.—The food value of any food is an important item when its usefulness as a food is taken into account, but of equal importance is the manner in which the body uses the food; that is, whether it digests the food with ease or with difficulty. Therefore, when the value of fish as a food is to be determined, its digestibility must receive definite consideration. As has already been explained, much depends on the cooking of the food in question. On the whole, fish is found to be more easily digested than meat, with the exception perhaps of a few kinds or certain cuts. That physicians recognize this characteristic is evidenced by the fact that fish is often used in the feeding of invalids or sick people when meat is not permitted.

16. The ease with which fish is digested is influenced largely by the quantity of fat it contains, for this fat, acting in identically the same way as the fat of meat, has the effect of slowing the digestion that is carried on in the stomach. It follows, then, that with possibly one or two exceptions the kinds of fish most easily digested are those which are lean.

17. In addition to the correct cooking of fish and the presence of fat, a factor that largely influences the digestibility of this food is the length of the fibers of the flesh. It will be remembered that the parts of an animal having long fibers are tougher and less easily digested than those having short fibers. This applies with equal force in the case of fish. Its truth is evident when it is known that cod, a lean fish, is digested with greater difficulty than some of the fat fish because of the length and toughness of its fibers. This, however, is comparative, and it must not be thought that fish on the whole is digested with difficulty.

18. Another factor that influences the digestibility of fish is the salting of it. Whether fish is salted dry or in brine, the salt hardens the fibers and tissues. While the salt acts as a preservative in causing this hardening, it, at the same time, makes the fish preserved in this manner a little more difficult to digest. This slight difference need scarcely be considered so far as the normal adult is concerned, but in case of children or persons whose digestion is not entirely normal its effect is likely to be felt.

PURCHASE AND CARE OF FISH

19. Purchase of Fish.—The housewife has much to do with the market price of fish and the varieties that are offered for sale, for these are governed by the demand created by her. The fisherman's catch depends on weather conditions, the season, and other uncertain factors. If the kinds of fish he secures are not what the housewife demands, they either will not be sent to market or will go begging on the market for want of purchasers. Such a state of affairs should not exist, and it would not if every housewife were

TABLE II
NAMES, SEASONS, AND USES OF FRESH FISH

Name of Fish	Season	Method of Cookery
Bass, black	All the year	Fried, baked
Bass, sea	All the year	Baked, broiled, fried
Bass, striped	All the year	Baked, broiled, fried
Bass, lake	June 1 to January 1	Baked, broiled, fried
Bluefish	May 1 to November 1	Baked, broiled
Butterfish	October 1 to May 1	Fried, sautéd
Carp	July 1 to November 1	Baked, broiled, fried
Catfish	All the year	Fried, sautéd
Codfish	All the year	Boiled, fried, sautéd, baked, broiled
Eels	All the year	Fried, boiled, baked
Flounder	All the year	Sautéd, fried, baked
Haddock	All the year	Steamed, boiled, fried
Halibut	All the year	Boiled, fried, creamed
Herring	October 1 to May 1	Sautéd, fried, broiled
Kingfish	May 1 to November 1	Boiled, steamed, baked
Mackerel	April 1 to October 1	Baked, broiled, boiled, fried
Perch, fresh water	September 1 to June 1	Fried, broiled
Pike, or pickerel, fresh water	June 1 to January 1	Fried, broiled, baked
Porgies, salt water	June 15 to October 15	Fried, sautéd
Red snapper	October 1 to April 1	Boiled, steamed
Salmon, Kennebec	June 1 to October 1	Broiled, baked, boiled
Salmon, Oregon	October 1 to June 1	Broiled, baked, boiled
Shad	January 1 to June 1	Baked, broiled, fried
Shad roe	January 1 to June 1	Broiled, fried
Sheepshead	June 1 to September 15	Boiled, fried
Smelts	August 15 to April 15	Fried, sautéd
Sole, English	November 1 to May 1	Baked, broiled, fried
Sunfish	May 1 to December 1	Fried, sautéd
Trout, fresh water	April 1 to September 1	Baked, broiled, fried, boiled, sautéd
Weakfish, or sea trout	May 15 to October 15	Baked, broiled
Whitebait	May 1 to April 1	Fried, sautéd
Whitefish, fresh water	November 1 to March 1	Baked, fried, sautéd, broiled

to buy the kind of fish that is plentiful in her home market. So that she may become familiar with the varieties that the market affords, she should carefully study Tables II and III, which give the names, seasons, and uses of both fresh fish and salt and smoked fish. With the information given in these tables well in mind, she will be able not only to select the kind she wants, but to cooperate better with dealers.

TABLE III
NAMES, SEASONS, AND USES OF SALT AND SMOKED FISH

Name of Fish	Season	Method of Cookery
Salt Fish		
Anchovies	All the year	Served as a relish, stuffed with various highly seasoned mixtures, used as flavor for sauce
Codfish, dried	All the year	Creamed, balls
Herring, pickled	All the year	Sautéd
Mackerel	All the year	Broiled, fried, sautéd
Salmon, salt	All the year	Fried, broiled, boiled
Smoked Fish		
Haddock, or finnan haddie	October 15 to April 1	Broiled, baked, creamed
Halibut	October 1 to April 1	Baked, broiled, fried
Herring	All the year	Served as a relish without cooking
Mackerel	October 1 to November 1	Baked, boiled, fried
Smoked salmon	All the year	Baked, boiled, fried
Shad	October 1 to May 1	Baked, boiled, fried
Sturgeon	October 1 to May 1	Baked, boiled, fried
Whitefish	October 1 to May 1	Baked, boiled, fried

20. Another point to be considered in the purchase of fish is the size. Some fish, such as halibut and salmon, are so large that they

Fig. 1

must usually be cut into slices or steaks to permit the housewife to purchase the quantity she requires for immediate use. Other fish are of such size that one is sufficient for a meal, and others are so small that several must be purchased to meet the requirements. An idea of the difference in the size of fish can be gained from Figs. 1 and 2. The larger fish in Fig. 1 is a medium-sized whitefish and the smaller one is a smelt. Fish about the size of smelts lend themselves readily to frying and sautéing, whereas the larger kinds, like whitefish, may be prepared to better advantage by baking either with or without suitable stuffing. The larger fish in Fig. 2 is a carp and the smaller one is a pike. Much use is made of pike, but carp has been more shunned than sought after. However, when carp is properly cooked, it is a very palatable food, and, besides, it possesses high food value.

21. In the purchase of fish, the housewife, provided she is not obliged to have fish for a particular day, will do well also to get away from the one-day-a-week purchasing of fish; that is, if she is

Fig. 2

not obliged to serve fish on Friday, she should endeavor to serve it on some other day. Even twice a week is not too often. If such a plan were followed out, fishermen would be able to market their catch when it is procured and the waste of fish or the necessity for keeping it until a particular day would be overcome.

22. Another way in which the housewife can help herself in the selection of fish is to become familiar with all the varieties of edible fish caught in or near her community. When she has done this, it will be a splendid plan for her to give those with which she is unfamiliar a trial. She will be surprised at the many excellent varieties that are obtained in her locality and consequently come to her fresher than fish that has to be shipped long distances.

23. Freshness of Fish.—In the purchase of fish, the housewife should not permit herself to be influenced by any prejudice she may have as to the name or the appearance of the fish. However, too much attention cannot be paid to its freshness.

Several tests can be applied to fish to determine whether or not it is fresh; therefore, when a housewife is in doubt, she should make an effort to apply them. Fish should not give off any offensive odor. The eyes should be bright and clear, not dull nor sunken. The gills should have a bright-red color, and there should be no blubber showing. The flesh should be so firm that no dent will be made when it is touched with the finger. Fish may also be tested for freshness by placing it in a pan of water; if it sinks, it may be known to be fresh, but if it floats it is not fit for use.

24. Care of Fish in the Home.—If fish is purchased in good condition, and every effort should be made to see that it is, the responsibility of its care in the home until it is presented to the family as a cooked dish rests on the housewife. If, upon reaching the housewife, it has not been cleaned, it should be cleaned at once. In case it has been cleaned either by the fish dealer or the housewife and cannot be cooked at once, it should be looked over carefully, immediately washed in cold water, salted slightly inside and out, placed in a covered enamel or porcelain dish, and then put where it will keep as cold as possible. If a refrigerator is used, the fish should be put in the compartment from which odors cannot be carried to foods in the other compartments. In cold weather, an excellent plan is to put the fish out of doors instead of in the refrigerator, for there it will remain sufficiently cold without the use of ice. However, the best and safest way is to cook the fish at once, so that storing it for any length of time after its delivery will not be necessary.

Salt and smoked fish do not, of course, require the same care as fresh fish. However, as many of these varieties are strong in flavor, it is well to weaken their flavor before cooking them by soaking them or, if possible, by parboiling them.

PREPARATION OF FISH FOR COOKING

25. Cleaning Fish.—Fish is usually prepared for cooking at the market where it is purchased, but frequently a fish comes into the home just as it has been caught. In order to prepare such a fish properly for cooking, the housewife must understand how to clean it. The various steps in cleaning fish are illustrated in Figs. 3 to 6.

The first step consists in removing the scales. To do this, place the fish on its side, as shown in Fig. 3, grasp it firmly by the tail, and

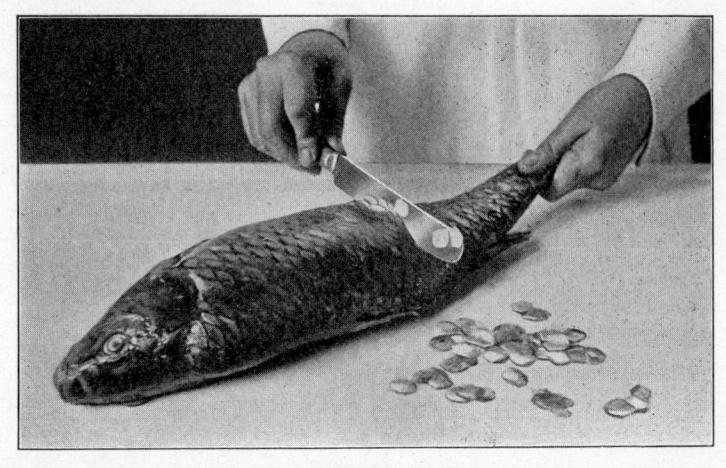

Fig. 3

then with the cutting edge of a knife, preferably a dull one, scrape off the scales by quick motions of the knife toward the head of the fish. When one side has been scraped clean, or *scaled,* as this operation is called, turn the fish over and scale the other side.

With the fish scaled, proceed to remove the entrails. As shown

Fig. 4

in Fig. 4, cut a slit in the belly from the head end to the vent, using a sharp knife. Run the opening up well toward the head, as Fig. 5

§ 13　FISH AND SHELL FISH　13

shows, and then through the opening formed draw out the entrails with the fingers.

If the head is to be removed, it should be cut off at this time.

Fig. 5

When a fish is to be baked or prepared in some other way in which the head may be retained, it is allowed to remain on, but it is kept

Fig. 6

more for an ornament than for any other reason. To remove the head, slip a sharp knife under the gills as far as possible, as Fig. 6

shows, and then cut it off in such a way as not to remove with it any of the body of the fish.

Whether the head is removed or not, make sure that the cavity formed by taking out the entrails is perfectly clean. Then wash the fish with cold water and, if desired, cut off the fins and tail, although this is not usually done. The fish, which is now properly prepared, may be cooked at once or placed in the refrigerator until time for cooking.

FIG. 7

26. Boning Fish. In the preparation of some kinds of fish, it is often desired to bone the fish; that is, to remove the backbone and the ribs. Figs. 7 to 10 show the various steps in the process of boning. After the fish has been thoroughly cleaned, insert a sharp-pointed knife in the back where it is cut from the head, as shown in Fig. 7, and loosen the backbone at this place. Then, as in Fig. 8, slip the knife along the ribs away from the backbone on both sides. After getting the bone well loosened at the end, cut it from the flesh all the way down to the tail, as shown in Fig. 9. When thus separated from the flesh, the backbone and the ribs, which comprise practically all the bones in a fish, may be lifted out intact, as is shown in Fig. 10.

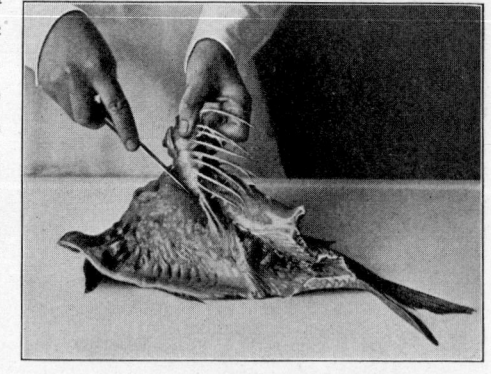

FIG. 8

27. Skinning Fish.—Some kinds of fish, especially those having no scales, such as flounder, catfish, and eels, are made more palatable by being skinned. To skin a fish, cut a narrow strip of the skin along the spine from the head to the tail, as shown in Fig. 11.

§ 13 FISH AND SHELL FISH 15

At this opening, loosen the skin on one side where it is fastened to the bony part of the fish and then, as in Fig. 12, draw it off around toward the belly, working carefully so as not to tear the flesh. Sometimes it is a good plan to use a knife for this purpose, working the skin loose from the flesh with the knife and at the same time pulling the skin with the other hand.

FIG. 9

After removing the skin from one side,

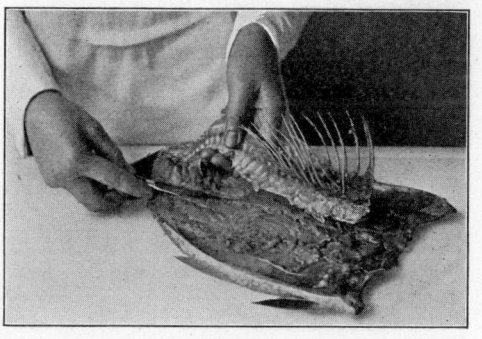

FIG. 10

turn the fish and take off the skin from the other side in the same way. Care should be taken to clean the fish properly before attempting to skin it. If the fish is frozen, it should first be thawed in cold water.

28. Filleting Fish. As many recipes require fish to be cut into *fillets*, that is, thick, flat slices from which the bone is removed, it is well for the housewife to understand just how to

FIG. 11

accomplish this part of the preparation. Figs. 13 to 15 show the filleting of a flounder. While this process varies somewhat in the

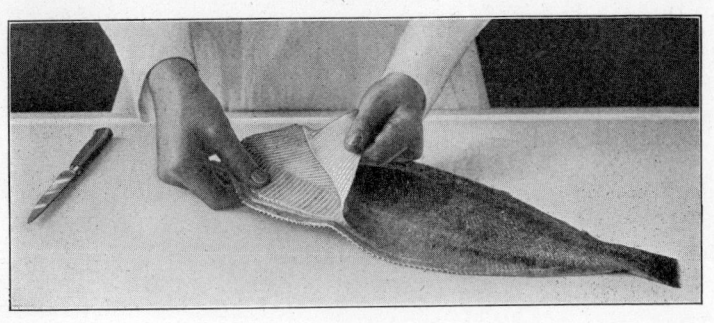

Fig. 12

different varieties of fish, the usual steps are the ones here outlined. After thoroughly cleaning the flounder and removing the skin, lay the fish out flat and cut the flesh down through the center from the head end to the tail, as shown in Fig. 13. Then, with a knife, work each half of the flesh loose from the bones, as in Fig. 14. With these two pieces removed, turn the fish over, cut the flesh down through the center, and separate it from the bones in the same manner as before. If a meat board is on hand, it is a good plan to place the fish on such a board before removing the flesh. At the end of the filleting process, the flounder should appear as shown in Fig. 15, the long, narrow strips on the right being the flesh and that remaining on the board being the bones intact. The strips thus produced may be cut into pieces of any preferred size.

Fig. 13

§ 13　　　FISH AND SHELL FISH　　　17

RECIPES FOR FISH AND FISH ACCOMPANIMENTS

METHODS OF COOKING FISH

29. As Tables II and III show, practically all methods of cookery are applicable in the cooking of fish. For instance, fish may be boiled, steamed, baked, fried, broiled, sautéd, and, in addition, used for various kinds of bisques, chowders, and numerous other made dishes. The effect of these different methods is exactly the same on fish as on meat, since the two foods are the same in general construction. The cookery method to select depends largely on the size, kind, quality, and flavor of the fish. Just as an old chicken with well-developed muscles is not suitable for broiling, so a very large fish should not be broiled unless it can be cut into slices, steaks, or thin pieces. Such a fish is usually

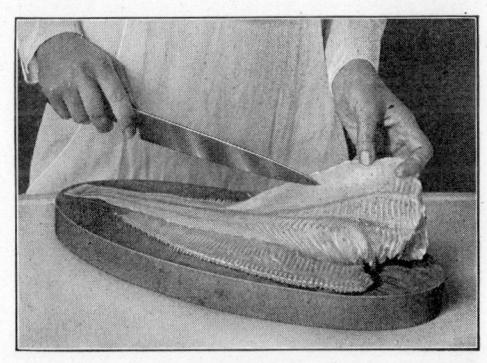

FIG. 14

FIG. 15

either stuffed and baked or baked without stuffing, but when it is cut into slices, the slices may be sautéd, fried, broiled, or steamed.

Some varieties of fish are more or less tasteless. These should be prepared by a cookery method that will improve their flavor, or if the cooking fails to add flavor, a highly seasoned or highly flavored sauce should be served with them. The acid of vinegar or lemon seems to assist in bringing out the flavor of fish, so when a sauce is not used, a slice of lemon is often served with the fish.

RECIPES FOR FISH SAUCES AND STUFFINGS

30. As many of the recipes for fish call for sauce and stuffing, recipes for these accompaniments are taken up before the methods of cooking fish are considered. This plan will make it possible for the beginner to become thoroughly familiar with these accompaniments and thus be better prepared to carry out the recipes for cooking fish.

31. Sauces for Fish.—Sauces are generally served with fish to improve their flavor and increase their nutritive value. Some kinds of fish, such as salmon, shad, butterfish, Spanish mackerel, etc., contain more than 6 per cent. of fat, but as many of the fish that are used for food contain less than this, they are somewhat dry and are improved considerably by the addition of a well-seasoned and highly flavored sauce. Then, too, some fish contain very few extractives, which, when present, as has been learned, are the source of flavor in food. As some of the methods of cooking, boiling in particular, dissolve the few extractives that fish contain and cause the loss of much of the nutritive material, it becomes almost necessary to serve a sauce with fish so prepared, if a tasty dish is to be the result.

32. The sauces that may be used with fish are numerous, and the one to select depends somewhat on the cookery method employed and the preference of those to whom the fish is served. Among the recipes that follow will be found sauces suitable for any method that may be used in the preparation of fish. A little experience with them will enable the housewife to determine the ones that are most satisfactory as to both flavor and nutritive value for the different varieties of fish she uses and the methods of cookery she employs.

LEMON CREAM SAUCE

2 Tb. butter   Salt and pepper
2 Tb. flour   Juice of 1 lemon or 1 Tb.
1 c. thin cream   vinegar

Melt the butter in a saucepan, stir in the flour, and continue stirring until the two are well mixed. Add to this the thin cream and stir until the mixture is thick and boils. Season with salt, pepper, and the juice of the lemon or the vinegar.

Spanish Sauce

2 Tb. butter $\frac{1}{8}$ tsp. pepper
1 slice of onion 1 c. milk
2 Tb. flour $\frac{1}{4}$ c. tomato purée
1 tsp. salt $\frac{1}{4}$ c. chopped pimiento

Brown the butter with the onion, add the flour, salt, and pepper, and stir until well blended. Add the milk and allow the mixture to cook until it thickens. To this add the tomato and pimiento. Heat thoroughly and serve.

Nut Sauce

1 Tb. butter $\frac{1}{2}$ tsp. salt
2 Tb. flour $\frac{1}{8}$ tsp. pepper
2 Tb. peanut butter 1 c. meat stock

Melt the butter and add the flour and peanut butter. When they are well mixed, allow them to brown slightly. Add the salt and pepper to this mixture and pour into it the meat stock. Bring to the boiling point and serve.

Horseradish Sauce

$\frac{1}{2}$ c. cream $\frac{1}{2}$ tsp. salt
$\frac{1}{4}$ c. boiled salad dressing $\frac{1}{4}$ tsp. paprika
2 Tb. grated horseradish $\frac{1}{4}$ tsp. mustard

Whip the cream until stiff; then add the salad dressing, horseradish, salt, paprika, and mustard. When well blended, the sauce is ready to serve.

Egg Sauce

2 Tb. butter $\frac{1}{8}$ tsp. pepper
2 Tb. flour 2 Tb. vinegar
$\frac{3}{4}$ c. milk 1 egg
$\frac{1}{2}$ tsp. salt 1 Tb. chopped parsley

Melt the butter, add the flour, and stir until well blended. Add the milk, salt, and pepper, and cook until the mixture thickens. To this add the vinegar, the egg chopped fine, and the chopped parsley. Heat thoroughly and serve.

Tomato Sauce

2 c. tomato purée 2 Tb. butter
1 small onion, sliced 2 Tb. flour
1 bay leaf 1 tsp. salt
6 cloves $\frac{1}{8}$ tsp. pepper

Strain stewed tomato to make the purée. Put this over the fire in a saucepan with the sliced onion, the bay leaf, and the cloves.

Cook slowly for about 10 minutes. Strain to remove the onion, bay leaf, and cloves. Melt the butter, add the flour, salt, and pepper, and into this pour the hot tomato. Cook until it thickens and serve.

Mushroom Sauce

2 Tb. butter
1 slice of carrot
1 slice of onion
Sprig of parsley
½ tsp. salt
⅛ tsp. pepper
2 Tb. flour
1 c. meat stock
½ c. mushrooms
2 tsp. lemon juice

Put the butter in a frying pan with the carrot, onion, parsley, salt, and pepper, and cook together until brown. Remove the onion, carrot, and parsley. Stir in the flour, brown it slightly, and then add the meat stock. Cook together until thickened. Just before removing from the fire, add the mushrooms, chopped into fine pieces, and the lemon juice. Allow it to heat thoroughly and then serve.

Drawn-Butter Sauce

¼ c. butter
2 Tb. flour
½ tsp. salt
⅛ tsp. pepper
1½ c. hot water
2 hard-cooked eggs

Melt the butter, and add the flour, salt, and pepper. Pour into this the hot water, and cook until the mixture thickens. Slice the eggs into ¼-inch slices and add these to the sauce just before removing from the stove.

33. Stuffing for Fish.—As has been mentioned, fish that is to be baked is often stuffed before it is put into the oven. The stuffing not only helps to preserve the shape of the fish, but also provides a means of extending the flavor of the fish to a starchy food, for bread or cracker crumbs are used in the preparation of most stuffings. Three recipes for fish stuffing are here given, the first being made of bread crumbs and having hot water for the liquid, the second of cracker crumbs and having milk for the liquid, and the third of bread crumbs and having stewed tomato for the liquid.

Fish Stuffing No. 1

¼ c. butter
½ c. hot water
½ tsp. salt
⅛ tsp. pepper
1 tsp. onion juice
1 Tb. chopped parsley
2 c. fine bread crumbs

Melt the butter in the hot water, add the salt, pepper, onion juice, and parsley, and pour over the crumbs. Mix thoroughly and use to stuff the fish.

Fish Stuffing No. 2

½ c. milk
2 c. cracker crumbs
½ tsp. salt
⅛ tsp. pepper

¼ c. melted butter
1 Tb. chopped parsley
1 egg

Warm the milk and add it to the crumbs, together with the salt, pepper, melted butter, and parsley. To this mixture, add the beaten egg. When well mixed, use as stuffing for fish.

Fish Stuffing No. 3

2 Tb. butter
1 Tb. finely chopped onion
1 Tb. chopped parsley
½ tsp. salt

⅛ tsp. pepper
1 Tb. chopped sour pickles
½ c. stewed tomato
2 c. stale bread crumbs

Melt the butter and add the onion, parsley, salt, pepper, pickles, and tomato. Pour this mixture over the crumbs, mix all thoroughly, and use to stuff the fish. If the dressing seems to require more liquid than the stewed tomato, add a little water.

RECIPES FOR FRESH FISH

34. Boiled Fish.—Boiling extracts flavor and, to some extent, nutriment from the food to which this cookery method is applied. Therefore, unless the fish to be cooked is one that has a very strong flavor and that will be improved by the loss of flavor, it should not be boiled. Much care should be exercised in boiling fish, because the meat is usually so tender that it is likely to boil to pieces or to fall apart.

35. A utensil in which fish can be boiled or steamed very satisfactorily is shown in Fig. 16.

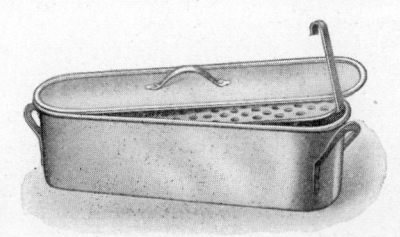

Fig. 16

This *fish boiler,* as it is called, is a long, narrow, deep pan with a cover and a rack on which the fish is placed. Attached to each end of the rack is an upright strip, or handle, that permits the rack containing the fish to be lifted out of the pan and the fish thus removed without breaking. To assist further in holding the fish together while it is cooking, a piece of gauze or cheesecloth may be wrapped around the fish before it is put into the pan.

36. When a fish is to be boiled, clean it and, if desired, remove the head. Pour sufficient boiling water to cover the fish well into the vessel in which it is to be cooked, and add salt in the proportion of 1 teaspoonful to each quart of water. Tie the fish in a strip of cheesecloth or gauze if necessary, and lower it into the vessel of slowly boiling water. Allow the fish to boil until it may be easily pierced with a fork; then take it out of the water and remove the cloth, provided one is used. Serve with a well-seasoned sauce, such as lemon cream, horseradish, etc.

37. Boiled Cod.—A fish that lends itself well to boiling is fresh cod. In fact, codfish prepared according to this method and served with a sauce makes a very appetizing dish.

Scale, clean, and skin a fresh cod and wrap it in a single layer of gauze or cheesecloth. Place it in a kettle or a pan of freshly boiling water to which has been added 1 teaspoonful of salt to each quart of water. Boil until the fish may be easily pierced with a fork, take from the water, and remove the gauze or cheesecloth carefully so as to keep the fish intact. Serve with sauce and slices of lemon.

38. Steamed Fish.—The preparation of fish by steaming is practically the same as that by boiling, and produces a dish similar to boiled fish. The only difference is that steamed fish is suspended over the water and is cooked by the steam that rises instead of being cooked directly in the water. Because the fish is not surrounded by water, it does not lose its nutriment and flavor so readily as does boiled fish.

If fish is to be cooked by steaming, first clean it thoroughly. Wrap in a strip of gauze or cheesecloth and place in a steamer. Steam until tender, and then remove the cloth and place the fish on a platter. As steaming does not add flavor, it is usually necessary to supply flavor to fish cooked in this way by adding a sauce of some kind.

39. Broiled Fish.—The best way in which to cook small fish, thin strips of fish, or even good-sized fish that are comparatively thin when they are split open is to broil them. Since in this method of cooking the flavor is entirely retained, it is especially desirable for any fish of delicate flavor.

To broil fish, sear them quickly over a very hot fire and then cook them more slowly until they are done, turning frequently to prevent burning. As most fish, and particularly the small ones used for broiling, contain almost no fat, it is necessary to supply fat for successful broiling and improvement of flavor. It is difficult to add fat to the fish while it is broiling, so, as a rule, the fat is spread over the surface of the fish after it has been removed from the broiler. The fat may consist of broiled strips of bacon or salt pork, or it may be merely melted butter or other fat.

40. Broiled Scrod With Potato Border.—Young cod that is split down the back and that has had the backbone removed with the exception of a small portion near the tail is known as *scrod*. Such fish is nearly always broiled. It may be served plain, but it is much more attractive when potatoes are combined with it in the form of an artistic border.

To prepare this dish, broil the scrod according to the directions given in Art. **39**. Then place it on a hot platter and spread butter over it. Boil the desired number of potatoes until they are tender, and then force them through a ricer or mash them until they are perfectly fine. Season with salt, pepper, and butter, and add sufficient milk to make a paste that is a trifle stiffer than for mashed potatoes. If desired, raw eggs may also be beaten into the potatoes to serve as a part of the moisture. Fill a pastry bag with the potatoes thus prepared and press them through a rosette tube in any desired design on the platter around the fish. Bake in a hot oven until the potatoes are thoroughly heated and are browned slightly on the top.

41. Broiled Fresh Mackerel.—Probably no fish lends itself better to broiling than fresh mackerel, as the flesh of this fish is tender and contains sufficient fat to have a good flavor. To improve the flavor, however, strips of bacon are usually placed over the fish and allowed to broil with it.

Clean and skin a fresh mackerel. Place the fish thus prepared in a broiler, and broil first on one side and then on the other. When seared all over, place strips of bacon over the fish and continue to broil until it is done. Remove from the broiler, season with salt and pepper, and serve.

42. Broiled Shad Roe.—The mass of eggs found in shad, as shown in Fig. 17, is known as the *roe* of shad. Roe may be purchased separately, when it is found in the markets from January 1 to June 1, or it may be procured from the fish itself. It makes a delicious dish when broiled, especially when it is rolled in fat and bread crumbs.

Wash the roe that is to be used and dry it carefully between towels. Roll it in bacon fat or melted butter and then in fine crumbs.

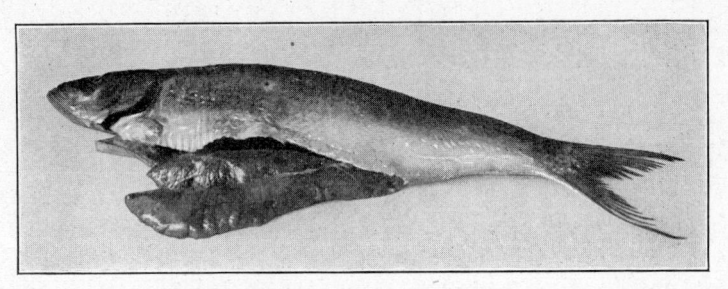

Fig. 17

Place in a broiler, broil until completely done on one side, turn and then broil until entirely cooked on the other side. Remove from the broiler and pour melted butter over each piece. Sprinkle with salt and pepper, and serve hot.

43. Baked Fish.—Good-sized fish, that is, fish weighing 4 or 5 pounds, are usually baked. When prepared by this method, fish are very satisfactory if they are spread out on a pan, flesh side up, and baked in a very hot oven with sufficient fat to flavor them well. A fish of large size, however, is especially delicious if its cavity is filled with a stuffing before it is baked.

When a fish is to be stuffed, any desired stuffing is prepared and then filled into the fish in the manner shown in Fig. 18. With the cavity well filled, the edges of the fish are drawn together over the stuffing and sewed with a coarse needle and thread, as Fig. 19 shows.

Fig. 18

Whether the fish is stuffed or not, the same principles apply in its baking as apply in the roasting of meat; that is, the heat of a quick, hot oven sears the flesh, keeps in the juices, and prevents the loss of flavor, while that of a slow oven causes the loss of much of the flavor and moisture and produces a less tender dish.

44. Often, in the baking of fish, it is necessary to add fat. This may be done by putting fat of some kind into the pan with the fish, by spreading strips of bacon over the fish, or by larding it. In the dry varieties of fish, larding, which is illustrated in Fig. 20, proves very satisfactory, for it supplies the substance in which the fish is most lacking. As will be observed, larding is done by inserting strips of bacon or salt pork that are about 3 inches long and ¼ inch thick into gashes cut into the sides of the fish.

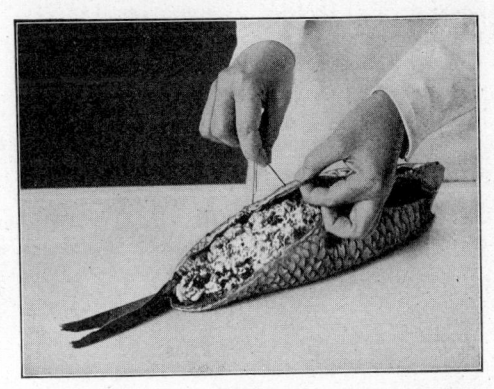

Fig. 19

45. Baked Haddock.—As haddock is a good-sized fish, it is an especially suitable one for baking. However, it is a dry fish, so

Fig. 20

fat should be added to it to improve its flavor. Any of the methods suggested in Art. **44** may be used to supply the fat that this fish needs.

When haddock is to be baked, select a 4- or 5-pound fish, clean it thoroughly, boning it if desired, and sprinkle it inside and out with salt. Fill the cavity with any desired stuffing and sew up. Place in a dripping pan, and add some bacon fat or a piece of salt pork, or place several slices of bacon around it. Bake in a hot oven for about 1 hour. After it has been in the oven for about 15 minutes, baste with the fat that will be found in the bottom of the pan and continue to baste every 10 minutes until the fish is done. Remove from the pan to a platter, garnish with parsley and slices of broiled bacon, and serve with any desired sauce.

46. Baked Halibut.—Because of its size, halibut is cut into slices and sold in the form of steaks. It is probably one of the most economical varieties of fish to buy, for very little bone is contained in a slice and the money that the housewife expends goes for almost solid meat. Halibut slices are often sautéd, but they make a delicious dish when baked with tomatoes and flavored with onion, lemon, and bay leaf, as described in the accompanying recipe.

BAKED HALIBUT
(Sufficient to Serve Six)

2 c. tomatoes	$\frac{1}{8}$ tsp. pepper
Few slices onion	2 thin slices bacon
1 bay leaf	1 Tb. flour
1 tsp. salt	2 lb. halibut steak

Heat the tomatoes, onion, and bay leaf in water. Add the salt and pepper and cook for a few minutes. Cut the bacon into small squares, try it out in a pan, and into this fat stir the flour. Pour this into the hot mixture, remove the bay leaf, and cook until the mixture thickens. Put the steaks into a baking dish, pour the sauce over them, and bake in a slow oven for about 45 minutes. Remove with the sauce to a hot platter and serve.

47. Baked Fillets of Whitefish.—When whitefish of medium size can be secured, it is very often stuffed and baked whole, but variety can be had by cutting it into fillets before baking it. Besides producing a delicious dish, this method of preparation eliminates carving at the table, for the pieces can be cut the desired size for serving.

Prepare fillets of whitefish according to the directions for filleting fish in Art. **28.** Sprinkle each one with salt and pepper, and dip it first into beaten egg and then into bread crumbs. Brown some butter in a pan, place the fish into it, and set the pan in a hot oven. Bake until the fillets are a light brown, or about 30 minutes. Remove to a hot dish, garnish with parsley and serve with any desired sauce.

FISH AND SHELL FISH

48. Fillet of Flounder.—In appearance, flounder is not so attractive as many other fish, but it is a source of excellent flesh and

Fig. 21

is therefore much used. A very appetizing way in which to prepare flounder is to fillet it and prepare it according to the accompanying recipe, when it will appear as in Fig. 21.

Secure a flounder and fillet it in the manner explained in Art. **28**. Cut each fillet into halves, making eight pieces from one flounder. Cut small strips of salt pork or bacon, roll the pieces of flounder around these, and fasten with a toothpick. Place in a baking dish with a small quantity of water, and bake in a hot oven until a good brown. Serve hot.

49. Planked Fish.—Like planked steak, planked fish, which is illustrated in Fig. 22, is a dish that appeals to the eye and pleases

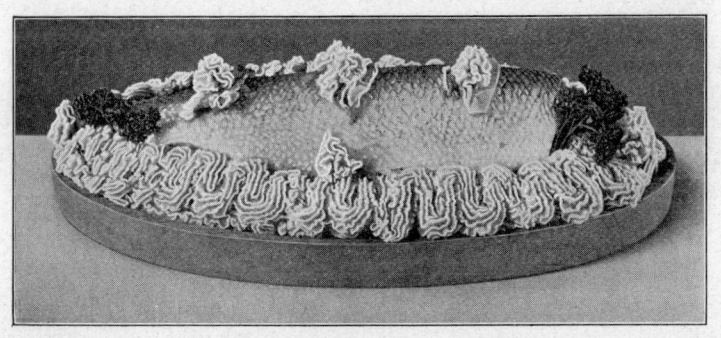

Fig. 22

the taste. The fish is baked on the plank and then surrounded with a border of potatoes, the fish and potatoes making an excellent food.

To prepare planked fish, thoroughly clean and bone a medium-size whitefish, shad, haddock, or any desired fish. Grease a plank and place the fish on it. Lay some strips of bacon across the top of the fish, place in a hot oven, and bake for about 30 minutes or a little longer if necessary. Boil potatoes and prepare them for piping by mashing them, using 4 tablespoonfuls of milk, 1 tablespoonful of butter, and one egg to each 2 cupfuls of potato. Then, with a rosette pastry tube, pipe a border of potatoes around the edge of the plank, so that it will appear as in Fig. 22. Likewise, pipe rosettes of potatoes on the strips of bacon placed on top of the fish. Then replace the plank with the fish and potatoes in the oven, and bake until the potatoes are brown. Garnish with parsley and serve.

50. Fried Fish.—Very small fish or slices of larger fish are often fried in deep fat. When they are prepared in this way, they are first dipped into beaten egg and then into crumbs or corn meal to form a coating that will cling to their surface. Coated with such a material, they are fried in deep fat until the surface is nicely browned. After being removed from the fat, they should be drained well before serving.

51. Fried Perch.—When fried in deep fat, perch is found to be very appetizing. To prepare it in this way, secure a perch and scale and clean it. Cut it crosswise into 2-inch strips, roll each piece in flour, and fry in deep fat until nicely browned. Serve hot with lemon or with a sauce of some kind.

52. Fried Eel.—If an appetizing way to cook eel is desired, it will be found advisable to fry it in deep fat. When it is to be cooked in this way, skin and clean the eel and cut it into thick slices. Pour some vinegar over the slices, sprinkle them with salt and pepper, and allow them to stand for several hours. Remove the pieces from the vinegar, dip each one into slightly beaten egg and then into flour, and fry in deep fat until well browned. Serve plain or with a sauce.

53. Sautéd Fish.—Without doubt, the most popular way to prepare fish is to sauté them. This method may be applied to practically the same kinds of fish that are fried or broiled, and it is especially desirable for the more tasteless varieties. It consists in browning the fish well in a small quantity of fat, first on one side and then on the other. If fat of good flavor is used, such as bacon or ham fat, the flavor of the fish will be very much improved. Before sautéing, the fish or pieces of fish are often dipped into slightly beaten egg and then rolled in flour, very fine cracker crumbs, or corn meal, or the egg is omitted and they are merely covered with the dry, starchy material. The effect of this method of cooking is very similar to that of deep-fat frying, except that the outside tissues are apt to become very hard from the application of the hot fat because of the coating that is generally used. Since most fish breaks very easily, it is necessary that it be handled carefully in this method in order that the pieces may be kept whole.

54. Sautéd Smelts.—To be most satisfactory, smelts are generally sautéd, as shown in Fig. 23. Fish of this kind are prepared for cooking by cutting off the heads and removing the entrails through the opening thus made; or, if it is desired to leave the heads

Fig. 23

on, the entrails may be removed through the gill or a small slit cut below the mouth. At any rate, these fish are not cut open as are most other fish.

With the fish thus prepared, roll them in fine cracker crumbs and sauté them in melted butter until they are nicely browned. Serve with slices of lemon.

55. Sautéd Halibut Steak.—Slices of halibut, when firm in texture and cut about ¾ inch thick, lend themselves very well to sautéing. Secure the required number of such slices and sprinkle each with salt and pepper. Then spread melted butter over each steak, and roll it in fine crumbs. Place fat in a frying pan, allow it to become hot, and sauté the halibut in this until well browned.

56. Sautéd Pickerel.—A variety of fresh-water fish that finds favor with most persons is pickerel. When this fish is to be sautéd, scale and clean it and cut it crosswise into 2-inch strips. Then roll each piece in flour, sprinkle it with salt and pepper, and sauté the slices in hot fat. When one side is sufficiently brown, turn and brown on the other side.

57. Stewed Fish.—Like boiling, stewing extracts flavor and nutriment from fish. The process differs, however, in that the fish is cooked gently by simmering. This cookery method is employed for fish that is inclined to be tough. Usually, vegetables, such as carrots and onions, are cooked with the fish in order to impart flavor. To prevent the fish from falling apart, it may be wrapped in cheesecloth or gauze.

58. Stewed Fresh Herring.—When fresh herring can be obtained, it can be made into a delicious dish by stewing it with onions, parsley, and carrots. In this method of preparation, the herring should not be permitted to stew rapidly; it will become more tender if it simmers gently. As herring are rather small fish, weighing only about ½ pound, it will usually be necessary to obtain more than one for a meal.

Clean the required number of fresh herring, place them in a saucepan, and sprinkle them with salt and pepper. Brown some slices of onion in butter, and add the same number of slices of carrots and a generous quantity of parsley. Add enough boiling water to these vegetables to cover them and the fish, and pour both over the fish. Place all on the fire and simmer gently until the fish is tender. Remove the fish from the water and serve. The vegetables are used merely to add flavor, and they will have practically boiled away by the time the fish is cooked.

59. Stewed Eel.—Eel is delicious when stewed. When allowed to simmer slowly with several slices of onion and a little parsley, it becomes both tasty and tender.

Skin and clean the eel that is to be stewed, remove all the fat, and cut into pieces about 2 inches long. Season well with salt and pepper and place in a saucepan with several slices of onion, 1 tablespoonful of chopped parsley, and 2 tablespoonfuls of butter. Add enough cold water to cover well, and allow the eel to simmer gently until it is tender enough to be pierced with a fork. Remove from the water and serve hot.

RECIPES FOR SALT AND SMOKED FISH

60. Place of Salt and Smoked Fish in the Diet.—In regions where fresh fish cannot be obtained or in seasons when they are scarce everywhere, the housewife will do well to use salt and smoked fish. These varieties of fish not only will give her a chance to vary the diet, but will enable her to provide at a more economical price, food that, pound for pound, contains more nutriment than the same fish when fresh. While some of the varieties of smoked and salt fish may not be obtainable in all communities, the housewife will do much toward bringing the supply to her community by requesting them from the dealer. When a dealer knows that there is a demand for certain kinds, he will make an effort to secure the varieties wanted.

61. Freshening Salt and Smoked Fish.—The cooking of salt and smoked fish is not a difficult matter, but it always involves the freshening of the fish before any cooking method can be applied. This consists in placing the fish in a large quantity of water and allowing it to stand until enough of the salt has been extracted to suit the taste. Some kinds of fish are so salty that they require considerable soaking, whereas others require only a little freshening. However, it is usually advisable to change the water several times. If it is desired to hasten the extraction of the salt, the fish should be raised above the bottom of the vessel by means of a wire rack or several clean sticks. In the case of very thick fish, several gashes may be cut into the flesh to permit the salt to pass out more readily.

62. Creamed Codfish.—Since codfish is a rather dry fish, containing little fat, it is usually combined with some other food to make it more appetizing. In the case of creamed codfish, the cream sauce supplies the food substances in which the fish is lacking and at the same time provides a very palatable dish. When codfish is prepared in this way, boiled potatoes are usually served with it.

To make creamed codfish, freshen the required amount of codfish by pouring lukewarm water over it. Shred the fish by breaking it into small pieces with the fingers. Pour off the water, add fresh warm water, and allow the fish to stand until it is not too salty. When it is sufficiently freshened, drain off all the water. Melt a little butter in a frying pan, add the fish, and sauté until slightly browned. Make a medium white sauce and pour it over the codfish. Serve hot with boiled potatoes.

63. Codfish Balls.—Another excellent way in which to serve codfish is to combine it with mashed potatoes, make these into balls, and fry them in deep fat. These give variety to meals and also afford an opportunity to serve a nutritious food.

Freshen the codfish as explained in Art. **61,** and then mince it very fine. Add an equal amount of freshly cooked hot potato that has been put through a potato ricer or mashed fine. Mix thoroughly and, if necessary, season with salt and pepper. Shape into balls and fry in deep fat. Drain well and serve hot.

64. Sautéd Salt Mackerel.—When an extremely tasty dish that will afford a change from the usual daily routine of meals is desired, sautéd salt mackerel will be found very satisfactory.

Freshen salt mackerel that is to be sautéd by putting it into a saucepan and covering it with cold water. Place this over the fire, and allow the water to heat to almost the boiling point. Pour off the water, and sauté the fish in butter or other fat until nicely browned. If desired, pour a small amount of thin cream over the mackerel just before removing it from the pan, allow this to heat, and serve it as a sauce with the mackerel.

65. Baked Finnan Haddie.—When haddock is cured by smoking, it is known as *finnan haddie*. As fish of this kind has considerable thick flesh, it is very good for baking. Other methods of cookery may, of course, be applied to it, but none is more satisfactory than baking.

To bake a finnan haddie, wash it in warm water and put it to soak in fresh warm water. After it has soaked for ½ hour, allow it to come gradually to nearly the boiling point and then pour off the water. Place the fish in a baking pan, add a piece of butter, sprinkle with pepper, and pour a little water over it. Bake in a hot oven until it is nicely browned. Serve hot.

66. Creamed Finnan Haddie.—The flavor of finnan haddie is such that this fish becomes very appetizing when prepared with a cream sauce. If, after combining the sauce with the fish, the fish is baked in the oven, an especially palatable dish is the result.

To prepare creamed finnan haddie, freshen the fish and shred it into small pieces. Then measure the fish, put it into a baking dish, and pour an equal amount of white sauce over it. Sprinkle generously with crumbs and bake in a hot oven until the crumbs are browned. Serve hot.

67. Boiled Salmon.—When smoked salmon can be secured, it makes a splendid fish for boiling. If it is cooked until tender and then served with a well-seasoned sauce, it will find favor with most persons.

Freshen smoked salmon in warm water as much as seems necessary, remembering that the cooking to which it will be subjected will remove a large amount of the superfluous salt. Cover the salmon with hot water, and simmer slowly until it becomes tender. Remove from the water, pour a little melted butter over it, and serve with any desired sauce.

RECIPES FOR CANNED FISH

68. Canned Fish in the Diet.—As a rule, canned fish is a comparatively cheap food and there is no reason why the economical housewife should not make frequent use of the various kinds. It should be bought, however, from a reputable firm, in order that the greatest value may be obtained for the money spent. In addition, it should be used as soon as possible after the can has been opened; if all of it cannot be utilized at one time, it should be placed in a covered receptacle—not a metal one—and kept cold to prevent it from spoiling. Often canned fish can be served without any further preparation than removing it from the can. However, as some varieties, particularly salmon and tuna fish, are much used in the preparation of both cold and cooked dishes, several recipes are here given for these varieties.

69. Creamed Tuna Fish.—Combining tuna fish with a cream sauce and serving it over toast makes a dish that is both delicate and palatable—one that will prove very satisfactory when something to take the place of meat in a light meal is desired.

CREAMED TUNA FISH
(Sufficient to Serve Six)

3 Tb. butter $\frac{1}{8}$ tsp. paprika
3 Tb. flour $1\frac{1}{2}$ c. hot milk
$\frac{1}{2}$ tsp. salt $1\frac{1}{2}$ c. tuna fish
$\frac{1}{8}$ tsp. pepper   1 egg

Melt the butter in a saucepan and add the flour, salt, pepper, and paprika. Stir well, pour in the milk, and when this has thickened add the tuna fish. Allow this to heat thoroughly in the sauce. Just before serving, add the slightly beaten egg and cook until this has thickened. Pour over toast and serve.

70. Salmon Mold.—A change from the usual way of serving salmon can be had by making a salmon mold such as is illustrated in Fig. 24. Besides being a delicious dish and providing variety in the diet, salmon mold is very attractive.

SALMON MOLD
(Sufficient to Serve Six)

2 c. salmon $\frac{1}{8}$ tsp. pepper
2 Tb. vinegar 1 Tb. gelatine
$\frac{1}{2}$ tsp. salt $1\frac{1}{2}$ c. boiling water

Remove all skin and bones from the salmon when it is taken from the can, and mince it thoroughly with a fork. Add the vinegar, salt,

FIG. 24

and pepper. Prepare the gelatine by dissolving it in the boiling water. Add the seasoned salmon to the prepared gelatine. With cold water, wet a ring-shaped mold having an open space in the center. Pour the salmon-and-gelatine mixture into this mold, and allow it to stand until it solidifies. Arrange a bed of lettuce leaves on a chop plate, turn the mold out on this, and fill the center with dressing. Serve at once. A very desirable dressing for this purpose is made as follows:

DRESSING FOR SALMON MOLD

1 c. cream 2 Tb. sugar
2 Tb. vinegar 1 c. finely chopped cucumber
$\frac{1}{4}$ tsp. salt

Whip the cream until it is stiff, and add the vinegar, salt, and sugar. Fold into this the finely chopped cucumber.

71. Salmon Patties.—Delicious patties can be made from salmon by combining it with bread crumbs and using a thick white sauce to hold the ingredients together. These may be either sautéd in shallow fat or fried in deep fat.

SALMON PATTIES
(Sufficient to Serve Eight)

2 c. finely minced salmon   ½ tsp. salt
1 c. fresh bread crumbs   ⅛ tsp. pepper
1 c. thick white sauce   Dry bread crumbs

With the salmon, mix the fresh bread crumbs and the white sauce. Season with salt and pepper. Shape into round patties, roll in the dry bread crumbs, and fry in deep fat or sauté in shallow fat. Serve hot with or without sauce.

72. Creamed Salmon With Rice.—A creamed protein dish is always more satisfactory if it is served on some other food, particularly one high in carbohydrate. When this is done, a better balanced dish is the result. Creamed salmon and rice make a very nutritious and appetizing combination.

CREAMED SALMON WITH RICE
(Sufficient to Serve Six)

1 c. salmon   Steamed rice
1 c. medium white sauce

Break the salmon into moderately small pieces and carefully fold these into the hot white sauce. Serve this on a mound of hot steamed rice.

RECIPES FOR LEFT-OVER FISH

73. So as not to waste any food material, it is necessary that all left-over fish be utilized in some way. This is not so simple a matter as in the case of meat, because fish is one of the foods that are not popular as a left-over dish. Still fish left-overs can be used if a little thought is given to the matter. Of course, it is a wise plan to prepare only the quantity of fish that can be consumed at the meal for which it is cooked, but should any remain it should not be thrown away, for some use can be made of it. A point to remember, however, is that fish is not satisfactory in soup of any kind except a fish soup; therefore, bits of left-over fish may be added to only such soups as clam chowder or other fish chowder.

Whether the fish has been boiled, steamed, baked, fried, sautéd, or prepared in any other way, it may always be made into croquettes. When used for this purpose, all the bones should be carefully removed. These may be easily taken out after the fish has become cold. If the fish has been stuffed and part of the stuffing remains, it may be broken into pieces and used with the flesh of the fish. A recipe for croquettes in which fish is combined with rice follows.

74. Fish Croquettes.—If any quantity of left-over fish is on hand, it may be combined with rice to make very tasty croquettes.

Fish Croquettes
(Sufficient to Serve Six)

1½ c. cold fish	Salt and pepper
1 c. cold steamed rice	1 egg
1 c. thick white sauce	Crumbs

Mince the fish into small pieces, mix with the rice, and add the white sauce. Season with salt and pepper and shape into croquettes. Dip into slightly beaten egg, roll in crumbs, and fry in deep fat. Drain and serve with any desired sauce.

75. Creamed Fish in Potato Nest.—Fish may also be combined with mashed potato to produce a most appetizing dish. Line a baking dish with hot mashed potato, leaving a good-sized hollow in the center. Into this pour creamed fish made by mixing equal proportions of left-over cold fish and white sauce. Season well with salt and pepper, sprinkle with crumbs, and dot the top with butter. Bake until the crumbs are brown. Serve hot.

SHELL FISH

NATURE, VARIETIES, AND USE OF SHELL FISH

76. Besides the varieties of fish that have already been considered, the general term fish also includes **shell fish.** Fish of this kind are different in structure from bony fish, for they are aquatic animals that are entirely or partly encased in shells. They include *mollusks,* or *bivalves,* such as oysters, clams, and scallops, and *crustaceans,* such as lobsters, crabs, and shrimp.

77. The popularity of the edible varieties of mollusks and crustaceans mentioned depends largely on whether they can be easily obtained and whether they are pleasing to the local or individual taste. As they are found in salt rivers, bays, and other shallow salt-water sources, their greatest use is among people living near the seashore, but they are much favored where they can be procured in edible condition. They are not so cheap as many other fish foods; that is, a certain amount of money will not purchase so great a quantity of shell fish, lobster for instance, as some of the well-known varieties of fish proper, such as halibut or whitefish. Lobsters and crabs are usually more expensive than oysters and clams; consequently, they are used more often to provide a delicacy or to supply something more or less uncommon for a special meal.

78. Several precautions should be observed in purchasing shell fish. For instance, crabs and lobsters should be purchased alive. They are usually shipped on ice so that they will remain in this condition for some time, and they are displayed on ice in the markets for the same reason. Such shell fish should be kept alive until they are plunged into boiling water to cook. Oysters and clams bought in the shell must also be alive when purchased. A tightly closed shell indicates that they are alive, whereas a slightly open shell proves that they are dead. If these two varieties are bought out of the shells, the fish themselves should not be accompanied by a great quantity of liquid. Considerable liquid is an indication that the oysters or clams have been adulterated by the addition of water. Formerly it was the custom to keep oysters in fresh water, as the water they absorb bloats or fattens them. This practice, however, has fallen into disfavor.

79. Shell fish lend themselves admirably to a large variety of dishes, including soups, entrées, salads, and substitutes for meat dishes. They possess a great deal of distinctive flavor, their food value is comparatively high, and, provided they are in good condition and are properly prepared, they are healthful and easily digested. It can therefore be seen that shell fish have much to recommend their use. There is considerable danger, however, in using any varieties that are not perfectly fresh or freshly cooked. In the case of mollusks, or bivalves, much harm has resulted from the use of those which have been grown or bred in unsanitary surroundings. Because of these facts, it is of the utmost importance that great care be exercised in selecting and preparing shell fish.

80. Composition and Food Value of Shell Fish.—In composition, the varieties of fish included under shell fish do not differ greatly from fish proper. Most of them, however, contain more waste and less of the food substances than fish, so that their food value is somewhat lower. Table IV will serve to give a good idea of the composition and food value of the several varieties of shell fish, and in studying it, a good plan will be to compare it with Table I, which gives the food value of fish. As will be observed,

TABLE IV
COMPOSITION AND FOOD VALUE OF SHELL FISH

Name of Fish	Water	Protein	Fat	Total Carbo-hydrates	Ash	Food Value per Pound Calories
Clams, removed from shell	80.8	10.6	1.1	5.2	2.3	340
Crabs, whole	77.1	16.6	2.0	1.2	3.1	415
Lobsters, whole	79.2	16.4	1.8	.4	2.2	390
Oysters, in shell	86.9	6.2	1.2	3.7	2.0	235
Scallops	80.3	14.8	.1	3.4	1.4	345

protein forms a very large proportion of the food substance of shell fish. Also, they contain more carbohydrates than fish, the amount ranging from .4 to 5.2 per cent., which is in the form of sugar.

TABLE V
SEASONS FOR SHELL FISH

Name of Fish	Season
Clams, hard shelled	All the year
Clams, soft shelled	May 1 to October 15
Crabs, hard shelled	All the year
Crabs, soft shelled	March 1 to October 15
Lobsters	All the year
Oysters	September 1 to May 1
Scallops	September 15 to April 1
Shrimp	March 15 to June 1, and September 15 to October 15

Although this amount is too small to warrant much consideration as a supply of carbohydrates, it is mentioned because it is an interesting fact.

81. Seasons for Shell Fish.—With the exception of clams and lobster, which can be obtained all the year around, shell fish have particular seasons; that is, there is a certain time of the year when they are not suitable for food. It is very important that every housewife know just what these seasons are, so that she will not include the foods in the diet of her family when they should not be used. Table V, which will furnish her with the information she needs, should therefore be carefully studied.

OYSTERS, CLAMS, AND SCALLOPS

OYSTERS AND THEIR PREPARATION

82. Oysters, clams, and **scallops** are salt-water fish that belong to the family of mollusks, or soft-bodied animals. They are entirely encased in hard shells, which, though of the same general

FIG. 25

shape, differ somewhat from each other in appearance. Fig. 25 shows a group of oysters and clams, the three on the left being oysters and the three on the right, clams. Oysters are larger than clams and have a rough, uneven shell, whereas clams have a smooth, roundish shell. The three varieties of mollusks are closely related in their composition and in their use as food, but as oysters are probably used more commonly than the others they are considered first.

83. Composition of Oysters.—Oysters occupy a prominent place among animal foods, because they are comparatively high in protein. In addition, they contain a substance that most flesh foods lack in any quantity, namely, carbohydrate in the form of glycogen, and for this reason are said to resemble milk closely in composition.

A comparison of the following figures will show how these foods resemble each other:

	Water	Protein	Fat	Carbo-hydrate	Mineral Salts
Milk	87.0	3.3	4.0	5.0	.7
Oysters	86.9	6.2	1.2	3.7	2.0

Oysters, as will be observed, contain only a small quantity of fat, and for this reason their total food value is somewhat lower than that of milk. A pint of milk has a value of 325 calories, while the same quantity of oysters has an approximate value of only 250 calories. Because of the difference in the cost of these two foods, oysters costing several times as much as milk, the use of oysters is not so cheap a way of supplying food material.

84. Digestibility of Oysters.—When merely the ability of the digestive tract to handle oysters is taken into consideration, they are said to be easily digested if they are served raw or are properly prepared. This is due to the fact that when taken as a food they are disposed of in a comparatively short time by the stomach. In addition, their absorption from the alimentary tract is quite complete; that is, they contain little or no waste material. But, just as cooking has much to do with the digestibility of other protein foods, so it has with oysters. For this reason, the housewife who wishes to feed her family this food in its most digestible form must thoroughly understand all phases of its cooking.

85. Healthfulness of Oysters.—Much illness has been attributed to oysters, and without doubt they have been the cause of some typhoid and some ptomaine poisoning. A knowledge of the reason for these diseases has done much to eliminate them. It is now definitely known that much of the typhoid caused from eating oysters was due to the conditions under which they were grown. In their growth, oysters fasten themselves to stationary things, such as rocks or piles driven into the ground underneath the water, and they obtain their food by simply opening the shell and making use of minute particles of plant and animal life that they are able to extract from the water. When the water was not clean or when sewage was turned into it, typhoid germs were transmitted to persons who took oysters as food. At present, there is scarcely any danger from such causes, for more care is now given to the conditions under which oysters grow. Ptomaine poisoning from oysters was caused by eating them when they had been improperly cared for in storage or had been taken from the shells after they were dead. Unless persons handling oysters know how to take care of them, this danger is still likely to exist.

86. Purchasing Oysters.—To be able to purchase oysters intelligently, the housewife should be familiar with the names of the various kinds. These names are dependent on the locality from which the oysters come, and include *Blue Points, Cape Cods, Cotuits, Lynn Havens,* and numerous other varieties. It should be remembered that the varieties raised in different localities are quite distinctive, differing to some extent in both size and appearance. Unless the purchaser is familiar with the different varieties, almost any of the small oysters are likely to be sold to her for one of the small varieties and, likewise, any of the large oysters for one of the large varieties. While this is of small consequence, provided the quality is satisfactory and the price is right, it is well for every housewife to familiarize herself with the names of the various kinds, so that she may know just what variety she is purchasing.

87. When oysters are bought in the shell, they should be alive, a fact that can be determined by the tightly closed shell, as has already been stated. If the shells are not closed or can be easily pried apart, it may be known that the oysters are not good and that they should be rejected. When it is possible to procure them, oysters that have been removed from the shells immediately after being taken from the beds are preferable to those which have not been removed from the shells before shipping. When purchased out of the shells, oysters should be grayish in color, should have no disagreeable odor, and should contain no excess water or liquid. After being purchased, oysters should be kept on ice unless they can be cooked at once.

The season for oysters is from September to April, inclusive. While in some localities they can be purchased at other times during the year, they are not likely to be so good. In fact, it is not safe to use oysters during the warm months.

88. Important Points in Cooking Oysters.—The protein of oysters, like that found in other foods, is coagulated by heat. Long heat, provided it is sufficiently intense, makes oysters tough, and in this condition they are neither agreeable to eat nor readily digested. When they are to be cooked at a high temperature, therefore, the cooking should be done quickly. If they are to be cooked at a temperature below the boiling point, they may be subjected to heat for a longer time without becoming so tough as when a high temperature is used. Cooking quickly at a high temperature, however, is preferable in most cases to long, slow cooking. For example, in the preparation of oyster stew, long cooking produces no better flavor than short cooking at a high temperature and renders oysters far less digestible.

89. Opening Oysters.—Unless oysters are bought already opened, it becomes necessary to open them in the home before they can be served raw or cooked. To open oysters is not difficult, and with a little experience the work can be done with ease. It will be well to note that the two shells of an oyster, which are called *valves*, are held together by a single muscle, known as the *adductor muscle*, that lies near the center, and that this muscle must be cut before the shell will open readily. Before attempting to open oysters, however, they should be scrubbed

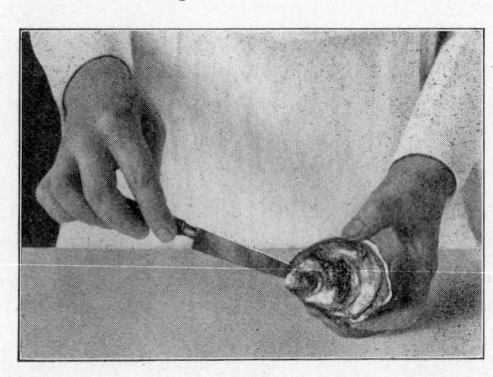

FIG. 26

with clean water, so as to remove any sand that may be on the shells. When the oysters are cleaned, proceed to open them in the manner shown in Figs. 26 and 27. First, as in Fig. 26, insert the point of a knife into the hinged, or pointed, end and push the blade between the valves until they appear to separate, when it will be known that the muscle has been cut. Then, as in Fig. 27, lay the valves open and loosen the oyster from the shell by slipping the knife under it.

If the oysters that are being opened are to be cooked before serving, simply drop them with their liquid into a suitable vessel and discard the shells. Before using the oysters, remove them from the liquid, look them over carefully to see that no small particles of shells cling to them, and wash them in clean, cold water to remove any sand that may be present. Also, strain the liquid through a cloth, so that it will be free from sand when used in the preparation

§ 13　　　　　FISH AND SHELL FISH　　　　　43

of the dish for which the oysters are to be used or for the making of soup or broth.

Oysters that are to be eaten raw are frequently served on the half shell. Therefore, if they are to be used in this way, place each oyster, as it is loosened in the process of opening, into the deeper shell, as Fig. 27 shows, and discard the other one. Very often good-looking oyster shells are saved in order that they may be used from time to time in serving raw oysters that are bought already opened.

90. Raw Oysters.—When an appetizer is desired in a meal that is to consist of several courses, raw oysters are often used for the first course. Oysters that are to be eaten raw may be served in the shells or removed from them. They are bland in flavor,

Fig. 27

however, and require some sharp, highly seasoned sauce in order to give them sufficient snap. The sauces commonly used for this purpose include cocktail sauce, chilli sauce, catsup, horseradish, and tobasco sauce. Sometimes, though, lemon juice or vinegar and pepper and salt are preferred to sauce. As a rule, crisp crackers, small squares of toast, or wafers and butter accompany raw oysters in any form, and sometimes celery and radishes are served, too.

91. When a cocktail sauce is served with raw oysters, they are generally referred to as **oyster cocktails.** Two methods of serving these are in practice. In one, as shown in Fig. 28, the cocktail sauce is put into a small glass placed in the center of a soup plate filled with cracked ice, and the oysters, usually six in half shells, are arranged around the glass, on the ice. In the other, as shown in Fig. 29, the desired number of oysters that have been removed from the shells are dropped into a stemmed glass containing the cocktail

Fig. 28

sauce, and the glass is placed in a bowl of cracked ice. An *oyster fork,* which is a small, three-pronged fork, is always served with raw oysters, and usually a piece of lemon is supplied in addition to the cocktail sauce.

92. Oyster Stew.—If an extremely nutritious way of preparing oysters is desired, oyster stew should be selected. This is perhaps the simplest way in which to cook oysters, and yet care must

Fig. 29

be exercised in making this dish, for the oysters should not be cooked too long and the milk, which must be brought to the boiling point, should not be allowed to burn. Oyster stew makes an excellent dish for lunch. It should not be served as the first course of a heavy meal because of the large amount of nutriment it contains.

Oyster Stew
(Sufficient to Serve Six)

1 qt. oysters	1 tsp. salt
1 qt. milk	$\frac{1}{8}$ tsp. pepper
2 Tb. butter	

Pour 1 cupful of water over the oysters, look them over carefully, and remove any pieces of shell that may cling to the oysters, making sure that any particles of sand are washed off. Heat this liquid to the boiling point and then strain it through a cloth. Put the milk on the fire to heat, and when hot, add the butter, salt, and pepper, and strained liquid. After the whole mixture has come to the boiling point, pour in the oysters and cook until they look plump and the edges begin to curl. Remove from the heat and serve with crisp crackers.

93. Creamed Oysters.—Another nutritious way in which to prepare oysters and at the same time produce a dish that is pleasing to most persons is to cream them. After being creamed, oysters may be served over toast or in timbale cases.

Creamed Oysters
(Sufficient to Serve Six)

2 Tb. butter	Salt and pepper
24 oysters	6 slices toast or 6 timbale cases
1½ c. medium white sauce	

Melt the butter in a frying pan, add the oysters, and heat them in the butter until the edges begin to curl slightly. Pour the hot oysters into the hot white sauce, season to taste with salt and pepper, and serve over toast or in timbale cases.

94. Scalloped Oysters.—No food makes a more palatable scalloped dish than oysters. Oysters so prepared are liked by nearly every one, and the ingredients with which they are combined help to give such a dish balance so far as the food substances are concerned. Care should be taken, however, in the baking of scalloped oysters, for they are likely to become tough if they are cooked too long.

Scalloped Oysters
(Sufficient to Serve Six)

1 c. bread crumbs	1 pt. oysters
2 Tb. butter	Salt and pepper
1 c. cracker crumbs	1 c. milk

Butter the bread crumbs with the butter, and then mix them with the cracker crumbs. Sprinkle the bottom of a greased baking dish with one-fourth of the crumbs, and over this put a layer of oysters that have been previously cleaned. Sprinkle with salt and pepper and add one-fourth more of the crumbs. Add another layer of oysters, sprinkle with salt and pepper, and place the remainder of the crumbs on top. Strain the liquid from the oysters through a piece of cloth, mix this with the milk, and pour over the dish thus prepared. Place in a hot oven, and bake until the mixture is thoroughly heated and the top is brown.

95. Fried Oysters.—Of all the dishes prepared from oysters, fried oysters undoubtedly find favor with the greatest number of persons. However, unless care is taken in frying the oysters, they are likely to be somewhat indigestible. Deep fat should be used for this purpose, and it should be hot enough to brown a 1-inch cube of bread a golden brown in 40 seconds.

Fried Oysters
(Sufficient to Serve Six)

24 large oysters	Fine cracker crumbs
1 egg	Salt
$\frac{1}{4}$ c. milk	Pepper

Thoroughly dry the oysters by laying them on one end of a soft cloth and patting them with the other. Beat the egg and add the milk to it. Dip the oysters into the cracker crumbs, then into the egg-and-milk mixture, and again into the crumbs. Fry in deep fat until brown. Remove from the fat, drain well, and place on oiled paper. Sprinkle with salt and pepper and serve hot.

96. Oyster Pie.—Baking oysters into a pie is another means of combining a protein food with foods that are high in other food substances. As oyster pie is somewhat hearty, it may be used as the main dish of a heavy meal.

Oyster Pie
(Sufficient to Serve Six)

1 pt. oysters	Salt and pepper
1 c. medium white sauce	Baking-powder biscuit dough

Cut each of the oysters into three or four pieces, and place them in a greased baking dish. Pour over them the hot white sauce and the juice from the oysters. Season with salt and pepper. Over the top, place a layer of the biscuit dough rolled about $\frac{1}{4}$ inch thick. Set in a hot oven and bake until the crust is brown.

97. Pigs in Blankets.—When something entirely different in the way of oysters is desired, pigs in blankets should be tried. This is a very good name for the dish given in the accompanying recipe, for the oysters are rolled up in a strip of bacon, which serves as a blanket. They are especially suitable for a light meal, such as luncheon or a dainty lunch that is to be served to company.

PIGS IN BLANKETS
(Sufficient to Serve Six)
18 large oysters   18 thin strips of bacon

After the oysters have been cleaned, roll each one in a strip of bacon. Fasten the bacon where the edges meet by running a toothpick through at this point. Place in a broiler and broil on one side until brown; then turn them and broil until the other side is brown. Serve hot.

98. Oyster Fritters.—Variety may also be secured in the use of oysters by making oyster fritters. When such fritters are nicely browned and served with an appetizing sauce, an attractive as well as a tasty dish is the result.

OYSTER FRITTERS
(Sufficient to Serve Six)
1 pt. oysters   1-egg muffin batter

Clean the oysters and cut each into four or five pieces. Make a one-egg muffin batter and to it add the cut oysters. Drop the mixture by spoonfuls into deep fat and fry until brown. Remove from the fat, drain, and sprinkle with salt and pepper. Serve with a desired sauce.

CLAMS AND THEIR PREPARATION

99. Nature and Digestibility of Clams.—Clams are bivalves similar to oysters in both form and composition. Because of the similarity in composition, they are utilized in much the same ways as oysters, being used extensively for food in parts of the country where the supply is large. There are numerous varieties of clams, and some of them differ slightly from each other in appearance, color, and flavor. Preference for the different varieties is largely a matter of individual taste.

Clams may be purchased loose or in the shell and they may be served in or out of the shell. However, when bought in the shell, they must be purchased alive and must be subjected to the same tests as are oysters. As in the case of oysters, they may be eaten raw or cooked. Their preparation for cooking is similar to that of oysters. In the raw state, they are easily digested, but upon the application of heat they become tough, and the longer they are cooked, the tougher they become. It can therefore be seen that the digestibility of clams is influenced very much by cooking.

100. Opening Clams.—If clams are to be opened in the home, the method illustrated in Fig. 30 may be employed. First wash the clams to remove the sand, and then place a clam on a hard surface so that the pointed edge is up. Insert the thin edge of a knife into the very slight groove between the shells, or valves, and with a heavy utensil of some kind strike the top of the knife several

Fig. 30

times so as to separate the valves. Then, as in opening oysters, spread the shells apart, as shown, and loosen the clam from the shell it adheres to.

101. Raw Clams.—Like oysters, raw clams are generally served as a cocktail, or an appetizer, at the beginning of a meal. If they are to be served in the half shell, place them in a dish of cracked ice; if they are to be served without the shells, place the required number in a stemmed glass that is set in a dish of cracked ice. In either case, lemon or a suitable sauce, or both, should be supplied.

102. Steamed Clams.—Steaming is the method generally adopted when clams in large numbers are cooked for a "clam bake," but there is no reason why it cannot be used by the housewife when she wishes to cook only enough for her family. When large quantities are to be steamed, use is generally made of a steamer, but the housewife will find that she can steam a few clams very satisfactorily in a saucepan or a similar vessel.

To prepare steamed clams, scrub the shells of the clams until they are perfectly clean. Place the desired number thus cleaned in a saucepan and add enough water to cover the bottom of the pan about 1 inch. Allow this to cook until the shells of the clams open. Remove the clams from the pan and serve them in the shells. Provide each person with a small dish of melted butter into which to dip the clams as they are removed from the shells to be eaten. The liquid found in the clams may be poured from the shell before the clams are served, and after being well seasoned may be served as clam broth.

103. Baked Clams.—Another very appetizing way in which to prepare clams is to combine them with bread crumbs, season them well, and then bake them until they are well browned. Select several good-sized clams for each person to be served. Scrub the shells well and open them. Remove the clams and chop them into small pieces. To each cupful of chopped clams, add 2 cupfuls of buttered bread crumbs, 1 tablespoonful of chopped parsley, 1 tablespoonful of chopped pimiento, and 1 tablespoonful of onion juice. Season the mixture with salt and pepper and fill the shells with it. Place these in a shallow pan and bake in a very hot oven until the crumbs are well browned on top. Serve hot.

104. Fried Clams.—As oysters make a very desirable dish when fried in deep fat, so clams may be treated in this way, too. Remove the desired number of clams from the shells, wash them thoroughly, and dry them on a clean towel. Dip them into beaten egg, and finally into the crumbs. Fry in deep fat until they are a golden brown. Serve with slices of lemon.

SCALLOPS AND THEIR PREPARATION

105. Nature of Scallops.—Scallops, which are another form of bivalves, are less commonly used for food than oysters and clams. Scalloped dishes get their name from the fact that scallop shells were originally used for their preparation. Not all of the scallop is used for food; merely the heavy muscle that holds the two shells together is edible. Scallops are slightly higher in protein than oysters and clams and they also have a higher food value than these two mollusks. The most common method of preparation for scallops is to fry them, but they may also be baked in the shells.

106. Fried Scallops.—If scallops are properly fried, they make an appetizing dish. As they are a rather bland food, a sauce of some kind, preferably a sour one, is generally served with them.

Select the desired number of scallops and wash thoroughly. Dip first into either fine bread crumbs or cracker crumbs, then into beaten egg, and again into the crumbs. Fry in deep fat until a golden brown, remove, and drain. Serve with lemon or a sour sauce, such as horseradish or tomato sauce.

107. Baked Scallops.—If a tasty as well as a slightly unusual dish is desired to give variety to the diet, baked scallops will undoubtedly find favor. As shown in the accompanying recipe, mushrooms are one of the ingredients in baked scallops and these not only provide additional material, but improve the flavor.

To prepare baked scallops, clean the desired number, parboil for 15 minutes, drain, and cut into small pieces. For each cupful of scallops, melt 2 tablespoonfuls of butter in a frying pan, sauté in it 1 tablespoonful of chopped onion, and add ½ cupful of chopped mushrooms. When these have browned, add 2 tablespoonfuls of flour and 1 cupful of milk. Cook until thick and then add the scallops. Fill the scallop shells with the mixture, sprinkle with buttered bread crumbs, place in the oven, and bake until the crumbs are brown.

LOBSTERS, CRABS, AND SHRIMP

GENERAL CHARACTERISTICS

108. The shell fish, **lobsters, crabs,** and **shrimp,** come under the head of crustaceans; that is, animals consisting of jointed sections, each of which is covered with a hard shell. Their flesh is similar in composition to that of other fish, but it is tougher and harder to digest. However, it is popular because of its unique and delicate flavor. In fact, whenever these varieties of fish can be obtained along the seacoast or within a reasonable distance from the place where they are caught, they are considered a delicacy. If they can be shipped alive to any point, they are perfectly safe to use, although quite high in price because of their perishable nature.

109. Unless such shell fish can be procured alive in the markets, the use of a good brand of any of them canned is recommended. In fact, canned lobster, crab, and shrimp are very satisfactory and may be substituted for any of the fresh cooked varieties in the recipes that follow. It is true that some persons object to canned food because ptomaine poisoning sometimes results, but it has been found that ptomaine poisoning is more liable to result from eating these foods when they are bought in the market in poor condition than when they are secured in canned form. Care must be exercised, however, whenever use is made of canned food of any kind. Upon opening a can of any of these varieties of fish, the entire contents should be removed from the can at once and used as soon as possible. It must be remembered that the ptomaine poisoning that is sometimes caused by eating canned foods is not due to the fact that the foods come in tin cans, but that they are allowed to stand in the cans after they are opened. Upon their being exposed to the air, putrefaction sets in and causes the harmful effect.

110. Lobsters, crabs, and shrimp are very similar in composition, shrimp being slightly higher in protein and total food value than the others. If they are not prepared in an indigestible way, they are comparatively easy to digest. It has been proved a fallacy that lobster and ice cream are a dangerous combination, for if both are in good condition they may be combined with no ill effects to the normal individual.

LOBSTERS AND THEIR PREPARATION

111. Distinguishing Features.—Of these three types of sea food, lobsters are perhaps the most popular. They are found along the North Atlantic and North Pacific seacoasts. Alive, they are mottled bluish-green in color, but upon being cooked they change to bright red. As soon as they are caught, many of them are packed in ice and shipped alive to various points, while others are plunged immediately into boiling water and sold cooked. A live lobster ready for cooking is shown in Fig. 31. Lobsters vary greatly in size. Only those 9 inches or more in length can be sold, the smaller ones being thrown back into the water. When they are purchased either raw or cooked, they should be heavy for their size; that is, they should be heavy because of their plumpness and good condition.

FISH AND SHELL FISH §13

112. Preliminary Preparation.—To prepare a lobster, which should be alive, grasp it firmly by the back, as shown in

Fig. 31

Fig. 32, plunge it quickly, head first, into a kettle of rapidly boiling water, and then submerge the rest of the body. Be sure to have a sufficient amount of water to cover the lobster completely. Boil rapidly for 5 minutes; then lower the flame or remove to a cooler part of the stove and cook slowly for $\frac{1}{2}$ hour. Remove from the water and allow to cool.

After being prepared in this way, a lobster may be served cold or it may be used in the preparation of various made dishes. If it is to be used without further preparation, it is often served from the shell, which is usually split open. Mayonnaise or some other sauce is generally served with lobster. The flesh is removed from the shell with a small fork as it is eaten.

Fig. 32

113. Removing Lobster From the Shell.—The majority of the dishes made from lobster require that the flesh be removed from the shell. To do this, first pull off the two large claws and the four pairs of small claws, as shown in Fig. 33, and break the tail

§ 13   FISH AND SHELL FISH   53

from the body. Then with scissors, as in Fig. 34, cut a single slit the entire length of the shell covering the under part of the tail and

Fig. 33

remove the flesh inside the tail in a whole, large piece, as shown in Fig. 35. The intestinal tract, which can be readily observed, will be found embedded in this piece and running the entire length. Slash the flesh and remove it. Next remove the flesh of the body from the shell, retaining only that part which appears to be fibrous, like the flesh of the tail. The stomach, which is called "the lady" because its inside appearance closely resembles a lady sitting in a chair, should not be removed from the shell. However, care should be taken to obtain all the flesh surrounding the bones in the bony part of the lobster. The coral substance, that is, the roe of the lobster, should also be removed, as it can be used for a garnish.

Fig. 34

With the flesh removed from the shell, proceed to take out that contained in the claws. Break open the large claws, using a nut cracker or a small hammer for this purpose, and, as in Fig. 36, remove the flesh that they contain. If the small claws are to be used for a garnish, as is often done, remove the flesh without breaking them; otherwise break them as in the case of the large ones.

114. Lobster Cocktail. — Practically all varieties of shell fish make most satisfactory cocktails, and lobster is no exception. To make a lobster cocktail, shred or cut into small pieces the flesh of a lobster that has been prepared according to the directions just given. Chill the shreds or pieces and then serve them in stemmed cocktail glasses with any desirable cocktail sauce.

FIG. 35

115. Scalloped Lobster.—Persons who care for the flavor

FIG. 36

of lobster will find scalloped lobster a very attractive dish. When prepared in this way, it is suitable either for luncheon or for dinner.

FISH AND SHELL FISH

SCALLOPED LOBSTER
(Sufficient to Serve Six)

1 c. lobster meat	1 hard-cooked egg
1 c. medium white sauce	Salt
⅔ c. buttered bread crumbs	Pepper

Mix the lobster with the medium white sauce. Butter a baking dish, place half of the crumbs in the bottom, and pour over them the lobster and white sauce. Slice the hard-cooked egg over the top of the lobster, season the whole well with salt and pepper, and sprinkle the remainder of the crumbs over the top. Place in a hot oven and bake until the crumbs are brown. Garnish with sprays of parsley and serve at once.

116. Deviled Lobster.—A dish that is delicious and at the same time very attractive is deviled lobster. After removing the flesh from the shell, the shell should be cleaned thoroughly, as it is to be used as a receptacle in which to put the lobster mixture for baking. When removed from the oven, this dish can be made more attractive by garnishing it with the lobster claws and tail.

DEVILED LOBSTER
(Sufficient to Serve Six)

1 Tb. chopped onion	⅛ tsp. pepper
2 Tb. butter	1 Tb. lemon juice
2 Tb. flour	1 Tb. chopped parsley
1 tsp. salt	1 c. milk
Dash of Cayenne pepper	2 c. lobster meat
⅛ tsp. paprika	¼ c. buttered cracker crumbs

Sauté the onion in the butter, and to this add the flour, salt, Cayenne pepper, paprika, pepper, lemon juice, and parsley. Mix well and add the milk. When the whole has cooked until it is thick, add the lobster. Pour the mixture into the clean shell of the lobster, sprinkle with cracker crumbs, and place in the oven long enough to brown the crumbs. Remove from the oven, place on a serving dish, garnish with the claws and tail of the lobster, if desired, and serve at once.

117. Lobster à la Newburg.—When lobster à la Newburg is mentioned, one naturally thinks of a chafing dish, for this is one of the dishes that is very often made in a chafing dish and served at small social gatherings. However, it can be made just as satisfactorily on the kitchen stove and is a dish suitable for a home luncheon or small dinner.

LOBSTER À LA NEWBURG
(Sufficient to Serve Six)

2 Tb. butter	½ c. milk
1 Tb. flour	½ c. thin cream
2 c. lobster	1 tsp. vinegar
½ tsp. salt	1 Tb. lemon juice
Few grains of Cayenne pepper	2 egg yolks

Melt the butter in a saucepan, add the flour, and into this pour the lobster meat cut into rather large pieces. Add the salt, pepper, milk, and cream; cook together until thick, and then pour in the vinegar and lemon juice. Beat the egg yolks and stir them into the cooked mixture, using care to prevent them from curdling. When the mixture has thickened, remove from the stove and serve over toast.

118. Lobster Croquettes.—Probably the most attractive dish that can be made out of lobster is the one explained in the accompanying recipe. As this is artistically garnished, and at the same time extremely appetizing, it is suitable for a meal that is intended to be very nice, such as a dainty luncheon. If the elaborate garnishing here suggested is not desired, the croquettes may be served with merely a suitable sauce.

LOBSTER CROQUETTES
(Sufficient to Serve Six)

1 c. thick white sauce	½ tsp. salt
2 eggs	⅛ tsp. pepper
2 c. diced lobster meat	Fine bread crumbs

Prepare the white sauce and allow it to cool. Add one beaten egg and the lobster meat. Season with the salt and pepper. Shape into croquettes, roll in beaten egg, then in crumbs, and fry in deep fat until an even brown. Drain, stick a lobster claw into the end of each, and arrange on a platter with the claws around the outside. Pour a medium white sauce over the opposite ends and the centers of the croquettes and over this sprinkle the lobster coral and hard-cooked egg yolks, which have been forced through a sieve. In the center of the platter, arrange a small mound of parsley and one of the large claws of the lobster.

CRABS AND THEIR PREPARATION

119. Nature of Crabs.—Numerous varieties of crabs are obtained along the seashores of the United States, and most of them measure not more than 5 or 6 inches across. Shell fish in this form are used for food both before the shells have hardened, when they are known as *soft-shelled crabs,* and after the shells have grown hard, when they are called *hard-shelled crabs.* To be at their best, crabs should be as heavy as lobsters in proportion to their size. Their flesh should be firm and stiff and their eyes should be bright. The male crab has a smaller body and longer claws than the female. In food value, crabs are quite similar to lobsters.

Tiny *oyster crabs* are found in the shells of crabs as well as in oysters. These are considered a great delicacy and are used chiefly for garnishing, because they are very small and, as a rule, are not found in large numbers.

120. Preliminary Preparation.—Before either soft-shelled or hard-shelled crabs can be used as food, a certain amount of preparation is necessary. In the case of hard-shelled crabs, plunge them alive into hot water, allow them to come to the boiling point, and cook slowly for $\frac{1}{2}$ hour. It is a good plan to add 1 tablespoonful of salt for each crab that is being boiled. While the crabs are cooking, remove the scum that rises to the top. When they are sufficiently cooked, open the shells and take out the meat, being careful to remove all the meat from the claws.

Soft-shelled crabs require a somewhat different kind of preparation. With this variety, lift up the points on each side of the back shell and remove the spongy substance that is found under them. In addition, take off the apron, which is the small piece that occurs at the lower part of the shell and that terminates in points. The crabs are then ready for frying, which is the method of cooking that is usually applied to this variety.

121. Crab-Flake Cocktail.—Crab meat is used for cocktails in the same way as oysters, clams, and lobster. In fact, no better appetizer to serve at the beginning of a meal can be found. To make crab-flake cocktail, remove the meat from the shells of cooked hard-shelled crabs in the way just explained, and chill it. Then place it in stemmed glasses and serve with cocktail sauce.

122. Deviled Crabs.—Variety in the cooking of hard-shelled crabs can be secured by deviling them according to the accompanying directions. As will be observed, this is done in practically the same way that lobster is deviled.

DEVILED CRABS
(Sufficient to Serve Four)

2 Tb. butter Dash Cayenne pepper
4 crabs $\frac{1}{8}$ tsp. pepper
1 c. cream sauce 1 egg
1 Tb. onion juice Cracker crumbs
$\frac{1}{2}$ tsp. salt

Put the butter in a frying pan, add the meat from the four crabs, and pour into this the cream sauce. Season with the onion juice, salt, Cayenne pepper, and pepper. Add the well-beaten egg and allow the mixture to cook until the egg has thickened, being careful not to let it curd. Fill the back shells of the crabs with this mixture, sprinkle with cracker crumbs, place in a hot oven, and bake until brown. Serve hot or cold.

123. Fried Soft-Shelled Crabs.—After soft-shelled crabs are prepared in the manner explained in Art. **120,** they are usually fried in deep fat. Egg and cracker dust or flour are used to make a coating for the crabs.

FRIED SOFT-SHELLED CRABS
(Sufficient to Serve Four)

4 soft-shelled crabs Cracker dust or flour
1 egg Salt and pepper

Prepare the crabs by removing the apron and the spongy substance under the shell of each crab. Beat the egg slightly. Roll the crabs first in the egg and then in the cracker dust or the flour. Fry in hot, deep fat until a golden brown. Remove from the fat, drain, and sprinkle well with salt and pepper to season. Serve hot or cold.

124. Creamed Crab Meat.—When the meat of hard-shelled crabs is creamed, it makes a very dainty dish, especially if it is served over toast or in timbale cases. To give a touch of color and at the same time add a little flavor, chopped pimiento is generally added.

Boil the desired number of hard-shelled crabs and remove the meat from the shells. For each cupful of crab meat, prepare 1 cupful of medium white sauce. Add the crab meat, season well, and, if desired, add some chopped pimiento. Serve hot over toast or in timbale cases.

SHRIMP AND THEIR PREPARATION

125. Nature of Shrimp.—Shrimp are similar to crabs and lobsters in composition and in the methods of preparation. They differ considerably in appearance, however, and are smaller in size.

When alive, shrimp are a mottled greenish color, but upon being dropped into boiling-hot water they turn red. When they have cooked sufficiently, the meat, which is very delicious, may be easily removed from the shells. After the meat of shrimp is thus prepared, it may be used cold in a salad or a cocktail or it may be utilized in a number of ways for hot dishes. Very often a chafing dish is used in the preparation of such dishes, but this utensil is not necessary, as they may be cooked in an ordinary utensil on a stove of any kind.

126. Creamed Shrimp.—The usual way of preparing shrimp is to cook it with mushrooms and then serve it over toast, or, as shown in Fig. 37, in timbale cases. Creamed shrimp is dainty in appearance, pleasing to the taste, and highly nutritious.

FIG. 37

CREAMED SHRIMP
(Sufficient to Serve Six)

1 c. medium white sauce $\frac{1}{2}$ tsp. salt
1 c. diced shrimp $\frac{1}{8}$ tsp. pepper
$\frac{1}{2}$ c. chopped mushrooms

Heat the white sauce, and to it add the shrimp, mushrooms, salt, and pepper. Beat a little butter into the mixture to improve the flavor, heat, and serve in timbale cases, as shown, or over toast.

127. Shrimp à La Salle.—Shrimp also makes an appetizing and attractive dish when combined with tomato and green pepper. The accompanying recipe gives directions for the preparation of such a dish, which is called shrimp à La Salle.

SHRIMP À LA SALLE
(Sufficient to Serve Six)

2 Tb. butter   1 Tb. chopped onion
1 c. shredded shrimp   1 tsp. celery salt
1 c. stewed tomato   1 tsp. salt
1 small green pepper, chopped $\frac{1}{8}$ tsp. pepper

Brown the butter in a saucepan, and add the shrimp, tomato, green pepper, onion, celery salt, salt, and pepper. Heat all together thoroughly, and serve over toast.

FISH AND SHELL FISH

EXAMINATION QUESTIONS

(1) (a) For what food may fish be substituted in the diet? (b) How does fish compare with meat as to its usefulness as food?

(2) (a) What food substances are present in fish? (b) How does the food value of fish compare with that of meat?

(3) (a) Discuss the digestibility of fish. (b) How does the salting of fish for preservation affect its digestibility?

(4) How does the housewife's purchase of fish affect the market price?

(5) What methods of cookery should be used in preparing: (a) large fish? (b) small fish?

(6) Mention the tests for determining the freshness of fish.

(7) Discuss the care of fish in the home.

(8) Give the steps in the preparation of a fish for cooking.

(9) Give the steps in the boning of a fish.

(10) (a) What are fillets? (b) Tell briefly how fillets are obtained.

(11) Why are sauces frequently served with fish?

(12) (a) What is larding? (b) How may fish be larded? (c) For what purpose is larding done?

(13) How may salt fish be freshened?

(14) (a) Mention the shell fish. (b) Discuss their usefulness in the diet.

(15) What precautions should be taken in the purchase of shell fish?

(16) Discuss the composition and food value of shell fish.

(17) Compare the composition of milk with that of oysters.

(18) (a) What is the season for oysters? (b) How are oysters opened?

(19) (a) How are clams opened? (b) What is the effect of long cooking on clams?

(20) (a) How are lobsters prepared? (b) Mention the two kinds of crabs. (c) How do these differ.

ADDITIONAL WORK

Mention the varieties of fish most common in your local market.

Compare the cost of a sufficient amount of fish to serve your family with the cost of beef and either veal or lamb served to the same number of persons at other times. Submit your results.

§ 13

INDEX

NOTE.—In this Volume, each Section is complete in itself and has a number, which, together with the section mark (§), is printed at the top of every page of the Section. To find a reference, glance along the inside edges of the headlines until you find the desired Section number and then along the outside edges until you find the desired page. Thus, to find the reference "Hard-shelled crabs, §13, p57," turn to the Section marked §13, and then to page 57 of that Section.

A

Adductor muscle of an oyster, §13, p42
American forcemeat balls, §9, p36
Apples, Bacon with sliced, §11, p34
    Cold pork with fried, §11, p37
Asparagus soup, Cream-of-, §9, p27

B

Bacon, §11, pp27, 33
    and eggs, §11, p34
    Calves' liver and, §11, p10
    combined with cereals, §11, p34
    combined with other foods, §11, p34
    with sliced apples, §11, p34
    with tomatoes, §11, p34
Baked clams, §13, p49
    fillet of whitefish, §13, p26
    finnan haddie, §13, p32
    fish, §13, p24
    haddock, §13, p25
    halibut, §13, p26
    ham, §11, p36
    poultry with rice, §12, p49
    scallops, §13, p50
Balls, American forcemeat, §9, p36
    Codfish, §13, p32
    Egg, §9, p35
    Forcemeat, §9, p35
Bass, Food value and composition of black, §13, p5
Basting of meat, §10, p36
Batter, Timbale-case, §11, p44
Bechamel, Chicken, §12, p45
Beef, §10, p17
    Boiled corned, §10, p41
    Braized, §10, p36
    Composition and food value of, §10, p5; §13, p5
    Cooking of, §10, p22
    Corned, §10, p40

Beef, Cuts of, §10, p18
    Fillet of, §10, p31
    for stewing and corning, Cuts of, §10, p38
    Frizzled, §10, p47
    General characteristics of, §10, p17
    hash, §10, p46
    Left-over, §10, p45
    loaf, §10, p37
    loaf, Recipe for, §10, p38
    loin, Steaks obtained from, §10, p22
    Mexican, §10, p45
    organs and their preparation, §10, p42
    pie, §10, p46
    Pot-roasted, §10, p37
    Preparation of stews and corned, §10, p38
    Roast, §10, p34
    stew, §10, p38
    Tenderloin of, §10, pp21, 24, 31
Beefsteak, Broiled, §10, p27
Beefsteaks and their preparation, §10, p22
Birds, Preparation of small, §12, p24
    Roast small, §12, p33
Biscuits, Creamed veal on, §11, p11
Bisques, §9, p4
Bivalves, §13, p36
Blue points, §13, p41
Bluefish, Composition and food value of, §13, p5
Bob veal, §11, p1
Boiled cod, §13, p22
    corned beef, §10, p41
    dinner, §10, p41
    fish, §13, p21
    ham, §11, p36
    salmon, §13, p32
    tongue, §10, p42
Boiler, Fish, §13, p21
Boiling, Cooking meat by, §10, p13
Bologna, §11, p39
Bone stock, §9, p6

INDEX

Boned chicken, §12, p35
Boning a chicken, §12, p35
  a fish, §13, p14
Borsch, §9, p5
Bouillon, §9, p4
  Tomato, §9, p21
Braized beef, §10, p36
  beef, Recipe for, §10, p37
  tongue, §10, p43
Braizing, §10, p15
Bread sticks, §9 p34
  stuffing, §12, p33
Broiled beefsteak, §10, p27
  fillet, §10, p31
  fish, §13, p22
  fresh mackerel, §13, p23
  ham, §11, p35
  pork, Sautéd or, §11, p31
  poultry, §12, p25
  scrod with potato border, §13, p23
  shad roe, §13, p23
  squirrel, §12, p55
  sweetbreads, §11, p9
  venison, §12, p55
  venison, Sauce for, §12, p55
Broiler, §12, p6
Broilers, Composition and food value of, §13, p5
Broiling, cooking meat by, §10, p12
Broth, §9, p4
Brown sauce, Veal cutlets in, §11, p5
Buying meats, Points to consider in, §10, p3

C

Cabbage, Scalloped pork and, §11, p37
Calves' liver and bacon, §11, p10
Canned fish in the diet, §13, p33
Cape Cods, §13, p41
Capons, §12, p4
Carbohydrate in fish, §13, p4
  in meat, §10, p7
Care, nature, and use of stock pot, §9, p7
  of fish in the home, §13, p11
  of meat, §10, p8
  of meat in the home, §10, p10
  of meat in the market, §10, p10
Carp, Composition and food value of, §13, p5
Carving meat, Serving and, §11, p38
  poultry, Serving and, §12, p49
Casserole, Chicken en, §12, p44
Catfish, Composition and food value of, §13, p5
Caul, §11, p15
Celery and radishes, §9, p32
Cereals, Bacon combined with, §11, p34
Chestnut purée, §9, p29
  stuffing, §12, p34
Chicken à la king, §12, p47
  Bechamel, §12, p45
  Boned, §12, p35

Chicken broilers, Composition and food value of, §13, p5
  Crop of a, §12, p15
  croquettes, §12, p47
  curry, §12, p44
  Cutting up a, §12, p19
  Definition of, §12, p6
  Determining the age of, §12, p8
  Determining the freshness of, §12, p9
  Drawing a, §12, p15
  Dressing a, §12, p13
  en casserole, §12, p44
  feet, Preparing, §12, p23
  Fricassee of, §12, p43
  Fried, §12, p27
  Frying, §12, p6
  General marks of good quality in, §12, p7
  giblets, §12, p18
  Gravy for fried, §12, p27
  Jellied, §12, p45
  Maryland fried, §12, p28
  pie, §12, p43
  Plucking a, §12, p13
  Poultry other than, §12, p9
  Preparation of, §12, p13
  Roast, §12, p29
  Roasting, §12, p6
  salad, §12, p47
  salad, Mock, §11, p37
  Selection of, §12, p7
  Singeing a, §12, p14
  stew with dumplings or noodles, §12, p42
  Wing tips of, §12, p23
  with paprika sauce, Fried, §12, p28
  with rice, §12, p48
Chickens, Live, §12, p9
Chops in tomato sauce, Pork, §11, p31
  Lamb and mutton, §11, p20
  Veal, §11, p4
Chowder, Clam, §9, p30
  Corn, §9, p31
  Fish, §9, p30
  Potato, §9, p30
Chowders, §9, pp4, 30
Chuck roasts, §10, p32
Clam chowder, §9, p30
Clams, and scallops, Oysters, §13, p39
  Baked, §13, p49
  Composition and food value of, §13, p38
  Fried, §13, p49
  Nature and digestibility of, §13, p47
  Opening of, §13, p48
  Preparation of, §13, p47
  Raw, §13, p48
  Steamed, §13, p48
Classes of soup, General, §9, p3
  of soups denoting consistency, §9, p4
Classification of poultry, §12, p3
  of soups, §9, p3
Cleaning fish, §13, p11

INDEX

Clear soup or bouillon, Stock for, §9, p19
  soups, §9, p4
  soups and stocks, §9, p19
Clearing soup, §9, p14
Cocktail, Crab-flake, §13, p57
  Lobster, §13, p54
  Oyster, §13, p43
Cod, Boiled, §13, p22
Codfish balls, §13, p32
  Creamed, §13, p31
Cold pork with fried apples, §11, p37
  -storage poultry, §12, p5
Comparison of fish and meat, Table showing the, §13, p5
  of fish with meat, §13, p3
  of mutton and lamb, §11, p12
Composition and food value of beef, §10, p5; §13, p5
  and food value of black bass, §13, p5
  and food value of bluefish, §13, p5
  and food value of canned salmon, §13, p5
  and food value of carp, §13, p5
  and food value of catfish, §13, p5
  and food value of chicken broilers, §13, p5
  and food value of clams, §13, p38
  and food value of crabs, §13, p38
  and food value of fowl, §13, p5
  and food value of halibut steak, §13, p5
  and food value of lake trout, §13, p5
  and food value of lamb, §10, p5
  and food value of leg of lamb, §13, p5
  and food value of lobsters, §13, p38
  and food value of mutton, §10, p5
  and food value of oysters, §13, p38
  and food value of pork, §10, p5
  and food value of pork chops, §13, p5
  and food value of red snapper, §13, p5
  and food value of scallops, §13, p38
  and food value of shell fish, §13, p37
  and food value of shell fish, Tables showing, §13, p38
  and food value of veal, §10, p5
  and food value of whitefish, §13, p5
  and structure of meat, §10, p3
  of fish, §13, p3
  of oysters, §13, p39
  of poultry, §12, p12
Connective tissue, §10, p4
Consommé, §9, pp4, 20
Cooking meat for soup, §9, p11
  meat, Methods of, §10, p11
  meat, Purposes of, §10, p11
  meat, Time required for, §10, p15
  meats, Time table for, §10, p16
  of beef, §10, p22
  of fish, §13, p17
  of giblets, §12, p46
  of mutton and lamb, §11, p17
  of pork, §11, p29
  of poultry, §12, p24

Cooking of veal, §11, p4
  oysters, Important points in, §13, p41
  Preparing rabbit for, §12, p53
Corn chowder, §9, p31
  soup, Cream of, §9, p26
Corned beef, §10, p40
  beef, Boiled, §10, p41
  beef, Preparation of stews and, §10, p38
Cottage pie, §10, p46
Cotuits, §13, p41
Crab, Deviled, §13, p57
  -flake cocktail, §13, p57
  meat, Creamed, §13, p58
Crabs, and shrimp, General characteristics of lobsters, §13, p50
  Composition and food value of, §13, p38
  Fried soft-shelled, §13, p58
  Hard-shelled, §13, p57
  Nature of, §13, p56
  Oyster, §13, p57
  Preliminary preparation of, §13, p57
  Preparation of, §13, p56
  Soft-shelled, §13, p57
Cracker stuffing, §12, p33
Crackers, §9, p33
Cream-of-asparagus soup, §9, p27
  -of-corn soup, §9, p26
  -of-onion soup, §9, p28
  -of-pea soup, §9, p27
  -of-potato soup, §9, p26
  -of-spinach soup, §9, p27
  -of-tomato soup, §9, p28
  sauce, Lemon, §13, p18
  soups, §9, pp4, 25
Creamed codfish, §13, p31
  crab meat, §13, p58
  finnan haddie, §13, p32
  fish in potato nest, §13, p36
  oysters, §13, p45
  salmon with rice, §13, p35
  shrimp, §13, p59
  sweetbreads, §11, p9
  tuna fish, §13, p33
  veal on biscuits, §11, p11
Crop of a chicken, §12, p15
Croquettes, §11, p41
  Chicken, §12, p47
  Fish, §13, p35
  Frying of, §11, p42
  Lobster, §13, p56
  Sweetbread, §11, p43
  Veal, §11, p42
Croutons, §9, p33
Crown roast of lamb, §11, p19
  roast of pork, §11, p30
Crustaceans, §13, p36
Cured pork, Preparation of, §11, p32
Curry, Chicken, §12, p44
Cutlets in brown sauce, Veal, §11, p5
  Pan-broiled veal steak or, §11, p5

INDEX

Cutlets, Veal steaks or, §11, p5
Cuts, Names and uses of beef, §10, p20
  Names of pork, §11, p24
  obtained from a side of beef and their uses, Table of, §10, p21
  of beef, §10, p18
  of beef for stewing and corning, §10, p33
  of beef, Method of obtaining, §10, p18
  of beef, Table of, §10, p21
  of beef, Uses of, §10, p20
  of mutton and lamb, Distinguishing features of, §11, p15
  of mutton and lamb, Method of obtaining, §11, p15
  of mutton and lamb, Names and uses of, §11, p15
  of mutton and lamb, Table of, §11, p17
  of pork, §11, p24
  of pork, Uses of, §11, p24
  of veal and their uses, §11, p2
  Preparation of veal, §11, p4
  Table of pork, §11, p28
  Table of veal, §11, p4
Cutting up a chicken, §12, p19

D

Daikan, §9, p5
Deep-fat frying, Principles of, §11, p40
Delmonico steak, §10, p22
Deviled crab, §13, p57
  lobster, §13, p55
Diet, Canned fish in the, §13, p33
  Fish in the, §13, p1
  Meat in the, §10, p1
  Salt and smoked fish in the, §13, p31
Digestibility of clams, Nature and, §13, p47
  of fish, §13, p6
  of oysters, §13, p40
Drawing a chicken, §12, p15
Drawn-butter sauce, §13, p20
Dressing a chicken, §12, p13
  for salmon mold, §13, p34
Dry plucking, §12, p5
Duck, Liver stuffing for, §12, p35
  Peanut stuffing for roast, §12, p35
  Preparation of, §12, p24
  Roast, §12, p32
  Spring, §12, pp10, 32
  Young, §12, p32
Ducks, Selection of, §12, p10
Dumplings, §10, p40
  or noodles, Chicken stew with, §12, p42

E

Economic value of soup, §9, p3
Economy in the purchase of poultry, §12, p2
Eel, Fried, §13, p28
  Stewed, §13, p30
Egg balls, §9, p35

Egg sauce, §13, p19
Eggs and bacon, §11, p34
Extractives, §10, pp4, 11
  in meat, §10, p7
Extracts, Meat, §9, p7
  Soup, §9, p7
  Vegetable, §9, p7

F

Fat in fish, §13, p4
  in meat, §10, p6
  Trying out suet and other, §10, p44
Feathers, Pin, §12, p8
Feeding and care on quality of poultry, Influence of, §12, p3
Fillet, Broiled, §10, p31
  mignon, §10, p32
  of beef, §10, p31
  of flounder, §13, p27
  of venison, Roast, §12, p55
  of whitefish, Baked, §13, p26
Filleting fish, §13, p15
Finnan haddie, Baked, §13, p32
  haddie, Creamed, §13, p32
First soup stock, §9, p6
Fish, §13, p1
  and meat, Relative nutritive value of, §13, p5
  and meat, Table showing the comparison of, §13, p5
  Baked, §13, p24
  Boiled, §13, p21
  boiler, §13, p21
  Boning a, §13, p14
  Broiled, §13, p22
  Carbohydrate in, §13, p4
  chowder, §9, p30
  Cleaning, §13, p11
  Composition and food value of shell, §13, p37
  Composition of, §13, p3
  Cooking of, §13, p17
  Creamed tuna, §13, p33
  croquettes, §13, p35
  Digestibility of, §13, p6
  Fat in, §13, p4
  Filleting, §13, p15
  Food value of, §13, p4
  Freshness of, §13, p10
  Fried, §13, p28
  in potato nest, Creamed, §13, p36
  in the diet, §13, p1
  in the diet, Canned, §13, p33
  in the diet, Salt and smoked, §13, p31
  in the home, Care of, §13, p11
  Left-over, §13, p35
  Mineral matter in, §13, p4
  Planked, §13, p27
  Protein in, §13, p3

INDEX

Fish, Purchase of, §13, p7
  Sauces for, §13, p18
  Scaling a, §13, p12
  Seasons for shell, §13, p38
  Shell, §13, pp1, 36
  Skinning, §13, p14
  Steamed, §13, p22
  Stewed, §13, p30
  stock, §9, p7
  Stuffing for, §13, p20
  Table showing composition and food value of shell, §13, p38
  Table showing names, seasons, and uses of fresh, §13, p8
  Table showing names, seasons, and uses of salt and smoked, §13, p9
  Table showing seasons for shell, §13, p38
  with meat, Comparison of, §13, p3
Flat-bone steak, §10, p24
Flavoring stock, §9, p12
Flounder, Fillet of, §13, p27
Food, Poultry as a, §12, p1
  Sea, §13, p1
  suitable for the stock pot, §9, p8
  value and composition of beef, §10, p5; §13, p5
  value and composition of black bass, §13, p5
  value and composition of bluefish, §13, p5
  value and composition of canned salmon, §13, p5
  value and composition of carp, §13, p5
  value and composition of catfish, §13, p5
  value and composition of chicken broilers, §13, p5
  value and composition of clams, §13, p38
  value and composition of crabs, §13, p38
  value and composition of fowl, §13, p5
  value and composition of halibut steak. §13, p5
  value and composition of lake trout, §13, p5
  value and composition of lamb, §10, p5
  value and composition of leg of lamb, §13, p5
  value and composition of lobsters, §13, p38
  value and composition of mutton, §10, p5
  value and composition of oysters, §13, p33
  value and composition of pork, §10, p5
  value and composition of pork chops, §13, p5
  value and composition of red snapper, §13, p5
  value and composition of scallops, §13, p38
  value and composition of veal, §10, p5
  value and composition of whitefish, §13, p5
  value of fish, §13, p4
  value of fish, Factors determining, §13, p4
  Value of meat as, §10, p1

Food value of shell fish, Composition and, §13, p37
  value of shell fish, Tables showing composition and, §13, p38
Forcemeat balls, §9, p35
Fore quarter of veal, §11, p3
Fork, Oyster, §13, p44
Fowl, Composition and food value of, §13, p5
  Definition of, §12, p6
Fowls, Selection of guinea, §12, p11
Frankfurters, §11, p39
Fresh fish, Table showing the names, seasons, and uses of, §13, p8
  herring, Stewed, §13, p30
  mackerel, Broiled, §13, p23
  pork, Preparation of, §11, p29
Freshening salt and smoked fish, §13, p31
Freshness of fish, §13, p10
Fricassee of chicken, §12, p43
Fricasseeing applied to meat and fowl, §10, p15
Fried apples, Cold pork with, §11, p37
  chicken, §12, p27
  chicken, Gravy for, §12, p27
  chicken, Maryland, §12, p28
  chicken with paprika sauce, §12, p28
  clams, §13, p49
  eel, §13, p28
  fish, §13, p28
  oysters, §13, p46
  perch, §13, p28
  scallops, §13, p50
  soft-shelled crabs, §13, p58
Fritters, Oyster, §13, p47
  Soup, §9, p35
Frizzled beef, §10, p47
Frying and sautéing applied to meat, §10, p13
  chicken, §12, p6
  of croquettes, §11, p42
  Principles of deep-fat, §11, p40

G

Gall bladder, §12, p18
Game, Definition of, §12, p1
  General description of, §12, p52
  stock, §9, p6
Garnishes, Soup accompaniments and, §9, p31
Geese, Selection of, §12, p10
Gelatine in meat, §10, p6
Giblets, Cooking of, §12, p46
  of a chicken, §12, p18
Glycogen, or muscle sugar, §10, p7
Goose, Preparation of, §12, p24
  Roast, §12, p32
Gravy for fried chicken, §12, p27
  Making, §10, p44
Green-pepper stuffing, §12, p34
Guinea fowls, Selection of, §12, p11

INDEX

H

Haddock, Baked, §13, p25
Halibut, Baked, §13, p26
  steak, Composition and food value of, §13, p5
  steak, Sautéd, §13, p29
Ham, §11, p34
  Baked, §11, p36
  baked in milk, §11, p36
  Boiled, §11, p36
  Broiled, §11, p35
Hamburger steak, §10, p29
Hard-shelled crabs, §13, p57
Hash, Beef, §10, p46
  Turkey, §12, p48
Headcheese, §11, p24
Healthfulness of oysters, §13, p40
Heart, Stuffed, §10, p43
  sweetbread, §11, p3
Heavy thick soups, §9, p21
Herring, Stewed fresh, §13, p30
Hind quarter of veal, §11, p3
Hip-bone steak, §10, p24
Home, Care of fish in the, §13, p11
Horseradish sauce, §13, p19
Household stock, §9, pp6, 19

I

Individual lamb pies, §11, p23
Influence of feeding and care on quality of poultry, §12, p3
Iron, Timbale, §11, p44

J

Jellied chicken, §12, p45
  veal, §11, p8
  veal, Left-over, §11, p11
Julienne soup, §9, p21

K

Keeping stock, §9, p15
Kidneys, §11, p10
Kouskous, §9, p5
Krishara, §9, p5

L

Lake trout, Composition and food value of, §13, p5
Lamb, §11, p12
  and mutton chops, §11, p20
  and mutton cuts, Distinguishing features of, §11, p15
  and mutton cuts, Names and uses of, §11, p15
  and mutton, Left-over, §11, p21
  and mutton stews, §11, p21
  Comparison of mutton and, §11, p12
  Composition and food value of, §10, p5
  Cooking of mutton and, §11, p17

Lamb, Crown roast of, §11, p19
  cuts, Method of obtaining mutton and, §11, p15
  cuts, Table of mutton and, §11, p17
  Food value and composition of leg of, §13, p5
  on toast, Minced, §11, p22
  or mutton, Scalloped, §11, p22
  pies, Individual, §11, p23
  Rack of, §11, p15
  Roast leg of, §11, p17
  Saddle of, §11, p15
  Spring, §11, p13
  Turkish, §11, p21
Lard, Leaf, §11, p24
Larding, §11, p33
Leaf lard, §11, p24
Lebaba, §9, p5
Left-over beef, §10, p45
  -over fish, §13, p35
  -over jellied veal, §11, p11
  -over lamb and mutton, §11, p21
  -over pork, §11, p37
  -over poultry, §12, p46
  -over veal, §11, p10
Leg of venison, Roast, §12, p56
Lemon cream sauce, §13, p18
Live chickens, §12, p9
Liver and bacon, §11, p10
  stuffing for roast duck, §12, p35
Liverwurst, §11, p39
Loaf, Beef, §10, p37
Lobster à la Newburg, §13, p55
  cocktail, §13, p54
  croquettes, §13, p56
  Deviled, §13, p55
  from the shell, Removing, §13, p52
  Scalloped, §13, p54
Lobsters, Composition and food value of, §13, p38
  crabs, and shrimp, §13, p50
  Distinguishing features of, §13, p51
  Preparation of, §13, p51
Loin, Steaks obtained from beef, §10, p22
Lynn Havens, §13, p41

M

Mackerel, Broiled fresh, §13, p23
  Sautéd salt, §13, p32
Making gravy, §10, p44
  soup, §9, p9
Market, Preparation of poultry for, §12, p4
Maryland fried chicken, §12, p28
Meaning and use of soup stock, §9, p5
Meat as food, Value of, §10, p1
  Basting of, §10, p36
  Carbohydrate in, §10, p7
  Care of, §10, p8
  Comparison of fish with, §12, p3
  Cooking of, §10, p11

INDEX

Meat, Creamed crab, §13, p53
  cuts, Names and uses of, §10, p20
  Definition of, §10, p1
  extracts, §9, p7
  Extractives in, §10, p7
  Fat in, §10, p6
  Gelatine in, §10, p6
  in the diet, §10, p1
  in the home, Care of, §10, p10
  in the market, Care of, §10, p10
  Methods of cooking, §10, p11
  Minerals in, §10, p7
  preparations, Sausages and, §11, p39
  Protein in, §10, p4
  Purchase of, §10, p8
  Purposes of cooking, §10, p11
  Relative nutritive value of fish and, §13, p5
  Serving and carving of, §11, p38
  Structure and composition of, §10, p3
  Time required for cooking, §10, p15
  used for soup making, §9, p9
  Water in, §10, p7
Meats, Points to consider in buying, §10, p3
  Time table for cooking, §10, p16
Method of obtaining beef cuts, §10, p18
  of obtaining mutton and lamb cuts, §11, p15
Methods of cooking meat, §10, p11
Mexican beef, §10, p45
Mignon, Fillet, §10, p32
Milk, Ham baked in, §11, p36
Minced lamb on toast, §11, p22
Mineral matter in fish, §13, p4
Minerals in meat, §10, p7
Minestra, §9, p5
Mint sauce, §11, p18
Mock chicken salad, §11, p37
Mock duck, or rolled steak, §10, p28
Mold, Salmon, §13, p34
Mollusks, §13, p36
Mulligatawny soup, §9, pp5, 22
Muscle sugar, Glycogen or, §10, p7
Mushroom sauce, §13, p20
Mutton, §11, p12
  and lamb chops, §11, p20
  and lamb, Comparison of, §11, p12
  and lamb, Cooking of, §11, p17
  and lamb cuts, Distinguishing features of, §11, p15
  and lamb cuts, Method of obtaining, §11, p15
  and lamb cuts, Names and uses of, §11, p15
  and lamb cuts, Table of, §11, p17
  Composition and food value of, §10, p5
  Left-over lamb and, §11, p21
  Rack of, §11, p15
  Roast leg of, §11, p17
  Roast saddle of, §11, p19
  Saddle of, §11, p15

Mutton, Scalloped lamb or, §11, p22
  stews, Lamb and, §11, p21

N

Noodle soup, §9, p23
Noodles, Chicken stew with dumplings or, §12, p42
  Vegetable soup with, §9, p24
Nut sauce, §13, p19
Nutritive value of fish, Relative, §13, p5

O

Onion soup, Cream-of-, §9, p28
Opening clams, §13, p48
  oysters, §13, p42
Organs, Veal, §11, pp3, 9
Ox-tail soup, §9, p22
Oyster, Adductor muscle of an, §13, p42
  cocktails, §13, p43
  crabs, §13, p57
  fork, §13, p44
  fritters, §13, p47
  pie, §13, p46
  stew, §13, p44
  stuffing, §12, p34
  Valves of an, §13, p42
Oysters, clams, and scallops, §13, p39
  Composition of, §13, p39
  Creamed, §13, p45
  Digestibility of, §13, p40
  Food value of, §13, p38
  Fried, §13, p46
  Healthfulness of, §13, p40
  Important points in cooking, §13, p41
  Opening, §13, p42
  Preparation of, §13, p39
  Purchasing, §13, p41
  Raw, §13, p43
  Scalloped, §13, p45

P

Pan-broiled steak, §10, p27
  -broiled veal steaks or cutlets, §11, p5
  broiling, Cooking meat by, §10, p12
Paprika sauce, Fried chicken with, §12, p28
Partridge, Selection of, §12, p12
Pastry strips, §9, p34
Pâté de fois gras, §12, p10
Patties, Rice and meat, §11, p43
  Salmon, §13, p35
Pea soup, Cream-of-, §9, p27
Peanut stuffing for roast duck, §12, p35
Perch, Fried, §13, p28
Pheasant, partridge, and quail, §12, p12
  Selection of, §12, p12
Pickerel, Sautéd, §13, p29
Pickled pig's feet, §11, p40
  tongue, §10, p42
Pie, Beef, §10, p46

WI—C3—18

INDEX

Pie, Chicken, §12, p43
  Cottage, §10, p46
  Oyster, §13, p46
  Rabbit, §12, p54
Pies, Individual lamb, §11, p23
Pig, Roast, §11, p30
Pigeons, Selection of, §12, p11
Pig's feet, Pickled, §11, p40
Pigs in blankets, §13, p47
Pin feathers, §12, p8
Planked fish, §13, p27
  steak, §10, p30
Plucking a chicken, §12, p13
  Dry, §12, p5
Poisoning, Ptomaine, §13, p51
Ponhasse, §11, p40
Pork, §11, p23
  and cabbage, Scalloped, §11, p37
  chops and tomato sauce, §11, p31
  chops, Composition and food value of, §13, p5
  Composition and food value of, §10, p5
  Cooking of, §11, p29
  Crown roast of, §11, p30
  Cuts of, §11, p24
  cuts, Table of, §11, p28
  cuts, Uses of, §11, p24
  General characteristics of, §11, p23
  Left-over, §11, p37
  Preparation of cured, §11, p32
  Preparation of fresh, §11, p29
  Roast, §11, p29
  Salt, §11, pp27, 33
  sausage, §11, p32
  Sautéd or broiled, §11, p31
  Sautéd tenderloin of, §11, p31
  Tenderloin of, §11, p27
  with fried apples, Cold, §11, p37
Porterhouse roast, §10, p33
  steak, §10, p24
Pot-au-feu, §9, p13
  -roasted beef, §10, p37
  Stock, §9, p7
Potato border, Broiled scrod with, §13, p23
  chowder, §9, p30
  nest, Creamed fish in, §13, p36
  soup, Cream-of-, §9, p26
Potpie, Veal, §11, p7
Potroka, §9, p5
Poulards, §12, p4
Poultry as a food, §12, p1
  Broiled, §12, p25
  Classification of, §12, p3
  Cold-storage, §12, p5
  Composition of, §12, p12
  Definition of, §12, p1
  Effect of sex on quality of, §12, p4
  for cooking, Preparation of, §12, p13
  for the market, Preparation of, §12, p4
  Indication of cold-storage, §12, p6

Poultry, Left-over, §12, p46
  other than chicken, §12, p9
  Selection of, §12, p2
  Serving and carving, §12, p49
  Stuffing for roast, §12, p33
  Table for the selection of, §12, p11
  with rice, Baked, §12, p49
Preparation of beef organs, §10, p42
  of beefsteak, §10, p22
  of chicken, §12, p13
  of clams, §13, p47
  of crabs, §13, p56
  of cured pork, §11, p32
  of duck, §12, p24
  of fresh pork, §11, p29
  of goose, §12, p24
  of lobsters, §13, p51
  of oysters, §13, p39
  of poultry for cooking, §12, p13
  of poultry for the market, §12, p4
  of roasts, §10, p31
  of scallops, §13, p49
  of shrimp, §13, p58
  of small birds, §12, p24
  of stews and corned beef, §10, p38
  of sweetbreads, §11, p9
  of turkey, §12, p23
  of veal cuts, §11, p4
Preparing chicken feet, §12, p23
  rabbit for cooking, §12, p53
Principles of deep-fat frying, §11, p40
Processes involved in making stock, §9, p11
Protein in fish, §13, p3
  in meat, §10, p4
Ptomaine poisoning, §13, p51
Purchase of fish, §13, p7
  of meat, §10, p8
  of poultry, Economy in the, §12, p2
Purchasing oysters, §13, p41
Purée, Chestnut, §9, p29
  Split-pea, §9, p29
Purées, §9, pp5, 29
Purpose of soup in the meal, §9, p1
Purposes of cooking meat, §10, p11

Q

Quail, Selection of, §12, p12
Quality in chicken, General marks of good, §12, p7
  of poultry, Effect of sex on, §12, p4
  of poultry, Influence of feeding and care on, §12, p3

R

Rabbit for cooking, Preparing, §12, p53
  pie, §12, p54
  Roast, §12, p54
  Sautéd, §12, p54
Rack of lamb, §11, p15
  of mutton, §11, p15
Radishes and celery, §9, p32

INDEX

Raw clams, §13, p48
  oysters, §13, p43
Red snapper, Food value and composition of, §13, p5
Relative nutritive value of fish, §13, p5
Removing grease from soup, §9, p14
  lobster from the shell, §13, p52
Rib roast, Standing, §10, p33
  roasts, §10, p32
Rice and meat patties, §11, p43
  Baked poultry with, §12, p49
  Chicken with, §12, p48
  Creamed salmon with, §13, p35
  Scalloped veal with, §11, p11
  stuffing, §12, p34
Rigor mortis, §10, p6; §12, p14
Roast beef, §10, p34
  chicken, §12, p29
  duck, §12, p32
  duck, Liver stuffing for, §12, p25
  duck, Peanut stuffing for, §12, p35
  fillet of venison, §12, p55
  goose, §12, p32
  leg of lamb, §11, p17
  leg of mutton, §11, p17
  leg of venison, §12, p56
  of lamb, Crown, §11, p19
  of pork, Crown, §11, p30
  pig, §11, p30
  pork, §11, p29
  Porterhouse, §10, p33
  poultry, Stuffing for, §12, p33
  rabbit, §12, p54
  saddle of mutton, §11, p19
  small birds, §12, p33
  Standing rib, §10, p33
  turkey, §12, p31
Roasting, §10, p12
  chicken, §12, p6
Roasts, Chuck, §10, p32
  Preparation of, §10, p31
  Rib, §10, p32
  Rump, §10, p34
  Veal, §11, p6
Roe, Broiled shad, §13, p23
Rolled steak, or mock duck, §10, p28
  steak, Stuffing for, §10, p28
Rolls, Veal, §11, p10
Rump roasts, §10, p34

S

Saddle of lamb, §11, p15
  of mutton, §11, p15
  of mutton, Roast, §11, p19
Salad, Chicken, §12, p47
  Mock chicken, §11, p37
  Veal, §11, p11
Salmon, Boiled, §13, p32
  Composition and food value of canned, §13, p5

Salmon mold, §13, p34
  mold, Dressing for, §13, p34
  patties, §13, p35
  with rice, Creamed, §13, p35
Salt and smoked fish, Freshening, §13, p31
  and smoked fish in the diet, §13, p31
  and smoked fish, Table showing names, seasons, and uses of, §13, p9
  mackerel, Sautéd, §13, p32
  pork, §11, pp27, 33
Sauce, Drawn-butter, §13, p20
  Egg, §13, p19
  for broiled venison, §12, p55
  Fried chicken with paprika, §12, p28
  Horseradish, §13, p19
  Lemon cream, §13, p18
  Mint, §11, p18
  Mushroom, §13, p20
  Nut, §13, p19
  Spanish, §13, p19
  Thin white, §9, p26
  Tomato, §13, p19
Sauces for fish, §13, p18
Sausage, Pork, §11, p32
Sausages and meat preparations, §11, p39
Sautéd fish, §13, p28
  halibut steak, §13, p29
  or broiled pork, §11, p31
  pickerel, §13, p29
  rabbit, §12, p54
  salt mackerel, §13, p32
  smelts, §13, p29
  tenderloin of pork, §11, p31
Sautéing and frying, §10, p13
Scaling a fish, §13, p12
Scalloped lamb or mutton, §11, p22
  lobster, §13, p54
  oysters, §13, p45
  pork with cabbage, §11, p37
  veal with rice, §11, p11
Scallops, Baked, §13, p50
  Composition and food value of, §13, p38
  Fried, §13, p50
  Oysters, clams, and, §13, p39
  Preparation of, §13, p49
Scrapple, §11, pp24, 40
Scrod with potato border, Broiled, §13, p23
Sea food, §13, p1
Seasons, and uses of fresh fish, Table showing the names, §13, p8
  and uses of smoked fish, Table showing the names, §13, p9
  for shell fish, §13, p38
  for shell fish, Table showing, §13, p38
Second soup stock, §9, p6
Selection of chicken, §12, p6
  of ducks, §12, p10
  of poultry, §12, p2
  of turkeys, §12, p9
Serving and carving meat, §11, p38

INDEX

Serving and carving poultry, §12, p49
  soup, §9, p16
Shad roe, Broiled, §13, p23
Shell fish, §13, pp1, 36
  fish, Composition and food value of, §13, p37
  fish, Seasons for, §13, p38
  fish, Tables showing composition and food value of, §13, p38
  fish, Table showing seasons for, §13, p38
Shrimp à La Salle, §13, p59
  Creamed, §13, p59
  General characteristics of lobsters, crabs, and, §13, p50
  Lobsters, crabs, and, §13, p50
  Nature of, §13, p58
  Preparation of, §13, p58
Simmering, or stewing, §10, p14
Singeing a chicken, §12, p14
Sirloin steak, §10, p25
Skinning fish, §13, p14
Skirt steak, §10, p29
Small birds, Preparation of, §12, p24
  birds, Roast, §12, p33
Smelts, Sautéd, §13, p29
Smoked fish, Freshening salt and, §13, p31
  fish in the diet, Salt and, §13, p31
  fish, Table showing the names, seasons, and uses of, §13, p9
Soft-shelled crabs, §13, p57
  -shelled crabs, Fried, §13, p58
Soljinka, §9, p5
Soup, §9, p1
  accompaniments and garnishes, §9, p31
  accompaniments, Recipes for, §9, p18
  and its place in the meal, §9, p1
  and soup accompaniments, §9, p18
  Clearing of, §9, p14
  Cooking meat for, §9, p11
  Cream-of-asparagus, §9, p27
  Cream-of-corn, §9, p26
  Cream-of-onion, §9, p28
  Cream-of-pea, §9, p27
  Cream-of-potato, §9, p26
  Cream-of-spinach, §9, p27
  Cream-of-tomato, §9, p28
  Definition of, §9, p1
  Economic value of, §9, p3
  extracts, §9, p7
  fritters, §9, p35
  General classes of, §9, p3
  in the meal, Purpose of, §9, p1
  in the meal, Value of, §9, p2
  Julienne, §9, p21
  making, Meat used for, §9, p9
  Making of, §9, p9
  making, Vegetables used for, §9, p10
  Mulligatawny, §9, p22
  Noodle, §9, p23
  Ox-tail, §9, p22

Soup, Principal ingredients of, §9, p9
  Recipes for, §9, p18
  Removing grease from, §9, p14
  Serving, §9, p16
  stock, Meaning and use of, §9, **p5**
  stock, Uses of, §9, p5
  stock, Varieties of, §9, **p6**
  Thickening, §9, p14
  Value of, §9, p1
Soups, Classification of, §9, p3
  Clear, §9, p4
  Cream, §9, pp4, 25
  denoting consistency, Classes of, §9, p4
  Heavy thick, §9, p21
  Thick, §9, p4
  typical of particular countries, §9, **p5**
Spanish sauce, §13, p19
  stew, §11, p22
Spinach soup, Cream-of-, §9, p17
Split-pea purée, §9, p29
Spring duck, §12, pp10, 32
  lamb, §11, p13
Squabs, §12, pp3, 11
Squirrel, Broiled, §12, p55
Standing rib roast, §10, p33
Steak, Club, §10, p24
  Delmonico, §10, p22
  Flat-bone, §10, p24
  Hamburger, §10, p29
  Hip-bone, §10, p24
  or cutlets, Veal, §11, p5
  Pan-broiled, §10, p27
  Planked, §10, p30
  Porterhouse, §10, p24
  Sautéd halibut, §13, p29
  Sirloin, §10, p25
  Skirt, §10, p29
  Stuffing for rolled, §10, p28
  Swiss, §10, p29
  Vegetables served with, §10, p30
Steaks obtained from the beef loin, §10, p22
  obtained from the round, §10, p25
  Preparation of beef, §10, p22
Steamed clams, §13, p48
  fish, §13, p22
Stew, Beef, §10, p38
  Oyster, §13, p44
  Spanish, §11, p22
  Veal, §11, p8
Stewed eel, §13, p30
  fish, §13, p30
  fresh herring, §13, p30
Stewing and corning, Beef for, §10, p38
  or simmering, §10, p14
Stews and corned beef, Preparation of, §10, p38
  Lamb and mutton, §11, p21
Sticks, Bread, §9, p34
Stock, Bone, §9, p6

INDEX

Stock, First, §9, p6
  Fish, §9, p7
  flavoring, §9, p12
  for clear soup or bouillon, §9, p19
  for soup, §9, p5
  Game, §9, p6
  Household, §9, pp6, 19
  Keeping, §9, p15
  Meaning and use of soup, §9, p5
  pot, §9, p7
  pot, Food suitable for the, §9, p8
  pot, Nature, use, and care of, §9, p7
  Second, §9, p6
  Varieties of soup, §9, p6
  Vegetable, §9, p6
  White, §9, p20
Stocks and clear soups, §9, p19
Stomach sweetbread, §11, p3
Strips, Pastry, §9, p34
Structure and composition of meat, §10, p3
Stuffed heart, §10, p43
  veal breast, §11, p7
Stuffing, Bread, §12, p33
  Chestnut, §12, p34
  Cracker, §12, p33
  for fish, §13, p20
  for roast duck, Liver, §12, p35
  for roast poultry, §12, p33
  for rolled steak, §10, p28
  for veal, §11, p7
  Green-pepper, §12, p34
  Oyster, §12, p34
  Rice, §12, p34
Suet, Trying out, §10, p44
Sweetbread croquettes, §11, p43
  Heart, §11, p3
  Stomach, §11, p3
  Throat, §11, p3
Sweetbreads, §11, p3
  Broiled, §11, p9
  Creamed, §11, p9
  Preparation of, §11, p9
Swiss steak, §10, p29

T

Table for the selection of poultry, §12, p11
  of cuts obtained from a side of beef and their uses, §10, p21
  of mutton and lamb cuts, §11, p17
  of pork cuts, §11, p28
  of veal cuts, §11, p4
  showing composition and food value of shell fish, §13, p38
  showing seasons for shell fish, §13, p38
  showing the comparison of fish and meat, §13, p5
  showing the names, seasons, and uses of fresh fish, §13, p8
  showing the names, seasons, and uses of smoked fish, §13, p9

Tarhonya, §9, p5
Tenderloin of beef, §10, pp21, 24, 31
  of pork, §11, p27
  of pork, Sautéd, §11, p31
Thick soups, §9, p4
Thickening soup, §9, p14
Thin white sauce, §9, p26
Throat sweetbread, §11, p3
Timbale-case batter, §11, p44
  cases, §11, p42
  iron, §11, p44
Time required for cooking meat, §10, p15
Tissue, Connective, §10, p4
Toast, Minced lamb on, §11, p22
Tomato bouillon, §9, p21
  sauce, §13, p19
  sauce, Pork chops and, §11, p31
  soup, Cream-of-, §9, p28
Tomatoes, Bacon with, §11, p34
Tongue, Boiled, §10, p42
  Braized, §10, p43
  Pickled, §10, p42
Trout, Food value of lake, §13, p5
Trying out suet, §10, p44
Tuna fish, Creamed, §13, p33
Turkey hash, §12, p48
  Preparation of, §12, p23
  Roast, §12, p31
Turkeys, Selection of, §12, p9
Turkish lamb, §11, p21

U

Use of soup stock, §9, p5
  of stock pot, §9, p7
Uses of beef cuts, §10, p20
  of fresh fish, Table showing the names, seasons, and, §13, p8
  of lamb and mutton cuts, §11, p15
  of smoked fish, Table showing the names, seasons, and, §13, p9
  of veal cuts, §11, p2

V

Value of fish, Food, §13, p4
  of fish, Relative nutritive, §13, p5
  of meat as food, §10, p1
  of shell fish, Tables showing composition and food, §13, p38
  of soup in the meal, §9, p2
Valves of an oyster, §13, p42
Varieties and uses of soup stock, §9, p5
  of soup stock, §9, p6
Veal, Bob, §11, p1
  breast, Stuffed, §11, p7
  chops, §11, p4
  Composition and food value of, §10, p5
  Cooking of, §11, p4
  croquettes, §11, p42
  cuts and their preparation, §11, p4
  cuts and their uses, §11, p2

INDEX

Veal cuts, Table of, §11, p4
  cutlets in brown sauce, §11, p5
  Fore quarter of, §11, p3
  Hind quarter of, §11, p3
  Jellied, §11, p8
  kidneys, §11, p10
  Left-over, §11, p10
  Left-over jellied, §11, p11
  Nature of, §11, p1
  on biscuits, Creamed, §11, p11
  organs, §11, pp3, 9
  potpie, §11, p7
  roasts, §11, p6
  rolls, §11, p10
  salad, §11, p11
  steak or cutlets, Pan-broiled, §11, p5
  stew, §11, p8
  Stuffing for, §11, p7
  sweetbreads, Broiled, §11, p9
  sweetbreads, Creamed, §11, p9
  with rice, Scalloped, §11, p11

Vegetable extracts, §9, p7
  soup with noodles, §9, p24
  stock, §9, p6
Vegetables served with steak, §10, p30
  used for soup making, §9, p10
Venison, Broiled, §12, p55
  Cuts of, §12, p55
  Roast fillet of, §12, p55
  Roast leg of, §12, p56
  Sauce for, §12, p55

W

Water in meat, §10, p7
White stock, §9, p20
Whitefish, Baked fillet of, §13, p26
  Composition and food value of, §13, p5
Wing tips of chicken, §12, p23

Y

Yearling, Meaning of, §11, p13
Young, or spring, duck, §12, p32

Set of 5
Great Britain
$15.00